God's Destiny
for
People of Color

DR. CLARENCE WALKER

UP

URIEL PRESS

An Imprint of UMI

Published in the United States by Uriel Press
P.O. Box 436987, Chicago, IL 60643
1-800-860-8642
www.urielpress.com

ISBN 978-0-9993326-2-7 (paperback)
ISBN 978-0-9993326-3-4 9 (eBook)

Library of Congress Control Number: 2017936726

Cover design by Laura Duffy
Book design by Astrid Lewis Reedy

Printed in the United States of America

Dedication

This book is dedicated to all the people of color who are discouraged and have lost hope given our history of oppression and the present state of affairs concerning race relations—to those who want to know the truth about who and what we are historically.

It is also dedicated to those who wonder if God left us out of Scripture or if He has a plan for people of color, especially those of African descent.

Furthermore, it is dedicated to all the people of color in the Americas, Africa, Latin America and the Caribbean who have shown remarkable resilience and fortitude in the face of seemingly overwhelming odds and despite often undergoing oppressive conditions. Somehow, they find the strength to keep on going and prove the doubters wrong time and time again.

To the families of those who have lost sons and daughters due to racist acts. To the families of the Charleston 9 who lost love ones because of one of the most horrific hate crimes in America.

To all those individuals both black and white who have gone before me and paid the price in blood, sweat, and tears to make life better for people of African heritage no matter the nation in which they reside. They have blazed a trail and left a legacy that successors can follow.

Finally, to the young people of color who have greatness locked inside of them that they need to release for the betterment of themselves and people of color in general. May this writing become a key to unleashing that greatness.

Table of Contents

Table of Contents

Genesis 10:8–10, KJV

"And Cush begat Nimrod: he began to be a mighty one in the earth. He was a mighty hunter before the LORD: wherefore it is said, Even as Nimrod the mighty hunter before the LORD and the beginning of his kingdom was Babel, and Erich, and Accad, and Canley, in the land of Shinar."

Isaiah 18:1–7, NCV

"How terrible it will be for the land beyond the rivers of Cush. It is filled with the sound of wings. That land sends messengers across the sea; they go on the water in boats made of reeds. Go, quick messengers, to a people who are tall and smooth-skinned, who are feared everywhere. They are a powerful nation that defeats other nations. Their land is divided by rivers. All you people of the world, look! Everyone who lives in the world, look! You will see a banner raised on a mountain. You will hear a trumpet sound. The Lord said to me, "I will quietly watch from where I live, like heat in the sunshine, like the dew in the heat of harvest time." The time will come, after the flowers have bloomed and before the harvest, when new grapes will be budding and growing. The enemy will cut the plants with knives; he will cut down the vines and take them away. They will be left for the birds of the mountains and for the wild animals. Birds will feed on them all summer, and wild animals will eat them that winter." At that time a gift will be brought to the Lord All-Powerful from the people who are tall and smooth skinned, who are feared everywhere. They are a powerful nation that defeats other nations. Their land is divided by rivers. These gifts will be brought to the place of the Lord All-Powerful, to Mount Zion."

Introduction

❧

Let me state from the outset that I am both a black Republican and a black evangelical in theology. Thus my scriptural presentation will come from that perspective.

However, I am not a radical fringe Republican. Let me also state that it is not my intent to address every issue facing African Americans and people of African descent or enter into every social controversy.

To start this literary journey, I would like to state some observations as it relates to black people:

1. We have seen, and in some measure experienced, the oppression, genocide, and poverty, of African people of color.
2. We continue to witness acts of overt and covert racism in America, Africa, Latin America, the Caribbean, Europe, and the world at large directed toward people of African descent.
3. There is a systematic destruction of young African American men and women (especially young Black men via murder, gun violence, drugs and AIDS).
4. The condition of many Africans, African Americans, Africans from the Caribbean, and that of people of African descent all over the world requires

interventions. It is my belief that these interventions must be based on certain spiritual convictions, and that these convictions are founded on the following statements:

1. There is a Divine Creator who is revealed in the Bible.
2. That this God is no respecter of nations (that is, He is without prejudice), as stated in Acts 10:34-35, GNT: **"Peter began to speak: "I now realize that it is true that God treats *everyone* on the same basis. Those who worship him and do what is right are acceptable to him, no matter what race they belong to."**
3. God has a predetermined purpose and destiny for all races. Acts 17:26, AMP:
4. **"And He made from one man [*common origin, one source, one blood*] every nation of mankind to live on the face of the earth, having definitely determined their appointed times and the boundaries of their lands and territories."**
5. Jesus Christ is the Son of God and it was through him, that is his death and resurrection that brought redemption for people of *all* nations. Revelation 5:9, GNT: **"They sang a new song: "You are worthy to take the scroll and to break open its seals. For you were killed, and by your sacrificial death you bought for God people from *every tribe, language, nation*, and race."**
6. Racism is sin and has no part in the body of Christ, God's purpose and redemptive plan is for all people from all nations and ethnicities, **"for God so loved the *world*."**

Therefore, it is not the aim of this book or any of the literature of the Destiny of H.O.P.E. Series to elevate Black Hamitic people of color or people of African descent above other ethnic groups, but rather to present God's truth about them knowing that truth will set free African people of color and those of other nationalities who receive this message.

The Motivation: It is necessary, and essential, that the reader read the entire book from cover to cover in order to receive the maximum benefit from the writing. There are some research findings and statistics presented. They are important. They are there to make a point, and to give credence to certain statements. *Don't* read selectively, excluding parts of the book. You may not complete the reading in one sitting, but stay with it.

The Mission: This book and the entire Destiny of H.O.P.E. series are designed to accomplish the following goals:

1. Address the hopelessness that hangs over many people of color throughout the world.
2. Inform people of African descent of their significant contributions and past achievements and their pivotal role in God's plan for the present and future.
3. Help set the record straight by correcting many misrepresentations and distortions about people of African descent due to the racism of European secular and biblical scholarship.
4. Provide a biblical foundation for the spiritual and emotional empowerment of African people.
5. Destroy racial barriers in the body of Christ due to ethnic, historical, and cultural ignorance, and provide a basis for true racial reconciliation.
6. Unveil the hidden mystery in prophecy concerning the destiny of African people of color.

7. Bring liberation to the families of African descent from their generational bondage.

8. Lay a foundation for the merging of efforts, finances, and resources from those of African descent in the Americas, Africa, the Caribbean, and throughout the world toward fulfilling our divine destiny.

9. Glorify our Father and the Son of God, the Lord Jesus Christ, as being truly the *LORD OF ALL*.

This book is part *history*, and therefore covers our *past*, it is part *prophecy* and covers our *future*, and it is part *sociology* and covers our *present*. More importantly, I have attempted to make it all biblical in both text and context. With these things in mind, we now embark on this literary trek.

How Did We Get Here?

How did African people of color get to where they are arguably the most oppressed group on the planet? Given the present social, economic, political, and spiritual state of affairs, is there any hope for them? The answer to the latter question is yes and the answer to the former question will be answered during this book.

I can further preface the latter question with the following statement: We had a glorious *history*—and we have been purposed by God to have a glorious *destiny*.

We go on record to say *we had it, we lost it, now it is time to get it back*. What did we have? Greatness, honor, respectability, notoriety, affluence, opulence, status, and distinction.

CHAPTER 1

Let's Go Black to the Beginning

꙾

"Once you go Black, you never go back."
— **AFRICAN-AMERICAN SAYING**

The history of people of color goes back to the beginning with the first two humans God created on the earth: Adam and Eve. They were both associated with the regions of Mesopotamia and Africa where the earliest people of color resided.[1]

African/Edenic Earth Historical Evidence

The Bible conveys some interesting details about the first man and woman. We can begin with the first man's name, Adam, which comes from *Adham,* meaning *red earth.* Adam comes from the same root as *Edom,* which means *brown* or *reddish brown.* Earth is usually blackish brown, brown or reddish brown.[2] The

---

1   Dr. Cain Hope Felder, editor, The Original African Heritage Study Bible: King James Version (World Bible Publishers, 1993).

2   Sean Brock, "Jews/Hebrew: Adam: What does it mean?," Yahoo Answers, 2006, https://answers.yahoo.com/question/index;_ylt=AwrC1C78doxZeXAAYjFPmolQ;_ylu=X3 oDMTEybTFvb2wxBGNvbG8DYmYxBHBvcwMxBHZoaWQDQjI1NTlfMQRzZWMDc3I-?qid=20080501092339AAbzLnQ.

name is also related to *Adamah,* which means red earth. Much of the soil of the Nile Valley is red or reddish brown due to the high levels of Chromic Cambisols.[3] W.E.B. Du Bois said primitive Africans varied in color from yellow to *reddish* brown. The Roman poet Statius spoke of *red* Negroes with copper-colored skin. Melville Herskovits, a notable anthropologist, said he saw Negroes from *brownish black* to *reddish brown* in his research of the earliest humans.[4]

Moreover, the Bible gives us the location of Eden as being near the rivers Pishon which compasseth the whole land of Havilah, in the "Table of Nations" of Genesis 10:6-7

> *"And the sons of Ham; Cush, and Mizraim, and Phut, and Canaan. And the sons of Cush; Seba, and Havilah, and Sabtah, and Raamah, and Sabtecha: and the sons of Raamah; Sheba, and Dedan.*

Thus, there are two Cushitic references in Genesis 2:10-14. The locations indicated are Africa and the Mesopotamia.[5]

African Eve

On March 23, 1986, the San Francisco Chronicle published a story titled "Mother of Us All." The story featured a black woman from East Africa nicknamed "Mitochondrial Eve" who is described as the most-recent common maternal ancestor of people

3 Alice C. Linsley, "The Christ in Nilotic Mythology," *Just Genesis,* 12 January 2011, http://jandyongenesis.blogspot.com/2011/01/christ-in-nilotic-mythology.html

4 "Race Noire Dans La Bible," Congoflash, 29 July 2013, http://www.congoflash.com/race-noire-dans-la-bible/

5 Felder, The Original African Heritage Study Bible, 15-16.

on Earth today. On May 11, 1986, Newsweek magazine published a story of a Black man eating a fruit from a Black woman. It was titled "The African Eve."[6]

In January 26, 1987, on January 11, 1988 an article entitled "The Search for Adam and Eve" in Newsweek and National Geographic pictured a black Adam and Eve. DNA researchers and *well-respected* scientists have traced back genetically to uncover evidence of what they believe was the first woman whom they called Eve. The evidence indicated that Eve was a *sub-Saharan African* woman and was most likely dark-haired and *dark-skinned*.

Time magazine had another photograph of a Black woman with the headline "Our Genealogical Mother from Africa." All the other Euro-American magazines, The Economist, Philadelphia, Science News, Organic, Inquirer, Natural History, Nature, and BJS and the New York Times wrote about the subject.[7]

African Adam

In 2004, IBM and National Geographic carried out a genealogical project that focused on the Y chromosome. This is the gene fathers pass directly to the child. By looking at who your grandfather was and who his grandfather was, you would eventually arrive at the father of us all, who is nicknamed *genetic Adam*.[8]

The IBM/National Geographic project led researchers to the Pate Island off the coast of Kenya in East Africa, where they found

---

6   Wikipedia contributors, "Recent African origin of modern humans," Wikipedia, The Free Encyclopedia, Wikipedia, The Free Encyclopedia, 20 August 2013, https://en.wikipedia.org/wiki/Recent_African_origin_of_modern_humans

7   Spencer Wells, producer, DNA Mysteries: The Search for Adam, National Geographic, 2008.

8   Kihura Nkuba, "The human race started in Africa," New Vision, 29 July 2007, http://www.newvision.co.ug/new_vision/news/1160123/human-race-started-africa.

the source of *all* genes, but one man did not fit the criteria. Then they moved further to the interior of Africa where they found the Hazabe tribe, the oldest people on the earth, who live near Lake Tanganyika. They have the original Y chromosome. The "scientific Adam" was compared to the Hazabe chief.

However, Professor Eske Willerslev of the University of Copenhagen led a study that concluded aboriginal Australians are descendants of the first people to leave Africa up to 75,000 years ago. This genetic study has found that aboriginal Australians may represent the oldest continuous culture on the planet.[9]

Therefore, according to molecular biology and archaeology, *humanity* started in *Africa*. Recent genetic studies have shown that the human group with the oldest sequence of genes is another African group.

The oldest genetic stream of humanity was discovered among the Khoi-San people of Southern and Central Africa. These genetic studies include a comparative analysis of select peoples of *all continents* and physical types.[10]

Since the mapping of the human genome in recent years, DNA samples from around the world have been compared. This has enabled scientists to establish a clear geographical chain of origin, descent, and migration for the human population globally.[11] The physical differences associated with some of these gene changes over thousands of years are expressed as differences in ap-

9   "DNA confirms Aboriginal culture one of Earth's oldest," Australian Geographic, 23 September 2011, http://www.australiangeographic.com.au/news/2011/09/dna-confirms-aboriginal-culture-one-of-earths-oldest/.

10   Dr. Orville Boyd Jenkins, "Peoples and Cultures Race and Ethnicity in the Horn of Africa," Orville Jenkins, 14 March 2015, http://orvillejenkins.com/peoples/raceandethnicity.html.

11   Science: "Neanderthal-Human Breeding Was Hard, But Yielded Benefits by Jason Mick (Blog) - January 31, 2014 4:48 PM.

pearance and body type between human populations. Yet these superficial differences also occur among humans whose DNA is 99.6 percent identical.[12]

In the book of Genesis, the boundaries of the Garden of Eden are given as the Tigris and Euphrates rivers on the north, the Zambezi on the south and the Nile on the east. This is the same area as the Great Rift Valley that runs from the Transjordan to Mozambique in Africa.

Archaeology is continuing to confirm that for five million years or more, all human beings were *Africans* and were living *only* in *Africa.* According to John Reader's book, *The Biography of Africa,* it was only 100,000 years ago when groups of human beings started leaving Africa to populate other continents.[13]

> Genesis 2:10-14, (CEB): "A river flows from Eden to water the garden, and from there it divides into four headwaters. The name of the first river is the Pishon. It flows around the entire land of Havilah, where there is gold. That land's gold is pure, and the land also has Sweet smelling resins and gemstones. The name of the second river is the Gihon. It flows around the entire land of Cush. The name of the third river is the Tigris, flowing east of Assyria; and the name of the fourth river is the Euphrates."

The first continent identified in Genesis is *Africa*, and the first nation mentioned by name in the Bible is Cush (*Sudan Africa*).

In the latest studies on human diversity, scientists identified sub-Saharan Africa as the place where the human migration

---

12   Dr. Orville Boyd Jenkins, "Peoples and Cultures Race and Ethnicity in the Horn of Africa," Orville Jenkins, 14 March 2015, http://orvillejenkins.com/peoples/raceandethnicity.html.

13   H.E. Yoweri Kaguta Museveni, "Grand Debate on the Union Government," The African Union Summit, 2 July 2007, Accra, Ghana, Ubuntu Platform, http://ayoubmzee.blogspot.com/2008/12/m7-at-9th-sssession-of-au_28.html.

phenomenon began about 80,000 years ago, when a small group of humans headed for North Africa and the Middle East and kept on going, gradually reaching the farthest continents of the Americas and Australia.[14]

Theories of a global migration with an African starting point had been circulating, but none of them brought the arguments and evidence this study did on the topic. "It's like looking back at the earth with a telescope a thousand times more powerful than what you had before," said Richard Myers of the Stanford University School of Medicine, as reported in the journal Science.[15]

Two studies have already been published in Science and Nature on the patterns of genetic mutations and human diversity, and based on the similar DNA samples, they both led to the same conclusion: The *modern human* left *Africa* (Addis Ababa, *Sudan Africa,* to be more precise), traversed Central Asia and continued heading east and west to Europe, Asia and the Americas.[16] All this information is a confirmation of Acts 17:26, AMPC:

> *"He made from one [common origin, one source, and one blood]*
> *all nations of men to settle on the face of the earth…"*

Science seems to confirm that the *original one blood* from which *all* mankind was made was *African blood.*[17]

---

14   Guy Gugliotta, "The Great Human Migration," Smithsonian.com, 1 July 2008, http://www.smithsonianmag.com/history/the-great-human-migration-13561/.

15   John Roach, "Massive Genetic Study Supports "Out of Africa" Theory," National Geographic News, 21 February 2008, http://news.nationalgeographic.com/news/2008/02/080221-human-genetics.html.

16   Roach

17   Roach

Thus, humanity, as we know, started in Africa and came out of Africa, but our discussion is about a group of Africans who descended from a patriarch whom the Bible refers to as Ham.

Discussion Questions

1. What is the evidence that Eden was in Africa/Mesopotamia?
2. Scientifically speaking, what do "African Adam" and "African Eve" mean?

CHAPTER 2

You're a Real Ham — Hamitic Peoples Contributions

ஜ

Until the story of the hunt is told by the lion, the tale of the hunt will always glorify the hunter.
~ AFRICAN PROVERB

Until the history of Africa is told by Africans, the story of greatness will always glorify the European and Euro-American imperialists. As a person of African descent, I seek to tell our story from our perspective.

Genesis 10 is a biblical record of the "Table of Nations." It cites the generations of the three sons of Noah. The three descendants of Noah produced the three streams of humanity. We won't use the term race because the Bible does not talk about race. That was a man-made invention created by European and Eurocentric scholars.

Genesis 10:2-5 records the genealogy of the descendants of Japheth—the Indo- Europeans, and Caucasoid people

Genesis. 10:21-32 records the descendants of Shem—Semitic, Hebrews, and descendants of Abraham

> *Genesis. 10:6-20 records the genealogy of the descendants of Ham—Canaanites, Egyptians, Arabians, Babylonians, Sumerians, and Africans.*[18]

Whom Did Noah Curse?

Ham, the youngest son of Noah, saw his father's nakedness and he cursed Canaan, the grandson of Ham.

> Genesis 9:22-25, KJV: *And Ham, the father of Canaan, saw the nakedness of his father, and told his two brethren without. And Shem and Japheth took a garment, and laid it upon both their shoulders, and went backward, and covered the nakedness of their father; and their faces were backward, and they saw not their father's nakedness. And Noah awoke from his wine, and knew what his younger son had done unto him. And he said, Cursed be Canaan; a servant of servants shall he be unto his brethren.*

Who is Canaan and what people did he represent? Canaanites were dwellers of the land of Canaan. They were Palestinian people of color. They were descendants of Ham's younger son.

Who Are the Hamitic Cushites?

The name Ham means "warm, dark and hot," which serves as a description of both the ethnic and cultural temperament of the people.[19]

---

18   Felder, The Original African Heritage Study Bible, 15-17

19   Felder, The Original African Heritage Study Bible, 15-16.

Dr. Arthur C. Custance, a Canadian anthropologist, scientist and author specializing on science and Christianity who is a renowned scholar, says of Ham:

> "Most of us have been brought up to believe that we indo Europeans are the most inventive people in the world. It is exceedingly difficult to escape from this culturally conditioned prejudice and take a fresh objective look at the origins of our technological achievements. One may take almost any essential element of our highly complex civilization, aircraft, paper, weaving, metallurgy, propulsion of various kinds, painting, explosives, medical techniques, mechanized principles, food, the use of electricity, virtually anything technological in nature, an examination of the history of its development leads us back to the Hamitic people, and exceedingly rarely to Japheth or Shem. The basic inventions by Shem and Japheth can it seem be numbered on the fingers of one hand. This can be supported by over 1,000 authoritative sources."[20]

Four Divisions of Ham

The following are the four divisions of the Hamitic people as presented in Scripture:

1. *Canaan*—the youngest son of Ham; Canaanites and Palestinians cursed by Noah to be under servitude to Shem and Semitic people
2. *Phut*—third-born son of Ham; the North African Libyans and Persians. He was a low achiever in

---

20 Arthur C. Custance, "Noah's Three Sons: Human History in Three Dimensions Vol.1: Part IV The Technology of Hamitic People," The Arthur C. Custance Centre for Science and Christianity, 1988, http://custance.org/Library/Volume1/#Part IV - Volume1.

comparison to his brothers. He did not accomplish much and had no descendants.

3. *Mizraim*—second-born of Ham; Egypt, Kemite Africans (Upper and Lower Nile). Each time Ham is mentioned in Scripture he is associated with his son, Mizraim (Egypt). He stayed close to his father and became a great nation.

4. *Cush*—(Afroid people) the Cushitic African, Afro-Asiatic and Sudanese African people who produced the Bible's first superhero, a man named *Nimrod*.

Birth Order Characteristics of the Four Sons of Ham

The descendants of Ham's four sons took on characteristics reflecting the birth order of their patriarch.

1. **Canaan**—youngest; rebellion, identity problems, negative image
2. **Phut**—middle child; low achievement and obscurity
3. **Mizraim (Egypt)**—second-born; Papa's boy, clinger, achiever
4. **Cush**—oldest; self-sufficient, independent, and achiever

Not only did the sons take on the nature of their father Ham in being warm dark and hot, they also took on the characteristics of their patriarch's birth order. We will focus primarily on Ham's oldest son, Cush, and we begin with some of his achievements.

Discussion Questions

1. What are the four divisions of Ham?
2. Who are the Hamitic Cushites?
3. What are the different ethnic names for Cush?

CHAPTER 3

When Life was "Cushy"
— Ancient Cushite Achievements

§

"What you learn is what you die with."

~ AFRICAN PROVERB

Scholars have come to recognize that there was more to the culture of Kush than was previously known. From Egyptian documents and modern archaeological research, it is now known that for five centuries in the second millennium B.C., the kingdom of Kush *flourished* with the political and military prowess to maintain power over a wide territory in Africa.[21]

We will focus on the Cushites because Africans, African Americans, Africans of the Caribbean, South America, Afro-Asiatic, and others of African heritage are descendants of Cush.

The significance of the events comes in Genesis 10 when we learn that Ham's descendants are the Cushites, who are linked geographically to Africa and the Middle East.

Throughout history, so-called Christians have justified slavery by citing the curse of Ham as proof that black Africans were destined and designated for such a station in life. This misin-

---

21   John Noble Wilford, "Scholars Race to Recover a Lost Kingdom on the Nile," The New York Times, 19 June 2007.

terpretation infiltrated the American South and, after the Civil War, was used heavily within the *church*. A civil war, the "curse of Ham," was used by clergymen to fight the notion of racial equality and the rights that would accompany such equality (voting, education, etc.).

For example, Richard River, editor of the Louisville Central Methodist, argued in an 1889 editorial for the popular view that, as long the two races must live together on American soil, the black man "must occupy the position of *inferiority*," and "Ham must be subservient to Japheth."[22]

That belief system is essentially *supremacy* belief and it subtly fuels the resurgence of overt racism in this season, particularly among many older evangelicals and religious conservatives. Especially those who feel threatened the most by the progress of Blacks.

Despite this, people of African descent are on course to fulfilling their purpose, and to that end Cushites take on the characteristics of Ham (warm, dark and hot) and the birth-order characteristics of Cush the first-born; *independence, self-sufficiency,* and *achievement*. This self-sufficiency and achievement can be seen in their technological superiority over other sons and descendants of Noah. How we know the Cushites are Black people:

We know from Their National Designation

The Name Cush, or Kush in Hebrew, means *"black," "dark skin,"* or *"burnt face:"*

---

22 Trillia Newbell, "People of All Color, United in the Image of God," Christianity.com, 2014, http://www.christianity.com/theology/people-of-all-color-united-in-the-image-of-god.html.

They were called:

> *Cushites* by Hebrews
> *Nubians* by Christians
> *Ethiopians* by Greeks
> *Negroes* by the Europeans and Euro-Americans

Cushite was the general term used by the Egyptians in 200 B.C. They were called Ethiopians by the Greeks, who replaced the name Cush with the name Ethiopia by the ninth century.[23]

However, Ethiopia today is not the Ethiopia of the Scripture. The Ethiopia of today is the kingdom of Abyssinia. Modern-day Ethiopia is an independent country in eastern Africa between Sudan and Somalia. Ethiopians claim they are descendants of the kingdom of Saba', which was in ancient southern Arabia, and they do not consider themselves wholly African.[24]

Historians point out that, prior to the 19th century, slave catchers were changing the names of people of these lands from "Cushites" and "Ethiopians" (of the Bible) to "Negroes" and "Coloreds."

This was done to obscure the identity of these African descendants in their own eyes, and in the eyes of the world community. The Cushite Empire was divided into sections and names were changed for political and sometimes for racist motives.

---

23 Timothy Kendall, "Racism and the Rediscovery of Ancient Nubia," PBS, 1999, http://www.pbs.org/wonders/Episodes/Epi1/1_rete1.htm.

24 "Ancient Ethiopia or Kush- Etymology." Taneter Foundation, http://www.taneter.org/ethiopia.html.

To the Jewish historian Josephus, Kush (a different spelling of Cush, the *former* designating the *country* and the latter its *people*) is the name given to the people located south of them.

The facts in the Book of Genesis, the real beginning, remain true. It was the children of Ham (*"Black One"* or *"Burned One"*) who migrated from Sumeria to Africa some time before 3000 B.C. Ham's sons, Egypt and Put (later replaced by Libya, one of Egypt's sons), possessed the lands closest to the entry point from the Middle East. Egypt took the choice Nile Valley. Descendants of Cush, who pushed further south to Nubia (Ethiopia-Sudan) and other parts of the upper Nile, still speak the remnants of the Hamitic and Cushite languages that they brought with them from the confusion of Babel. Kush was a significant civilization, with many ziggurats left behind as evidence. It was the original source culture of the Mesopotamia.

> *"He who is too sure of himself and acts*
> *without thinking is heading for his downfall."*
> **~ AFRICAN PROVERB**

Ancient Sumerian Achievements

The early Cushites were Sumerians from the Mesopotamia. The names of the places mentioned in Genesis 10:10-12—Babel, Erech, Accad, and Calneh, which are specifically linked to Nimrod biblically and historically speaking—were Cushite kingdoms made up of Cushite Sumerians and ruled by Nimrod, a Cushite Sumerian. They had significant achievements and exhibited *extraordinary* mental *ingenuity* and *scholarship*: The following are significant Babylonian/Sumerian contributions:

They were doing mathematical cube roots before 2000 B.C. They found the correct formula for calculating the area of a rectangle, had cuneiform multiplication tables from 1 through 19 and square roots written by 2000 BC.[25] They developed a complete grammar system using pronouns for scholars at the temple school. They developed signature seals to sign their letters.[26]

Specific Contributions of Accad

Accad, or agade, means "book town" and it was so named because of its *famous* libraries. It was the place where the sacred writings were buried before the flood. It had over 30,000 book volumes. They compiled the first grammar system and the first bilingual dictionary, and they had 50,000 tablets. A library of 20,000 volumes, archives of kings, schools with large reference cylinders on revolving stands, dictionaries, encyclopedias, and complete works of law, science, literature and religion. The Arcadians who came from the "mountains of the east" attained a *high* degree of civilization.

In the Babylonian inscriptions, they are called *"the black heads"* and *"the black faces,"* in contrast. They invented the form of writing presented in pictorial hieroglyphics, and the cuneiform system through which they wrote many books on papyrus and clay.[27]

---

25 Luke Mastin, "SUMERIAN/BABYLONIAN MATHEMATICS," The Story of Mathematics, 2010, http://www.storyofmathematics.com/sumerian.html.

26 B. Smith, "SUMERIANACCOMPLISHMENTS," Smithlife Science, 16 August 2015, http://www.smithlifescience.com/sumerian_accomplishments.htm.

27 "Accad," ChristianAnswers.net, http://www.christiananswers.net/dictionary/accad.html.

Some of Later Cushite Kingdom Contributions

Kush was the *first* African kingdom in Africa. The people of Kush developed one of the *oldest* and *greatest* civilizations in Africa. Around 5,000 years ago, a rich and powerful nation called the kingdom of Kush (also referred to as ancient Nubia) was a center of culture and military might in Africa. It was a country that lay to the south of Egypt, beginning at Syene on the First Cataract (Ezekiel 29:10; 30:6), and extending beyond the confluence of the White and Blue Nile. It corresponds generally with what is now known as Sudan (i.e., *"the land of the blacks"*).

This country was known to the Hebrews, and is described in Isaiah 18:1 and Zephaniah. 3:10. They carried on some commercial intercourse with it (Isaiah 45:14). Its inhabitants were descendants of Ham (Gen 10:6; Jer. 13:23; Nubia (Cush) was a land of *great* natural wealth, of gold mines, ivory, copper, frankincense incense, and ebony, which were always prized by her neighbors, but they also produced and traded a variety of goods.

The roots of "Western" civilization, culture, science, technology, and religion are to be found *not in Greece*, but in Black Egypt and Nubia/Kush. From as early as 10,000 B.C. to 1500 A.D., Blacks were in the *forefront* of the development of science, culture, and technology.

The Kingdom of Kush was a *redistributive* system. The state would collect taxes in the form of *surplus* produce and would (unlike our modern American system) *redistribute* it to the *people*. Others believe that most of the society worked on the land, required nothing from the state, and did not contribute to the state. Northern Kush seemed to be more productive and wealthier than the Southern area.[28]

Kush, or Nubia, is the homeland of Africa's *earliest* black culture with a history that can be traced from 3800 B.C. onward through Nubian monuments and artifacts, as well as written records from Egypt and Rome. In antiquity, the mathematical and astronomical sciences necessary for high technologies such as those used in *space technology* and industries were *first* began by Blacks in Khem (Egypt) and Kush (Sudan). These sciences were then passed on to the Sumerians and Babylonians.

Nubia, another name for Kush, an ancient region in northeastern Africa, extended approximately from the Nile River valley eastward to the shores of the Red Sea, southward to about Khartoum.

In what is now the Sudan and westward to the Libyan Desert, the southern part was called Cush (Kush) under the 18th-dynasty pharaohs of ancient Egypt and called Ethiopia by the ancient Greeks. With the rise of the first dynasty in Egypt (c. 2950 B.C.), the [first Nubian] culture and their hopes of independence were extinguished.[29]

The Cushites seized Buhen [in Egypt] and by 1650 B.C. had advanced northward to Aswan. The Cushite ruler Piankhi (Piye) completed the Egyptianization and about 730 B.C. The Cushite ruler Shabaka succeeded Piankhi and conquered all of Egypt

---

28 Wikipedia contributors, "Kingdom of Kush," Wikipedia, The Free Encyclopedia, Wikipedia, The Free Encyclopedia, https://en.wikipedia.org/wiki/Kingdom_of_Kush.

29 Wikipedia contributors, "Nubia," Wikipedia, The Free Encyclopedia, Wikipedia, The Free Encyclopedia,https://en.wikipedia.org/wiki/Nubia.

in about 715 B.C. Moving his capital to Memphis, he founded Egypt's 25th dynasty, which is called *Cushite* in the king lists.[30]

In 701 B.C., Shabaka backed the Hebrew king Hezekiah's revolt against Assyria, and in an Egyptian expedition sacked the capital of Cush, Napata, about 592 B.C. The Cushite capital was then transferred to Meroe, where the Cushite kingdom survived for another 900 years. The Egyptian culture of Nubia grew increasingly *Africanized*.[31] They didn't have to worry, as the Egyptians did, about the annual flooding of the Nile to bring good soil. They had *good* soil. They enjoyed plenty of rainfall all year long to keep things fresh and growing.

As mentioned, Kush had *tremendous* natural *wealth*. It had *gold* mines and *ivory* and *iron ore*. This was the Iron Age. Everyone wanted iron weapons and iron tools. It was the *center* of the iron trade in the ancient African world. Other kingdoms wanted to conquer it and keep the wealth for themselves. They did not allow this to happen. Kush was known as the *Land* of the *Bow* because of its many *expert* archers.[32]

The Contributions of the African Kingdoms of Ghana, Mali, and Songhai in West Africa

GHANA. The first of the great African empires of the Western Sudan to become known to the outside world was Ghana. It would later be developed into a state with a known history of more than a *thousand* years. The Empire was *well*-organized. The political

---

30 Wikipedia contributors, "Twenty-fifth Dynasty of Egypt," Wikipedia, The Free Encyclopedia, Wikipedia, The Free Encyclopedia, https://en.wikipedia.org/wiki/Twenty-fifth_Dynasty_of_Egypt.

31 "Nubia," Encyclopedia Britannica, Chicago: Encyclopedia Brittanica, 1999.

32 Lin Donn, "Ancient Kingdom of Kush (Nubia)," Mr. Donn.org, http://africa.mrdonn.org/kush.html.

progress and social well-being of its people could be favorably compared to the best kingdoms and empires that prevailed in Europe at this time.

The country had a military force of 200,000 men. They had a civil service, strong monarchy, a cabinet, an army, an effective justice system and a regular source of income from trade as well as tribute from vassal kings. Ghana became *wealthy* by collecting taxes from traders who passed through the kingdom.

The power of Ghana was based on the *superior* skill of the people in working iron. The old empire of Ghana is not located in the same place as the modern country of Ghana in West Africa. Two different places! Ancient Ghana was located about 400 miles northwest of the modern-day country of the same name. When the modern country of Ghana won independence, they took the name of a famous (and nearby) ancient kingdom—the kingdom of Ghana.[33]

Wealth through Trade: The king, ably assisted by his council of elders, headed the government. It was divided into districts. A district leader gently guided each district. They had laws that people mostly obeyed.[34]

Army: Ghana was a great military power. Legend says the king could order 200,000 warriors and 40,000 more with bows and arrows. That's a lot of manpower.[35]

Daily Life: The people were farmers, miners, and artists. They made the most wonderful fabrics. Using mud to make de-

33 Calvin R. Robinson, Redman Battle, and Edward W. Robinson, The Journey of the Songhai People, 1st ed. Farmer, 1987.

34 Robinson

35 Robinson

signs on dyed cloth and set in the sun made mud cloth. The sun baked the mud and created a design in the cloth.

They had fresh fruit and sweet potatoes. They had the Niger River, which provided water for farming, washing, bathing, and fish and waterfowl to eat. They worked very hard, but their life was good. They had ample food, and were protected. They sang. They laughed.

Griots: The griots were the storytellers. Kids did not go to school, as we know school. Rather, people collected in the evening to hear the wonderful stories of the griots who were responsible for passing on stories and traditions from one generation to another. They loved to hear any stories.[36]

The people were happy: The people of Ghana loved their life. They were ready for trouble. They had squabbles with their neighbors from time to time and had a huge army. But the king did not want to fight. He wanted to conduct public prayer in the big open plazas of his city, as he had always done.

The people in the villages wanted to hear the griots telling the stories they loved so much. All people, common and noble, wanted to dance at the festivals in the masks they so loved to make and wear, accompanied by the drums for which they were famous.[37]

Wealth through trade: Thanks to the cleverness of their king, the people of ancient Ghana were rich! Ghana never owned gold or salt mines. Salt came from the salt mines controlled by kingdoms to the north of Ghana, kingdoms in the north Sahara Des-

---

36 Donn

37 Robinson, 227

ert. Gold came from the gold mines controlled by kingdoms to the south of Ghana.

What they controlled was the *trade route* between the salt mines and the gold mines. Ghana offered the traders a deal. Their large army assured the traders of safe passage. In return, Ghana restricted trade to gold dust only. They kept the gold nuggets for themselves.

They became the guardians and the negotiators. As more and more traders braved the Trans-Sahara Trade Route, bringing spices and silks to Ghana, and taking gold in trade, the Kingdom of Ghana *flourished*. Ghana and other West African kingdoms soon became collectively known as the *Gold* Coast.[38]

MALI. Its great size made the African kingdom of Mali an even more diverse state than Ghana. Most the people lived in small villages and cultivated rice or sorghum and millet, while some communities specialized in herding and fishing.

Trade *flourished* in the towns, which housed a wide array of craftspeople, The Mali Empire *flourished* because of trade above all else. It contained three *immense* gold mines within its borders. Mali was the source of almost *half* the Old World's gold and salt exports.[39]

Mansa Musa, the 14th century emperor of Mali, was worth an astounding $400 billion, after adjusting for inflation, as calculated by Celebrity Net Worth. That would make him the *richest* man of *all* time, outpacing Carlos Slim Helu, the Mexican telecom giant, and Bill Gates.

---

38   Spokeo.com: Ancient African Kingdom of Ghana (Journey of Songhai

39   Robinson

Thus, the *richest* man of *all* time was not a European or an Asian. Not a Caucasoid or a Mongoloid but an African—a Negroid.[40]

SONGHAI. In the years when Timbuctoo was the great intellectual nucleus of the African Songhai Empire, African scholars were enjoying a *renaissance* that was known and respected throughout most of Africa and in *Europe.*

At this period in African history the University of Sankore was the *educational* capital of the Western Sudan. Askia the Great was one of the *most brilliant* and enlightened administrators of all times. He reorganized the army of Songhai, improved the system of *banking* and *credit,* and made the city-states of GAO, Walta, Timbuctoo, and Jenne into intellectual centers.

Timbuctoo during his reign was a city of more than 100,000 residents, "people filled to the top," says a chronicler of that time, "with gold and dazzling women. Askia encouraged *scholarship* and literature. Students from *all* over Africa and Europe came to Timbuctoo to study *grammar, law,* and *surgery* at the University of Sankore. Scholars came from North Africa and Europe to confer with learned historians and writers of this black empire. A Sudanese literature developed and *many* books were written.

In Scripture Cush was considered the land of Africa below Egypt. To Israel it was the southern part of Africa lying as far as possible. They were the people living on the edge of the southern horizon and they knew no other people.

---

40 Meredith Bennett-Smith, "Mansa Musa Of Mali Named World's Richest Man Of All Time; Gates And Buffet Also Make List," The Huffington Post, 12 October 2012, http://www.huffingtonpost. com/2012/10/17/mansa-musa-worlds-richest-man-all-time_n_1973840.html

Cush was between the second and third cataracts of the Nile Valley. A cataract was a steep waterfall over rock formations. This area was north of Khartoum. They were the people who were due east of and equally south of a location in Africa that was the site of the ancient great kingdom of Ghana that area *flourished* from 300 to 1200 AD.[41]

West African people have traditions that say their ancestors came from another homeland in the distant east or north. Many West African tribes say they came from the east, a reference to a time when blacks settled in the Babylonian region but migrated down through Africa.[42] There are also historical indicators that Cushite Africans also had a Jewish connection.

African Cushites of Brazil, Caribbean, and Latin America

Afro-Latin Americans, or Black Latin Americans, refers to Latin American people of significant African ancestry. The term may also refer to historical or cultural elements in Latin America thought to have emanated from this community.

The term Afro-Latin American refers specifically to people of African ancestry and not to European ancestry. The term is not widely used in Latin America outside academic circles. Normally Afro-Latin Americans are called "black" (Spanish: negro; Portuguese: negro or preto; French: negre or noir).[43]

---

41   Robinson

42   Robinson

43   Wikipedia contributors, "Afro-Latin Americans," Wikipedia, The Free Encyclopedia, Wikipedia, The Free Encyclopedia, https://en.wikipedia.org/wiki/Afro-Latin_Americans.

More commonly, when referring to cultural aspects of African origin within specific countries of Latin America, there are Africans in Latin (Central and South) America and the Caribbean. These western regions were among the first areas of the Americas to be populated by African immigrants. But African immigration to the Americas may have begun before European exploration of the region. African slave trading began before Columbus, and the earliest Spanish and Portuguese explorers. The most direct route from West Africa to the (then) New World was to what we now know as Brazil. Through the 15th and 16th centuries, slavery then moved up the coast of South America through the Caribbean. Today the largest population of African people outside of the African continent is in Brazil. The explorers were likewise accompanied by Black Africans who had been born and reared in Iberia. Over the following four centuries, millions of immigrants from Africa were brought to the New World in servitude.

Today, their descendants form significant ethnic minorities in several Latin American countries, and they are the dominant element in many of the Caribbean nations. Through the centuries, Black people have added their original contributions to the cultural venue of their societies and have exerted a deep influence on all areas of life in Latin America and Caribbean. A dominant African influence is evident in music, dance, the arts, literature, speech forms, and religious practices in Latin America and the Caribbean. Africans, whether as slaves or free immigrants, brought a variety of African cultural influences to the New World.[44]

---

44 "Blacks in Latin America, A Brief History," African American Registry, http://www.aaregistry.org/historic_events/view/blacks-latin-america-brief-history.

Brazil has an interesting history as it relates to Cushite black people. In the jungles of Brazil an important and surprising site was found, a prehistoric rock shelter with thousands of strange pictographs and paintings. Human skeletons that *weren't* European or Indian were found.

Archeologist dated the remains to the ice age. These people were in the Americas *before* the "native" Americans. Archeologists found fragments of bone and charcoal that were 50,000 years old. Next to the charcoal they found the remains of animals those people had eaten.

According to the 1999 BBC documentary on the program *Ancient Voices*, archaeologist discovered among them the oldest skull of a woman they named Lucia. They found it at Serra Da Capivara in remote northeast Brazil, dating between 9,000 and 12,000 years ago, although stone tools and charcoal from the site show evidence of human habitation dating back 50,000 years.

Forensic artist Richard Neave from the University of Manchester UK, who performed the facial reconstruction for the skull, found that the shape and dimensions of the skull, and the face that was reconstructed from it, show it to be the face of a *black* woman.

Neave says: "It has all the features of a *Negroid* face - a descendant from Australian aborigines." He stated that the result was *surprising*." This discovery provides evidence that the *first* Americans were *not* Native Americans, but *blacks*.

Secondly, the other unique history of Brazil concerning Cushite black people, as stated, is that their population includes the *largest* number of people of *African descent* in the *entire* Western Hemisphere.

How did Africans get to Brazil, a country in South of America? As in Mexico and India, in Brazil Africans were transported to the country as slaves. Here, slavery lasted *longer* than in any other country in the New World.[45]

Most slaves entered the country through the port cities of Salvador, Rio de Janeiro, and Santos, which were among the last countries to end the slave trade and slavery. The end of slavery came with difficulty because the Brazilian economy depended on African slave labor.

Brazil abolished the trade in slaves in 1850, and in 1888, all slaves in the country were emancipated, or set free. The slaves themselves took the lead in their fight for freedom by escaping slavery and organizing revolts. But after earning their freedom, slaves faced severe economic hardship and racial discrimination. They did not own any of the land they had worked, and immigrants who came to Brazil were often given jobs *before* black Brazilians.[46]

The African Cushite/Jewish Connection

Historically, there has been a strong affinity between Africans and Jews. That relationship has spanned throughout the continent of Africa. Two examples are the West African and African connection to Judah.

---

45 "How did they get to Brazil?" Exploring Africa. Michigan State U, 2017, http://exploringafrica. matrix.msu.edu/module-fifteen-activity-three/.

46 "How did they get to Brazil?"

West African/Jewish Connection: the *Ashanti* Tribe

An example of the Jewish/African connection were "The *Ashanti* people of West Africa which are descendants of a people who used to live in an ancient city named Ashan. The "ti" on the end of the name of Ashan means "children of," therefore the Ashanti people were *children of Ashan*. This city was mentioned in the Bible in the book of Joshua.

> *Joshua 15:42, GOD'S WORD® Translation: "An additional nine cities with their villages were given to* Judah: *Libnah, Ether,* Ashan"

This city is first referenced in Joshua chapter 15. It is also interesting that a region with Africans was given to and related to *Judah*. It discusses the territory of cities of the kingly tribe of Judah. Verse 1 (KJV) says: "This then was the lot of the tribe of the children of Judah by their families."

Joshua goes on to give the borders and boundaries of Judah. Verse 20 says: "This is the inheritance of the tribe of the children of Judah according to their families." Joshua named the families that make up the kingly tribe of Judah. In verse 42, the city of Ashan is listed as one of the families.

The people of Ashan left Israel between the years 70 and 135 C.E. to flee Roman persecution. The children of Ashan traveled southwest across the North African desert (i.e. the Sinai) down through *Kush* and then west across Chad, Nigeria and finally settling in the "*Gold Coast* of West Africa" south of the Upper Volta.

Throughout their travels and encounters with other kingdoms, the Ashanti people lost portions of their Judaic faith including the Torah, the Prophets and the Holy Writings. When the Ashanti arrived in West Africa, they had the remaining oral laws and a remnant of traditions. The Ashanti formed a West African Jewish kingdom that stretched below the Upper Volta to modern-day Angola. The Ashanti are not the only African tribe of people who share this *extraordinary* history with Jews.

There is also the *Yoruba, Ewe, Bantu, Fulani,* the people of the Songhai kingdom, and the *Ibo* of Nigeria as well as others.[47] This African connection with Judah will be rather significant when I discuss Yadah praise later and the relation to Jesus and Christ unique relation with Judah and Cushites.

Albeit, these Jewish connections suggests that Cushitic people of African descent are also related to, if not part of, God's chosen people. The tribe of Judah had an extraordinary connection to Cushitic people of African descent.

Cushite Africans, Egypt, and the Tribe of Judah

The Tribe of Judah, which is the tribe that Jesus descended from, was a *dark-complexioned* tribe of Hebrews. Historian Wilson Armistead states quite plainly: "The descendants of a colony of Jews, originally from Judea, settled on the coast of *Africa,* and were *black.*"[48]

Judah was the largest Israelite tribe to leave Egypt, which means that of the mixed multitude that left with Moses, Judah was the tribe that was *most* mixed. Biblical scholar J. Daniel Hays Ph.D., of Southwestern Baptist Theological Seminary says that although Cushites had been in Egypt for *centuries* it was during the time of the Exodus story (eighteenth and nineteenth dynas-

---

47 Silas, "The Israelites Went to West Africa Part 1 of 4," Gleanings in Hebrew, 31 July 2010, http://gleaningsinhebrew.blogspot.com/2010/07/israelites-went-to-west-africa-part-1.html.

48 Wilson Armistead, A tribute for the Negro. New York: Manchester, 1848.

ty) that they arrived in Egypt in *great* numbers, and while some of them were slaves like the Hebrews, certainly not all of them, although many Euro-American Bible interpreters try to paint them that way.

Cushites were found in other sectors of society. There is clear documentation that Cushites worked in Egyptian society up until the establishment of the 19th dynasty and the coming of King Ramses in 1292 B.C.

They not only ruled Egypt for thousands of years, but they also constituted the majority of those who made up the Egyptian middle class and intelligentsia including the clerics, theologians, artists, writers, poets, medics, artisans, builders, architects, mathematicians and professionals."[49]

Egypt and Cush had a close relationship historically, genetically and culturally. The two nations are mentioned *more* than any other nations in the Bible. The Egyptians and Cushites were ethnically the closest in the region, often exchanging people, genes, resources, and culture over many centuries—and, to reiterate, the 25th dynasty of Egypt was the Cushite dynasty ruled by Cushite pharaohs like Piankhy and Tarhaka.

It is almost certain that among the large group of persons designated as the *"mixed multitude"* would have been many Cushites. The tribe of Judah was a Semitic/Hamitic people but during their time in Egypt they intermarried with the Hamitic Africans of Cush and Mizraim (Egypt).

---

49 Femi Fani-Kayoke, "Who Are The Yoruba People? (Part 3)," Premium Times, 3 June 2013, http://www.premiumtimesng.com/opinion/137358-who-are-the-yoruba-people-part-3-by-femi-fani-kayode.html

Of the 12 tribes of Hebrews that left Egypt, Judah was the *largest* tribe. There were over 74,000 people in the tribe of Judah. Large numbers left Egypt with the Hebrews during the Exodus, but Judah had the highest population of all the tribes, so it certainly stands to reason that there were large numbers of Cushite *Africans* among the populace of Judah.

When God called the people of Israel out of Egypt, He designated the nation as a son. Judah would have been the most sizable tribe to be called out.

> Hosea 11:1 NIV: *"When Israel was a child, I loved him, and out of Egypt I called my son."*

When Christ the Lion of Judah was a *child*, the angel of the Lord once again called *Judah* out of *Egypt* by calling Jesus out of Egypt, where He had gone to hide from Herod's infanticide campaign.

> Matthew 2:13-15, NIV: *"When they had gone, an angel of the Lord appeared to Joseph in a dream. "Get up," he said, "take the child and his mother and escape to Egypt. Stay there until I tell you, for Herod is going to search for the child to kill him." So he got up, took the child and his mother during the night and left for Egypt, where he stayed until the death of Herod. And so was fulfilled what the Lord had said through the prophet: "Out of Egypt I called my son."*

The tribe of Judah had this affinity with Africa through the tribe itself and also through Christ. That affinity would have been inclusive of both Khemite and Cushite Africans.

Adding to this evidence for Cushites in Egypt as part of the *"mixed multitude"* is the fact that Moses, a Hebrew, married a *Cushite* African woman from Sudan in Numbers 12. When Miriam and

Aaron spoke against Moses making racist comments about the woman, and criticizing Moses for marrying this *African* female, Miriam received severe punishment from God by being struck with leprosy (Numbers 12:1-10). Since she criticized the woman because of the *color* of her skin, Miriam received God's judgment through a disease that *discolored* her skin.

For the leader of the Israelis to marry a Sudanese African woman was significant. It suggests that a precedent had already been set in Egypt. Such a marriage between African Cushites, Hebrews,[50] and Khemite Africans would have been probably more common than not.

Hebrew scholar Shaul Bar says many of the mercenaries (many of whom would have been Cushites) intermarried with Hebrews in Egypt.[51] This interbreeding partly explains why Judah was the *largest* and *most* ethnically *mixed* tribe coming out of Egypt.

Further proof is the fact that Moses' great nephew and priest was named *Phinehas* a name that means the *"Nubian," "Cushite,"* or the *"Negro,"* a clear reference to *Cush*. There is strong evidence that Cushites were part of the mixed crowd that came out of Egypt, a group of people who were the byproduct of miscegenation both ethnically and culturally.

Part of the Cushitic people come from the tribe of Judah. Cush was regarded as a large portion of Eastern Africa—not merely what we know as Ethiopia today. It also covered the Sudan, Somalia, and further.

---

50 J. Daniel Hays, From Every People and Nation: A Biblical Theology of Race (New Studies in Biblical Theology), Westmont: IVP Academic, 2003.

51 Shaul Bar, "WHO WERE THE 'MIXED MULTITUDE'?" Hebrew Studies, vol. 49, 2008, pp. 27–39. JSTOR, www.jstor.org/stable/27913875.

So, when we see in Genesis 10:6 and the sons of Ham; Cush, Mizraim, Phut, and Canaan. Cush is the eastern part below Mizraim (Egypt), and Phut is Libya. Canaan is the land of Africa to the north. A segment of Cush is from Ham, but another portion is related to the tribe of Shem. They are the true descendants of the tribe of Judah.[52] This interbred tribe of Judah that included *Hamitic* and *Shemitic* blood produced *Jesus Christ* the Savior. Hebrews 7:14, NIV, says:

> *"For it is clear that our Lord descended from* Judah ...*"*

In the genealogy of Christ, *Tamar*, the daughter-in-law of Judah as well as the mother of two of his children, was also a Hamitic Canaanite. Canaan was Ham's younger son and *Cush's* younger brother. Their children along with Tamar are mentioned in Matthew 1:1-3, The Message, as part of the genealogy of Christ.

> *The family tree of* Jesus Christ, *David's son, Abraham's son:*
> *2 Abraham had Isaac, Isaac had Jacob, Jacob had* Judah *and his brothers, 3* Judah *had Perez and Zerah* (the mother was Tamar)."

Thus, Perez and Zerah who are listed in Jesus genealogy from Judah, were mixed-race children, having both *Hamitic* and *Shemitic* blood, so the blood of Christ came from this first admixture. As previously stated, the Hebrews of Judah intermarried with Cushite Sudanese Africans, who were in large numbers at that time, as well as some Kemitic Africans from Egypt becoming the mixed multitude that left in the exodus.

---

52   The WikiAnswers Community, "What tribe of Judah do Ethiopian people come from?," Answers. com, http://www.answers.com/Q/What_tribe_of_Judah_do_Ethiopian_people_come_from.

> Deuteronomy 10:22, MSG: *"When your ancestors entered*
> *Egypt, they numbered a mere seventy souls. And now look*
> *at you—you look more like the stars in the night skies in number.*
> *And your God did it."*

This intermingling with Hamitic blood continued with the birth of *Salmon* to Obed and *Hamitic* Canaanite named Rahab. The increased Hamitic intermingling of blood also came when David and Bathsheba, possibly a Hamitic Hittite, sexually intermingled. I don't' think David would have been attracted to Bathsheba if she had been your typical Hebrew woman; he had seen a number of them. No, there was something extra special about her, say, like her dark-complexioned skin and anatomy.

This may have been the reason why most of Solomon's wives were also women of *color*. *No European* districts or tribes were mentioned as being part of Solomon's harem. The Song of Solomon tells how Solomon fell madly in love with a woman who referred to herself as being *black*, stating, *"I am black but comely [beautiful]."* (**Song of Solomon 1:5, KJV**)

Yet many of the commentaries on this woman's color argue that she was a white maiden sporting a deep tan. Scriptures detail the lineage of Solomon's many wives. Remember that Solomon had 700 wives and 300 concubines, and many of these women were from the land of Ham called Egypt and from other descendants of Ham. The Scriptures in 1 Kings 11:1-4, KJV, relate that:

> *"King Solomon loved many strange [foreign] women, together*
> *with the daughter of Pharaoh, women of the Moabites,*
> *Ammonites, Edomites, Zidonians, and Hittites; of the nations*
> *concerning which the LORD said unto the children of Israel,*
> *Ye shall not go in to them, neither shall they come in unto you:*
> *for surely they will turn away your heart after their gods: but*

Solomon clave unto these in love. And he had seven hundred wives, princesses, and three hundred concubines: and his wives turned away his heart. For it came to pass, when Solomon was old, that his wives turned away his heart after other gods ..."

One group of women Solomon was attracted to was *Hittite* women. Bathsheba was originally married to a *Hittite* named Uriah. Could it be that he was drawn to these Hamitic Hittites because his mother was a *dark-complexioned* Hittite?

It would explain why her son, King Solomon, would have an attraction and penchant for dark-complexioned women like Shulamith in Song of Solomon 1:5 "who by her own words says, "**I am black**" since men are often attracted to women like their mother, including their color.[53]

All this means that Jesus had both the Shemitic and Hamitic blood of Judah flowing through his veins. The blood he shed was for all men, but genealogically it came particularly *from* two men, *Shem* and *Ham*. (Genesis 10:6).

The blood he bled at Calvary was *spiritually* Holy blood, but *naturally* it was *Hamitic* and *Shemitic* blood. God chose the line of *Shem* and *Ham* to bring his Son into the world it was a royal line that produced the *King* of *Kings* – the *Prince* of Peace - the *Messiah* of Israel.

Thus, the people of African descent—the Cushites—are related to the tribe of Judah, ethnically through the miscegenation of Hamites and Shemites over time, but prophetically through Yadah (Judah) praise with their hands, which I will discuss more in-depth in a later chapter.

---

53 "King Solomon's Penchant for Dark-Skinned Women," *Blacks in the Bible*, http://www. blacksinthebible.net/Shulamitebridedoc.htm.

That reality alludes to the fact that these Cushite Africans were created for *greatness* that was consummated with Christ but began with the exploits of another notable Cushite named Nimrod, and he started out as one bad, awesome brother.

Discussion Questions

1. How are the Sumerians related to Cush?
2. What were the three major kingdoms of Africa and some their achievements?
3. How is Cush related to Jews?
4. How does Christ relate to Shem and Ham?

CHAPTER 4

One Bad Brother – The Legacy of Nimrod

❧

"He who is called a man must behave like a man"

~ **AFRICAN PROVERB**

We will use different translations of Genesis 10:8-10 in our discussion of the man Nimrod. The Scriptures state:

> **KJV:** *"And Cush begat* Nimrod: *he began to be a* mighty one *in the earth. He was a mighty hunter before the LORD: wherefore it is said, Even as Nimrod the* mighty hunter *before the LORD. And the beginning of his kingdom was Babel, and Erech, and Accad, and Calneh, in the land of Shinar."*

> **GNT:** *"Cush had a son named Nimrod, who became the world's* first great conqueror. *By the Lord's help he was a great hunter, and that is why people say, "May the Lord make you as great a hunter as Nimrod!" At first his kingdom included Babylon, Erich, and Accad, all three of them in Babylonia."*

> **MSG:** *"Cush also had Nimrod. He was the* first great warrior *on Earth. He was a* great hunter *before GOD. There was a saying, "Like Nimrod, a great hunter before GOD." His kingdom*

> got its start with Babel; then Erech, Akkad, and Calneh in the
> country of Shinar."

> **YLT:** "And Cush hath begotten Nimrod; he hath begun to be a
> hero in the land; he hath been a hero in hunting before Jehovah;
> therefore it is said, `As Nimrod the hero [in] hunting before
> Jehovah.' And the first part of his kingdom is Babel, and Erech,
> and Accad, and Calneh, in the land of Shinar"

Genesis 10, in accounting for the descendants of Japheth and
Shem, doesn't state anything significant.

However, when it comes to Ham, it pauses to state a great
achievement of a Cushitic descendant of Ham. This one man sur-
passed *all* the others in his day.

Dr. Henry Hampton Halley, author of *Halley's Bible Handbook*,
says of Nimrod:

> "He was the most outstanding leader for some 400 years between
> the flood and Abraham."

Albeit, let's review some factors concerning Nimrod in our
endeavor to understand him better.

His Name (Nimrod) may have come from the Mesopota-
mian Ninurta, a name that came to be applied to a war god who
was also called the *arrow* (the name arrow will be become significant in the chapter titled "Come Out With Your Hands Up." The
mighty hero is probably of foreign origin, although in Hebrew, it
can mean rebellion or can mean *valiant, strong,* the *arrow* ... the
mighty *hero*.

Euro-centric Bible scholars try to associate his name only
with rebellion, but the Sumerians and the Babylonians wrote

about this person as well as the Assyrians and the Hittites. Even in Palestine, tablets have been found with his name on them.

He was to them the most popular *hero* in the Ancient near East. He was a descendent of Cush through Noah's son Ham and, according to the book of Genesis, he was the founder of Sumerian kingdoms (Genesis 11:6-10).[54]

The Significance of Nimrod

If the name NIMROD were an acronym, the letters of his name could represent the following a (**N**aturally **I**nfluential **M**ighty **R**escuer of **D**ominion)

He was the first great conqueror, and warrior hero. Many Euro-centric Bible scholars portray him as primarily negative; some of that is true.

However, we can no longer permit Euro-centric scholars to be the final authority on the Bible or Black history given their legacy of racist interpretation. We now have scholars of African descent who can more accurately reflect who we are in Scripture.

Nimrod and his descendants had the greatest impact upon the world next to Abraham. He and his descendants had a great positive influence on the world technologically and had an important influence on the world spiritually.

He exemplifies important spiritual principles and God's agenda for Black people. He was supposed to depict the prototype warrior *archer* of the Cushites and deliverer of people. He

---

54 Reinhold Warttig Mattfeld y de la Torre Walter, "Identifying Genesis' Mid-First Millennium BCE Origins via Onomastic Research on Cain and Nimrod," BibleOrigins.net, 9 March 2002, http://www.bibleorigins.net/CainNimrod.html.

was a sign of things to come, particularly for God's purpose for people of African descent in the last days. He was an example of the endowments God imparted to them, some of which are the following:

Physical Capability

Now the Scriptures state *"and Cush begat Nimrod: and he began to be a mighty one in the earth."* (*Genesis 10:8, KJV*)

Cush was the father of Nimrod. Nimrod grew up to be a *mighty hero* on the earth. He was a mighty hunter in the Lord's eyes. That's why people sometimes compare others with Nimrod. They would say, "They are like Nimrod."

The Bible is saying the first man to become a superhero on the earth was a *Cushite*, a black man.

> *Cush was the father of Nimrod, who became a mighty warrior on the earth* NIV
>
> *Cush was also the ancestor of Nimrod, who was the first* heroic warrior *on earth* NLT
>
> *Cush fathered Nimrod; he was the* first *on earth to be a* mighty man. *ESV*
>
> *"He hath begun to be a* hero *in the land; he hath been a* hero *in hunting before Jehovah; therefore it is said, 'As Nimrod the* hero *in hunting before Jehovah.' YLT*

The original language word for *mighty* is *Gibbor*, which means *powerful warrior, champion, strong valiant man, strong man, able man, chief, and superhero.* It is a term that denotes a person of extraordinary physical appearance and ability.

Vocational Continuity

> Genesis 10:9 further states that Nimrod was "a mighty hunter." The word hunter suggests he was a protective fighter. Dr. Halley of Halley's Bible Handbook says his fame as a mighty hunter meant he was a food provider and protector of the people at a time when wild animals were a continual menace. Early Babylonian seals depict Nimrod as a warrior king in combat with a lion.

Moreover, this term also suggests that Nimrod was an objective setter. Nimrod was a hunter by nature; that is, he persistently set goals concerning the game he wanted to catch and went after it; he pursued it until he achieved it. He was a purpose-driven and goal-oriented Cushitic black man.

Theological Affinity

The passage says that Nimrod was a mighty hunter *before* the *Lord*. This statement *"before the Lord"* although brief has significant spiritual implications as seen when we translate some words in the statement. The word *before Paniym* comes from the word *Panaw* which means to face, to look, prepare, to regard, to appear, to have respect for, to *favor*, to be in sight of, to be in the presence of, or *honor*.

The term Lord is *Yâhovah* [/yeh•ho•vaw/] or *Yahweh*: the proper name of the one true God, "the existing One." His relationship with God was so well-known it became a colloquial expression and adage, "Wherefore it is said even as Nimrod the mighty hunter *before* the *Lord*." Good News translation says, "By the *Lord's help* he was a great hunter."

> *Holman Christian Standard says, "He was a powerful hunter*
> *in the sight of the Lord. That is why it is said, 'Like Nimrod, a*
> *powerful hunter in the sight of the Lord.'"*

Nimrod was a mighty hunter in *God's sight* and in *God's presence* who was blessed to receive favor and help from the Lord to become an extraordinary archer hunter. He had a relationship with God *before* Abraham.

Nimrod was also a great kingdom builder in Genesis 10:10 we read and the beginning of his kingdom' The word *beginning* [*re'shiyth* /ray•sheeth/] means *first* in place, time, or order, first in rank, first regarding dignity, best, chief, choice part, that which is superior in value to all others in the same class or kind.

It comes from a word *roche*, which means chief, excellent, highest, the head, or principal. The word implies that not only did Nimrod start kingdoms, but that those kingdoms were the *first* and the *best* of their kind.

Nimrod gets blamed for the tower of Babel by many Euro-American Bible scholars, but nowhere is his name mentioned in the episode. As related in Genesis 11:1-4, KJV:

> *"And the whole earth was of one language, and of one speech.*
> *And it came to pass, as they journeyed from the east, that they*
> *found a plain in the land of Shinar; and they dwelt there. And*
> *they said one to another, go to, let us make brick, and burn them*
> *thoroughly. And they had brick for stone, and slime had they for*
> *morter. And they said, Go to, let us build us a city and a tower,*
> *whose top may reach unto heaven; and let us make us a name, lest*
> *we be scattered abroad upon the face of the whole earth."*

In the Nov. 5, 1990, edition of U.S. News and World Report, an article entitled "Mother Tongue" reported that scientists had reconstructed language from a family tree based on world-wide comparisons of human genes. The human tree mirrored the branching of the world's 5,000 languages.

They traced the languages backed to a *mother tongue* from which *all* other languages originated. There was one language from which all other languages emerged and it was an *African* mother tongue.

They concluded that the mother tongue originated in Africa. Adam and Eve were the first humans on earth with language that passed from generation to generation.[55]

Thus, the African mother language had to start with Adam and Eve, who were created in Africa/Mesopotamia, and from there earth and apparently spoke an African mother language that became the linguistic heritage of the people of the earth for generations up to the point at which God confounded the language at the tower of Babel (Genesis 11:1-9, KJV).[56]

> "And the whole earth was of one language, and of one speech. And it came to pass, as they journeyed from the east, that they found a plain in the land of Shinar; and they dwelt there. And they said one to another, Go to, let us make brick, and burn them thoroughly. And they had brick for stone, and slime had they for morter. And they said, Go to, let us build us a city and a tower, whose top may reach unto heaven; and let us make us a name, lest we be scattered abroad upon the face of the whole earth. And the LORD came down to see the city and the tower, which the children

---

55 "The Mother Tongue," U.S News and World Report, 5 November 1990, 60-70.

56 "The Mother Tongue", pp. 60-70

of men builded. And the LORD said, Behold, the people is one, and they have all one language; and this they begin to do: and now nothing will be restrained from them, which they have imagined to do. Go to, let us go down, and there confound their language, that they may not understand one another's speech. So the LORD scattered them abroad from thence upon the face of all the earth: and they left off building the city. Therefore, is the name of it called Babel; because the LORD did there confound the language of all the earth: and from thence did the LORD scatter them abroad upon the face of all the earth."

Combining science with Scripture we conclude the following. Science says there was an original *one* language from which *all* other languages emerged and that this language was an African mother tongue. The Scripture says that there was a time that the whole earth spoke *one* language and *one* speech.

Therefore, we surmise that the one language spoken in Genesis by the whole earth was the original African mother tongue. This language was, in fact, the language that God confounded.

There is no mention of Nimrod's name in Genesis 11. The building of the tower was a people's decision based on how many times the words *they* and *us* are used. There is no clear leader in this passage; it is the *people* making this decision. The Scripture says, *"they said to one another."*

How can someone as powerful and prominent as Nimrod not be mentioned at all? This was raw democracy gone awry. It was people engaging in anarchy against God.

Babel is where God confused the language of the people. It was the name given to the tower, probably a Ziggurat, after God confounded the language, scattering the peoples of the earth.

However, Scripture says that the *beginning* of Nimrod's kingdom was *Babel*. His kingdom did not begin *before* Babel; it began
with Babel. The name *Babel* means *"confusion;"* essentially Nimrod, a Cushitic black man, took a world in confusion and political
chaos that had lost language—unity—and built his kingdom out
of it, establishing order where there was none.

He replaced the people's *anarchy* with his own *autocracy* to
bring order.

A sentence from the Akkadian language concerning the people means **"All of them were lord."** Some scholars have suggested that this may have been intended to signify the absence of a
central authority in Kish for a time.[57] The time was probably before Nimrod and the confounding of the languages of the people
at Babel.

Kish was an ancient city of Sumer, the Sumerians were Cushites, and Nimrod was a Sumerian Cushite. He was called Nim-ra-
da, Lord of Marada town southwest of Kish. The Sumerians of
Kish, founded around 3200 B.C., had a dynasty including 23 kings.

The name *Kish* is a form of *Kush*. The first kingdom of ancient
Sumeria and Sumerians called themselves Kishites/Kish or Cush.

Nimrod colonized Assyria and gained renown as an empire
builder. The cities of Babylon, Erech (Uruk) and Accad (Agade)
are among the oldest in the world known to man. His kingdom
consisted of Akkad and Babylon in the northern part and Erech
and Sumer in the southern part.

He was the father and founder of Nineveh and Calah. His
name is perpetuated in several places including Birs Nimrud,

---

57 Wikipedia contributors, "Kish (Sumer)," Wikipedia, The Free Encyclopedia, Wikipedia, The Free
    Encyclopedia https://en.wikipedia.org/wiki/Kish_(Sumer).

Southwest of Babylon and Nimrud in Assyria; his name is preserved in many cities.

A common feature found in tribes all down through East Africa to the farthest reaches of Southern Africa (e.g. the Zulus) is the appearance of rulers dressed identically to the Greek versions of Nimrod, the black Hercules wearing a lion or leopard skin. If the truth be told Hercules was modeled after Nimrod.[58]

Yes, Cush became a great people, and Nimrod was a strong valiant leader, but his idolatry was the beginning of our downfall and thus the people of Cush sustained several losses as a people and as a civilization.

We lost physical capability—Although we maintain some of that athletic prowess, people of African descent still lead several mortality rates concerning diseases. Africans in various countries are being devastated by AIDS, malaria, ebola, and other infectious diseases.[59]

We lost political sovereignty—The Cushite Sumerian/Acadian kingdom collapsed around 2002 B.C.;[60] Cushite West African Kingdoms all ended. By the 19th century much of Africa was dominated, controlled, or colonized by Europeans.[61]

---

58 Wikipedia contributors, "Nimrod," Wikipedia, The Free Encyclopedia, Wikipedia, The Free Encyclopedia, https://en.wikipedia.org/wiki/Nimrod.

59 Kerri Henderson, "Health Promotion and the African American Community," Minority Nurse Writer, Winter 2013.

60 Wikipedia contributors, "Babylonia," Wikipedia, The Free Encyclopedia, Wikipedia, The Free Encyclopedia, https://en.wikipedia.org/wiki/Babylonia.

61 Sanderson Beck, "Africa and the British 1700-1950," San.Beck.org, 2010, http://www.san.beck.org/16-10-WestAfricaBritish.html.

We lost technological credibility—It was lost, stolen, or adopted without giving us recognition. Many of the black inventions' patents were not obtained or were sold without credit.

Given European and Euro-American dominance and influence, history has not been kind to people of African descent when it comes to acknowledging our inventions and achievements.

These losses were direct consequences of the spiritual idolatry of our original African parents, Nimrod and the Cushitic people.[62]

Discussion Questions

1. What was the significance of Nimrod?
2. What was the theological impact of Nimrod?
3. What were the other impacts of Nimrod?
4. Did we lose because of Nimrod?
5. How do these losses impact people of African descent?

---

62 Mary Bellis, "Colors of Innovation," Thought Co, 6 August 2016, https://www.thoughtco.com/colors-of-innovation-1991281.

CHAPTER 5

An Idol Mind is the Devil's Workshop

☙

"One falsehood spoils a thousand truths."
~ **AFRICAN PROVERB (ASHANTI, GHANA)**

All the stories of Nimrod describe him as *dark*-skinned or *black*, and a mighty hunter. As mentioned. Genesis 10 describes Nimrod as a mighty hunter both meaning a warrior as well as animal hunter. He was worshipped as a God.

Nimrod's spouse also became immortalized. She was also known by multiple names: Aphrodite, Venus, Istar, Ishtar, Easter, Semiramis (*Sumeria comes from her name*), Freya, etc. Cush was also immortalized as Zeus, Kissos, Shiva, and Siva.

The gods of the ancient world were the Cushite kings and queens who were worshipped. Clearly this was a direct violation of the original priestly purpose of our African father, Adam, who was supposed to worship the true God, and it was a deviation from Nimrod's original purpose of being a warrior archer with God's favor.

In addition, many of the gods of Nimrod and the Cushites were also more or less personifications of Satan. Several of the Babylonian, Sumerian gods correspond to Satan:

Idol God	Satan's Name
Babylonian Serpent	the serpent
Enlil, god of wind and air	Prince of power of Air
Bel Marduk Meradach, chief over world	God of this world
Nergal, god of destruction	Abaddon, Apollyon destroyer
Utu, god of sun and light	Lucifer: Light bearer, bright shining
Ishtar, goddess of temptation	the Tempter

Moreover, the principal state deity was Amun, whose cult was celebrated at the great state temples of Napata and Meroe, and at many other places. In the Meroitic period (c. 350 BCE– 350 CE) the Kushite pantheon came to include several deities. The most important of them was Apedemak, a lion-headed warrior god worshiped in Nubia by Meroitic peoples. Several Meroitic temples dedicated to Apedemak are known from the Butana region: Naqa, Meroe, and Musawwarat es-Sufra, which seems to be his chief cult place.

In the temple of Naqa built by the rulers of Meroe, Apedemak was depicted as a three-headed lion god with four arms, but he is also depicted as a single-headed lion deity who was a special tutelary of the ruling family; (in 1 Peter 5:8, Satan is called a lion). He was a god of victory and also of agricultural fertility. There were temples of Apedemak at Meroe and at several other towns in the southern part of Kush.[63]

Because of the idolatry of Nimrod and his followers, it appears these early Cushite kingdoms produced a *false* worship, political, and religious system that affected the world for the next 3,000 years.

So then, based on my interpretation of Genesis 10–11, we see that Cushitic African people were greatly impacted by idolatry, which started with our original parents; moved to Nimrod and carried over even into our worship practices today. The idolatry of Nimrod and the Cushites was not only a transgression against Yahweh, it became Satan's ultimate distraction to our divine destiny.

However, this was not the conclusion of the story. For God had a plan for the people of Cush, and the people of African descent that would bring about restoration in these modern times, and that will result in a promotion of Cushitic people to a place of prominence. Although the plan has included some chastening, God's message to the Cushitic people of African heritage is this: Jeremiah 29:11 (NIV)

> "For I know the plans I have for you, declares the Lord, plans to prosper *you and not to harm you, plans to give you* hope *and a* future"

Those plans have been etched in prophecy, but because of racist biblical scholarship they have been hidden. We will unravel the prophetic destiny of the people of African descent, for we are

---

63   Wikipedia contributors, "Apedemak," Wikipedia, The Free Encyclopedia, Wikipedia, The Free Encyclopedia, https://en.wikipedia.org/wiki/Apedemak.

on God's timetable. He has determined that what we lost we'll recover.

❧

"However long the night may last, there will be a morning"
~ **AFRICAN PROVERB**

The good news for people of African descent is that what we lost was by no means the conclusion of our journey. God has an exciting destiny for our people and has unveiled that plan in this season of human history. A season many Bible scholars refer to as the end times or the last days.

God is presently positioning us for a gloriously significant purpose, and has lodged the truth of what He is going to do in prophetic predictions of Scripture. Euro-American scholarship has prevented us from seeing God's plan, some of which was intentional, and some of which was inadvertent.

Nevertheless, one such prophecy for review is Isaiah 18:1-7. We must first present the misrepresented translation and then the more accurate translation.

Discussion Questions

1. What is the relationship between Satan, worship, and idolatry?
2. Why is worship important for people of African descent?

CHAPTER 6

Translation Misrepresentation – The Concealing of Isaiah Prophecy

❧

"A false story has seven endings. It can be told in many ways. Like a snowball grows as it rolls along."

~ **AFRICAN PROVERB (SWAHILI)**

A definition of the word *conceal* means to hide or withdraw from observation; to cover or keep from sight; to prevent the discovery of; and to withhold the knowledge of.

Concerning the history and destiny of people of African descent there has been an attempt to conceal the truth concerning who we really are and where we are going.

This endeavor to conceal has largely been the practice of Euro-American historians, theologians, teachers and the media. The following is a prophecy concerning people of African heritage and God's purpose, for them in the last days: This is what I refer to as *Afro-eschatology*: the study of Gods purpose for those of African descent in the present and the future.

Isaiah 18:1-7, KJV: "Woe to the land shadowing with wings, which is beyond the rivers of Ethiopia: that sendeth ambassadors by the sea, even in vessels of bulrushes upon the waters, saying, Go, ye swift messengers, to a nation scattered and peeled, to a people terrible from their beginning hitherto; a nation meted out and trodden down, whose land the rivers have spoiled! All ye inhabitants of the world, and dwellers on the earth, see ye, when he lifteth up an ensign on the mountains; and when he bloweth a trumpet, hear ye. For so the LORD said unto me, I will take my rest, and I will consider in my dwelling place like a clear heat upon herbs, and like a cloud of dew in the heat of harvest. For afore the harvest, when the bud is perfect, and the sour grape is ripening in the flower, he shall both cut off the sprigs with pruning hooks, and take away and cut down the branches. They shall be left together unto the fowls of the mountains, and to the beasts of the earth: and the fowls shall summer upon them, and all the beasts of the earth shall winter upon them. In that time shall present be brought unto the LORD of hosts of a people scattered and peeled, and from a people terrible from their beginning hitherto; a nation meted out and trodden under foot, whose land the rivers have spoiled, to the place of the name of the LORD of hosts, the mount Zion."

This is a prophetic word concerning God's redemptive plan and restoration destiny for Cushitic people of African descent in the last days.

'Woe to the land.' Hoi says this interjection should be translated "ho' for it is properly a particle of calling: 'Ho land' Attend, give ear. The heading in the English version, "God will destroy the Cushites," is a mistake arising from the wrong rendering "woe," whereas the Hebrew does not express a threat, but is an appeal, a calling, attention "Ho." He is not speaking against but to the Cushites, calling on them to hear his prophetic announcement.

This passage has a dual meaning *historically* and *prophetically*. Historically the passage refers to the time just before the great invasion of Sennacherib (about 700 B.C.), when Tirhakah was the Cushitic African King and ruled at Napata, capital of the Cushitic Kingdom of Africa.[64]

However, many Eurocentric Bible scholars admit that this chapter is one of the most obscure in Scripture; meaning so faintly perceptible as to lack clear delineation; indistinct, hard to make out, not easily understood.[65]

There is a reason this passage is obscure to those scholars. It is because there is also a *prophetic* meaning of the passage that relates to the destiny and last day move of God concerning Cushitic African people, which can only be understood by revelation from the Spirit of God.

Therefore, this passage is a study and an interpretation based on *Afro-eschatology*. Eschatology is theology concerned with the final events in the history of the world or of humankind.[66] And the term African refers to a native or inhabitant of Africa, a person and especially a black person of African ancestry.[67] '*Afro-eschatology*' would be theology that is concerned with and focused on the final events in the history of persons from African ancestry.

Regrettably, Eurocentric scholars want to be the last word on Scripture interpretation because if they can control biblical interpretation then they will control the biblical narrative, and if they control the narrative then they will control the identity of

---

64 "Matthew Henry's Commentary," Bible Hub, http://biblehub.com/commentaries/mhc/matthew/6.htm.

65 "Matthew Henry's Commentary"

66 "Eschatology," Merriam-Webster.com, Merriam-Webster.

67 "African," Merriam-Webster.com, Merriam-Webster.

biblical characters, cultures, and ethnic groups mentioned in scripture.

When they reference a so-called expert they simply quote other Eurocentric scholars with the same ethnocentric bias that they have. This is often the case with scholars with a conservative evangelical predisposition.

Often when it comes to recognizing people of color in the Bible or prophecy, Eurocentric scholars' racially tainted approach to Scripture interpretation prevents them from seeing things that are veiled in the text. *Prejudice* inhibits *revelation* and distorts *interpretation*.

There is an interpretive remedy and that is revelation from God: Although racism can also impede revelation, if a scholar earnestly searches for the untainted truth, he or she will be open to true revelation.

> *Amos 3:7, ESV: "For the Lord God does nothing without* revealing *his* secret *to his servants the* prophets."

> *1 Corinthians 2:9-10, NLT: "No eye has seen, no ear has heard, and no mind has imagined what God has prepared for those who love him." but it was to us that God* revealed *these things by his* Spirit. *For his Spirit searches out everything and shows us God's* deep secrets."

The King James translators, in translating this passage, did a disservice to the Cushitic Africans who are the subject of the text. Let's review a few of the issues with the passage as translated from the King James Version when you look at the meanings of the English words in the text.

a. **Ethiopia:** Translators used this term instead of the ancient term Cush. The ancient Greeks referred to Ethiopia as Cush. The problem was they were not referring to ancient people of color in the Bible but rather a people of their day of Abyssinia who didn't see themselves as black (although to see them is to behold a people who are obviously a people of color).

b. **Scattered:** means to cause to separate widely, to cause to vanish, to fling away heedlessly, squander, to separate and in various directions. Merriam Webster's *scattered* has a negative connotation compared to the positive Biblical meaning.

c. **Peeled:** means to strip off an outer layer of to remove by stripping, to take off one's clothes, to break away from a group or formation. Again, English has a negative connotation but the Biblical meaning is different.

d. **Trodden down:** means to step or walk on or over, to beat or press with the feet, trample, to subdue or repress as if by trampling, crush. Negative English connotation is different from original Hebrew meaning.

e. **Terrible:** defined as extremely bad, strongly repulsive, obnoxious, notably unattractive or objectionable, of very poor quality. English meaning gives negative connotation from original Hebrew meaning.

f. **Spoiled:** meaning damaged seriously, or ruined. This word in English has negative connotation different from original Hebrew word.

Discussion Questions

1. What is Afro-eschatology and why is it important?
2. What are some of the mistranslated words in the text?
3. Why is the prophetic Scripture in Isaiah 18:1-7 significant?

CHAPTER 7

The Translation Revelation – The Revealing of Isaiah 18 Prophecy

❧

"Speaking the truth is no disgrace"
~ **AFRICAN PROVERB (SWAHILI)**

Isaiah 18:1-2 'Woe to the land shadowing with wings, which is beyond the rivers of Ethiopia: That sendeth ambassadors by the sea, even in vessels of bulrushes upon the waters, saying, Go, ye swift messengers, to a nation scattered and peeled, to a people terrible from their beginning hitherto; a nation meted out and trodden down, whose land the rivers have spoiled!'

We will focus on the text prophetically contextualized to our modern time. The following is a more accurate biblical translation of key words from the original language of the text and as such it reveals some wondrous things about Cushite people of African descent. The following are the meanings from some of the key words within the text.

    a. *Ethiopia* [**Kuwsh** /koosh/] Cush meaning black, the Cushites settled in Mesopotamia, Arabia and Africa

b. *Scattered* [**mashak** /**maw•shak**/] means to be *tall*, or stretched out. Herodotus, the great Greek historian, describes Cushites as "the tallest and *handsomest* of men."

c. *Peeled* [**mowrat** /**mo•rawt**/] polished, smooth.

d. *Trodden down* [**mebusah**] a trampling down, an *aggressiveness* and subduing others.

e. *Terrible* [**yare'** /**yaw•ray**/] causing fear, reverence, *honor*, *respect*, astonishment or *awe*. Cushite Africans were famed for their warlike prowess.

f. *Spoiled*: *divided* (referring to rivers) Cush is divided by rivers, that is, by branches of the Nile. The land is known for rivers, which were very important to their culture and livelihood.

When the Nile and its tributaries flooded, the silt that was deposited was essential for farming.

Other more accurate translations of the text:

"*Go, quick messengers, to a people who are* tall *and* smooth-skinned, *who are* feared *everywhere. They are a powerful nation that* defeats *other nations. Their land is divided by rivers*" NCV

"*Go, swift messengers, go to this people* tall *and* handsome, *this people held in* respect *everywhere, this people* mighty *and* merciless, *from the land crisscrossed with rivers*" The Message

"*Go back home, swift messengers! Take a message back to your land divided by rivers, to your* strong *and* powerful nation, *to your* tall *and* smooth-skinned *people, who are* feared *all over the world*" GNT

Isaiah 18:1 'has correctly identified this nation as Cush in Darby, Amplified, Holman Christian Standard, New American

Standard, New International Version, New Century Version and Young's Literal Translation.

God's Divine Chastisement of Cush

> Isaiah 18:3-6, KJV: "*All ye inhabitants of the world, and dwellers on the earth, see ye, when he lifteth up an ensign on the mountains; and when he bloweth a trumpet, hear ye. For so the LORD said unto me, I will take my rest, and I will consider in my dwelling place like a clear heat upon herbs, and like a cloud of dew in the heat of harvest. For afore the harvest, when the bud is perfect, and the sour grape is ripening in the flower, he shall both cut off the sprigs with pruning hooks, and take away and cut down the branches. They shall be left together unto the fowls of the mountains, and to the beasts of the earth: and the fowls shall summer upon them, and all the beasts of the earth shall winter upon them.*"

1. **'I will take my rest'**

   a. *Rest:* [*shaqat /shaw•kat/*] translates to be quiet, be tranquil, be at peace, lie still, be undisturbed, be inactive, to show quietness, be in a favorable circumstance, implying ease, security, and satisfaction, with lack of tumult or strife.

   b. *Consider:* [*nabat /naw•bat/*] pay attention to, look upon, show regard to, think about an object, implying an appropriate *caring* response, to *regard* with pleasure, *favor* or *care*

   c. *Clear:* [*tsach /tsakh/*] dazzling, glowing radiant, sunny, beaming, shining beauty

d. **Herbs:** [*owr*]: illumination, luminary, light, that which is contrasted to darkness sun, sunshine, light of day, or daylight

e. **Dew:** [*tal*]: night-mist, moisture condensed on surfaces, especially at night, with the associative meanings of *prosperity* and *abundance* (The farmers depended on early morning dew to keep their crops alive during the hot months of summer. In Bible times the absence of dew was considered a sign of God's disfavor)

Translation: I will rest and be quiet from any intervention with them for a season, but will then show regard and favor to the Cushites that will be like radiant light and dew in the hot season. Given what people of African blood suffered at the hands of their oppressors it seemed to appear that God was inactive, and had taken a *rest* from intervening to help us as a people.

2. **When:** "*Afore Harvest*" (some scholars think this refers solely to events of that historical day with Israel, Assyria, and Cush. Some think it may refer to a future millennial reign. The AMP, ESV, NAS, NKJV, ASV, and Darby translate afore harvest as '*before harvest*' is key to the timing of the prophecy. What is harvest?

> **Harvest:** [*qatsir*] *refers to a time of reaping and gathering crops from the field as a definite unit of time. When is harvest?*

To interpret this word *harvest* we should remember that Christ is the standard and the final authority on Scripture. Hebrews 1:1-2, AMP:

> "In many separate revelations [each of which set forth a portion of the Truth] and in different ways God spoke of old

to [our] forefathers in and by the prophets, [But] in the last of these days He has spoken to us in [the person of a] Son, Whom He appointed Heir and lawful Owner of all things, also by and through Whom He created the worlds and the reaches of space and the ages of time [He made, produced, built, operated, and arranged them in order].

As the final authority on Scripture, Jesus teaching in the New Testament *harvest* is a metaphor that represents the *end* time, the *consummation* of the *age* as seen in the gospel of Matthew 13:39:

> *"The* harvest *is the* close *and* consummation *of the* age, *and the reapers are angels"* AMP

> *"The* harvest *is the* end *of the age, and the harvest workers are angels"* GNT

We now place our attention on the next portion of the prophecy in Isaiah 18:5:

> *"When the bud is perfect, and the sour grape is ripening in the flower"* KJV

The translation of key words in this portion of the verse is as follows:

1. **Bud [*perach*]**: the beginning stage of a blossom growing
2. **Perfect [*tamam*]**: complete, finish, bring an event or activity to a successful end
3. **Ripening [*gamal* /*gaw•mal*]**: to deal bountifully with.

Blossom here is referring to the Cushites' power and glory and grape is symbolic of prosperity. Ripening grape is bountiful prosperity. Just before the end of the world and the consummation of the age when the Cushite people feared all over the world are blossoming in power and becoming bountiful in their prosperity, God is going to bring chastisement because of their idolatry. Probably the period just before the slave trade during the seasons of the great kingdoms of Songhai, Mali, and Ghana.

God's divine chastening was designed to correct our destiny and to get us back on track in fulfilling our purpose. His chastening was out of his love and was meant to be more *corrective* than *punitive*. Hebrews 12:6-7, Contemporary English Version (CEV):

> "*The Lord* corrects *the people he* loves *and disciplines those he calls his own. Be patient when you are being corrected! This is how God treats his children. Don't all parents correct their children?*"

God's intervention was not merely a chastisement for our *course*, but a re-establishment with our *source*. It was to bring us back to God. It was to end the satanic detour that took us away from God's purpose and caused us to stray from God's agenda.

The next portion of this prophecy deals with the method of that chastisement as we review key words in the text

> What: "*shall both cut off the sprigs with* pruning *hooks, and take away and cut down the branches. They shall be left together unto the* fowls *of the mountains, and to the* beasts *of the earth: and the* fowls *shall* summer *upon them, and all the* beasts *of the earth shall* winter *upon them*"

Translating some key words:

a. **Cut off** [*karat*]: *sever* from its source, or cut into parts, implying a *violent* action, to be *excluded* from an *association* or membership, to banish

b. **Sprigs** [*zalzal*]: shoots, the new tender, flexible tendrils of a vine

c. **Branches** [*nâtiyshah /net•ee•shaw*]: a spreading vine as a new, and tender growth

d. **Pruning hooks** [*mazmerah*]: a vine-knife, a husbandman's pruning iron tool to cut tendrils.

In the text God uses *pruning hooks* on the branches, not an *ax* on the *root*. One destroys the plant; the other makes it more *fruitful*. If God was alluding to the total destruction of Cushite African people, He would have used the symbol of the ax instead of pruning hooks, but in this passage, that was not the case.

The reasons a gardener uses pruning tools to prune plants include dead wood removal, shaping (by controlling or directing growth), improving or maintaining health, and both harvesting and increasing the yield or quality of fruits.[68]

Every year in Palestine, gardeners prune their vines with a trained eye, spotting the unfruitful branches and chopping them off in one stroke. The gardener spends more time on the fruitful branches, going over them inch by inch, looking for spots of disease, and looking for less promising fruit clusters, looking for extra leaves.

All of these, he cuts off with expert precision, so that the few fruits that he leaves behind may *mature* into the *largest* and *sweetest* grapes. Christ highlighted the pruning principle in John 15:2

God used the slave trade and slavery to *prune* Cushite Africans to cut them off from Africa severing them from their re-

---

68 Wikipedia contributors, "Pruning," Wikipedia, The Free Encyclopedia, Wikipedia, The Free Encyclopedia, https://en.wikipedia.org/wiki/Pruning.

ligious idolatry. He did this with the aim of making them more fruitful spiritually and economically.

> ."*Any branch in me that does not bear fruit [that stops bearing] He takes away (trims off, takes away); and every branch that continues to bear fruit, He [repeatedly] prunes, so that it will bear more fruit [even richer and finer fruit]." AMP*

The next three important words in Isaiah 18:5-6 text are:

a. *Cut down* [**tazaz**] cut away, cut off an object so, as to cause a separation

b. *Left* [**Azab**] abandon, reject, desert, to leave a former association, or forsaken

c. *Fowl* [`**ayit** /ah•**yit**/] bird of prey, a swooper, carrion birds, birds that eat dead things, such as vulture birds of prey, birds that hunt for living victims to kill.

Once again Jesus the final authority explains the *fowl* meaning in the following passages of Matthew 13:4, KJV:

> "*Behold, a sower went forth to sow and when he sowed, some seeds fell by the way side, and the fowls came and devoured them up.*"

> Matthew 13:19 "*When any one heareth the word of the kingdom, and understandeth it not, then cometh the wicked one, and catcheth away that which was sown in his heart. This is he who received seed by the way side.*'

Here in Matthew 13:19 Jesus explains that the *fowl* mentioned in verse four represents Satan. Fowl are symbolic of Satan thus when the Scripture says in Isaiah 18:6, KJV:

> "*They shall be left together unto the fowls of the mountains.*"

A mountain is an elevated place; these mountains represent high places. Ephesians reminds us that we wrestle against spiritual wickedness in *high places* (Ephesians 6:12). It is saying that as part of their chastisement the Cushites were left to Satan. God allowed Satan to attack them. Similarly, to God's permission for Satan to attack Job. In Job 2:6-7 GOD'S WORD Translation (GW) says:

> "*The LORD told* Satan, 'He is in your power, *but you must spare his life!' Satan left the LORD's presence and* struck *Job with painful boils from the soles of his feet to the top of his head.*"

Regardless of who he used or what he used, the enemy was behind the assault of the Cushites. It was not the flesh and blood, but the evil one who was behind them. God used what Satan did to us as both a means of *chastisement* and *development*.

Vs. 6 "And the fowls *shall summer upon them,"*

Summer: [*quwts /koots/*] *this means to cut off, to clip off, tear apart, separate a geographical area considered a whole into parts or sections implying violence in the process.*

This means that God allowed Satan (the Fowl) to cut them off, tear them away and separate a populace from the Motherland of Africa into the Americas, Caribbean, Latin America including some parts of Europe and Asia. This was essentially a Cushitic '*African Diaspora*'; a scattering, and separation of a people from their native homeland.

Beasts: [*bâhemah /be•hay•maw/*] *Ecclesiastes 3:18, ESV, says*

> *"I said in my heart with regard to the children of man that*
> *God is testing them that they may see that they themselves are*
> *but* beasts. *"*

Wild beasts is a reference to those who engage in enslaving others for their own profit or personal gain regardless of the race of the oppressors. This reference to the wild beasts in Isaiah 18:6 is symbolic of the character and behavior, but not necessarily the ethnicity, of a people. A description of such people is given in the following passage: 2 Peter 2:12-14, The Message (MSG)

> *"These people are nothing but brute* beasts, *born in the* wild, *predators on the prowl. In the very act of bringing down others with their ignorant blasphemies, they themselves will be brought down, losers in the end. Their evil will boomerang on them. They're so despicable and addicted to pleasure that they indulge in wild parties, carousing in broad daylight. They're obsessed with adultery, compulsive in sin,* seducing *every* vulnerable *soul they come upon. Their* specialty *is* greed, *and* they're experts *at it. Dead souls!*
>
> *They've left the main road and are directionless, having taken the way of Balaam, son of Beor, the prophet who turned* profiteer, *a connoisseur of evil." 2 Peter 2:12-15, The Message.*

In 2 Peter 2:3 it says they will make *"merchandise of you"* (KJV) As part of the character of those described as beasts is this term *merchandise: emporeuomai* [em●por●yoo●om●ahee/], which means to *traffic a thing,* to *import for sale,* to *deal in,* to *use a person* or a thing *for gain.*

These Scriptures are referring to profiteering people motivated by greed who *exploit, sell,* and *traffic,* others for their own profit.

This fits the description of those who orchestrated and operated the slave trade. Speaking deception to vulnerable Africans who trusted Europeans.

No race has a monopoly on producing "brute or wild beasts." They come in an assortment of colors, ethnicities, and nationalities. The slave trade was particularly the exploitation of *beastly* acting men.

Albeit, contrary to the popular myth mostly believed by many Euro-Americans, Europeans, and even some misinformed black folks, Africans did not sell their brothers into slavery as such. Like other continents and nations, Africa had wars, but in Africa they were tribal wars. The difference between *tribal* wars in Africa and the wars in the outside world was that, in the outside world, the conquered were often *butchered* whereas the conquered in Africa (excluding Arabs/Muslims in the north) became *part* of the conqueror.

In other words, while no enemy was left standing in the outside world, the conquered enemies were left to *live* and *serve* in Africa. So it is true there were slaves in Africa in those days before the White man came.

However, those slaves were *not* taken by force purposely to become slaves of another kingdom or empire. They were just victims of tribal wars, and the treatment by their African captors was *better* than what was happening in the outside world where no enemy could live.

Regrettably, Africans were deceived and manipulated by the Europeans who came to their land—with the bogus notion "we come in peace."

When the Europeans first came to Africa, most African communities drove them away from there, but the Europeans managed to convince some of the traditional rulers that they had not come to cause any harm, but just to preach the Good News (the Bible), and also to trade with the local people.

Some of the local chiefs along the coast started accepting the Europeans by giving them a place to reside. The foreigners started establishing missionary centers where they stayed and preached the Gospel, and traded with the local people.

However, they later expanded those missionary centers (including churches and cathedrals) into forts and castles where they packed slaves before shipping them abroad.

Instead of killing those captives, local rulers came up with the idea they could actually give those captured in the tribal wars to the strangers so they could preach the Good News to them since they said they came to preach to those captives, and also train them in the foreign language in order to aid communication.[69]

The local rulers concluded that this was a more humane response that was better than killing them. So the traditional rulers gave those captives out to them and, to show appreciation, those Europeans gave gifts to the traditional rulers.[70]

That was how they got their first "local servers." Those local people lived and served the Europeans in the castles and forts and learned their language, which enabled them to serve as mediators translating the local language for them, and the foreign language to the local people. This facilitated communication between the foreigners and the locals.

---

69 "Africans did NOT sell their own people into slavery," Africa and the World, 9 November 2011, http://www.africaw.com/africans-did-not-sell-their-own-people-into-slavery.

70 "Africans did NOT sell their own people into slavery," Africa and the World, 9 November 2011, http://www.africaw.com/africans-did-not-sell-their-own-people-into-slavery.

The foreigners also realized they could sell some of those "local servers" to their friends and relatives and make more money and that was why most of them returned with the intention of picking more local servers (this time around, slaves).

So they returned for slaves but no local ruler was willing to sell their people out except those captured as prisoners of war. The Europeans needed slaves and more slaves, but there was no easy way of getting slaves in Africa. So they engaged in a divide and conquer strategy inciting more tension among the tribes and created confusion so that there would be increased tribal wars and more war enabling them to acquire more slaves and prisoners of war.[71] These prisoners of war became oppressed captives treated inhumanely. This brings us to the next important word in the prophecy.

> **Winter** [*charaph*]: *the term means to scorn, to defame, treat with contempt, insult, reproach, taunt, ridicule, speak words that harm another, say sharp things to, and speak evil of another, to count one's life as of little worth, to expose one's life to great danger.*

Such was the treatment of slaves. This definition of winter is very descriptive of the treatment of people of African blood in the United States, Africa, and other parts of the world by their foreign oppressors.

This prophecy is a description of what happened to the Cushitic people of Africa brought to the Caribbean, the Americas, and other parts of the globe from the gold coast of West Africa.

Moreover, the last great African kingdoms of West Africa; Songhai, Mali, and Ghana collapsed. Ghana fell in 1087 A.D. from

---

71 "Africans did NOT sell their own people into slavery," Africa and the World, 9 November 2011, http://www.africaw.com/africans-did-not-sell-their-own-people-into-slavery.

an invasion of Moslems, Almoravids and Berbers, Mali fell due to conquests of the Woloffs, Songhai fell by the invasion of Moroccans in 1591 A.D. Like *sprigs* and *branches*, they were cut from the main vine of their lineage and people.

In the slave trade: 20-22 million slaves were moved. More than a third to about half died during the voyage; that amounts to between 7 and 11 million people. Most slaves on a plantation had a life expectancy of seven years and even less if the plantation was run by a church. Now isn't that a paradoxical concept that the word church and the word plantation are used in the same sentence?[72]

That the children of Ham through Cush have suffered greatly in slavery under the descendants of Noah's other sons is undeniable. Long before the Muslims or Europeans arrived in Africa.

Kings ruled, witchdoctors invoked spirits, and various tribes raided each other's territories, taking goods, cattle and prisoner of war slaves.

This tribalism and religious divisions are still rampant in Africa, a discrimination that denies the rights of other tribes within a nation and sometimes results in genocide, as evidenced in Nigeria (1967-70, mainly Muslim Hausa and Yoruba tribes vs. Christian Ibo tribe, 2,000,000 killed) and Rwanda (1994, Hutu vs. Tutsi, 900,000 killed).

Today violent Islamic extremists are killing their fellow countrymen, essentially targeting other Africans if they are Christians. One example of this was the killing of 147 non-Muslim students

---

72 BBC news Monday, 3 September, 2001, 13:45 GMT 14:45 UK

in Garissa University of Kenya. The Somalia-based Al-Shabaab militant group claimed responsibility for the assault.[73]

Another example was the killing of 21 Coptic *Christian* Egyptians by the ISIS terrorist group,[74] and finally, a third example was the throwing overboard of 12 Nigerian and Ghanian Christians by Muslim migrants.

The motive was that the victims "professed the Christian faith while the aggressors were Muslim."[75] Citing these examples is not done to put down Islam but to highlight violent extremism.

Hardly a year passes in Africa without an insurrection ousting a country's tribally dominated government, and then in turn decimating another ethnic group. In the realm of ancient Cush today (Sudan and Ethiopia) tribalism is an integral part of the war in which the *Islamic extremists* are attempting to wipe out the Christians.[76]

Albeit, Cushites of African heritage have played a major role throughout biblical history in the plan of God. Isaiah 18:7 (WEB)

> *"In that time, a* present *will be brought to Yahweh of Armies from a people tall and smooth, even from a people awesome from their beginning onward, a nation that measures out and treads down, whose land the rivers divide, to the place of the name of Yahweh of Armies, Mount Zion."*

---

73 Josh Levs and Holly Yan, "147 dead, Islamist gunmen killed after attack at Kenya college," CNN, 2 April 2015, http://www.cnn.com/2015/04/02/africa/kenya-university-attack/index.html.

74 "Coptic Church Recognizes Martyrdom of 21 Coptic Christians," Vatican Radio, 21 February 2015, http://en.radiovaticana.va/news/2015/02/21/coptic_church_recognizes_martyrdom_of_21_coptic_christians_/1124824

75 "Muslim migrants arrested for allegedly throwing Christians into sea after brawl," Fox News World, 17 April 2015, http://www.foxnews.com/world/2015/04/17/muslim-migrants-arrested-for-allegedly-throwing-christians-into-sea-after-brawl.html.

76 Peter Dunstan, The Dark Powers That Bind (CreateSpace Independent Publishing Platform, 2007).

The above translation clearly identifies the Cushites as the nation this passage is referring to. We continue to review the remainder of some key words and phrases in the translation of this prophecy. We begin with those that deal with the *when, what, who, how, why*, and *where* of the destiny of Cushitic African people.

> **When?** – At that time [eth /ayth/] *season, right time, appointed time. This refers to a period just before harvest or the end of the world- the last days—the end times—just before the return of Christ.*

> **What?** – "shall a present" [shay /shah•ee/] *a gift offered as tribute, a present given to a governmental head as an act of homage, submission, or respect.*

The English translation says the *"present"* refers to the Cushite African people *converted* to *Christ*. Cushitic people will not only bring gifts to God; they are a *gift* from God to the church and the world.

Gill's Bible commentary says, "This explains what the *present is*, that shall be brought to the Lord; *'it is a people,'* Isaiah 18:2 says, who, being converted, shall *stretch out their hands* to *God*, submit unto him, and present themselves soul and body as an acceptable sacrifice unto him."[77]

> **Who?** – A people [`am /am/] *army, troops, a nation [gowy, /go•ee/] larger group based on various cultural, physical, geographical ties, often extended clan relationships. The word people here relates to Cushites – people of African descent— African people of color—Negroid black people. They are "gift" of*

---

77   John Gill, "Isaiah 18:7 Gills Exposition," Biblehub, http://biblehub.com/commentaries/gill/isaiah/18.htm.

people—a special group of black warriors chosen, and purposed
by God to lead the church army into last day spiritual warfare

The Cushite Africans were a people; a large national army of troops, and a nation with these ties, but there is something else that they were. For they were more than an army; they were an army with *attitude,* for Isaiah 18:7 says that they were: ***"Terrible from their beginning onward."***

A nation powerful and treading down

The Cushite Africans were described as being terrible from their *beginning.* We have stated earlier that the original word *terrible* [*yare' /yaw•ray/*] meant to incite fear, reverence, honor, respect, to cause astonishment and awe. These Cushites prompted fear and awe from their adversaries, but that fear and awe not only came from their earthly adversaries, but also from their spiritual adversary as well, for Satan also feared these Cushites.

It must be remembered that Nimrod, a Cushite, had a favored relation with the Lord even before Abraham did, and that favored relation with God is what made him the successful warrior archer that he was, according to Genesis 10:8-10, GNT:

> *"Cush had a son named Nimrod, who became the* world's first great conqueror. *By the* LORD's help *he was a great hunter, and that is why people say, 'May the Lord make you as* great *a hunter as Nimrod!' At first his kingdom included Babylon, Erech, and Accad, all three of them in Babylonia."*

This high anxiety concerning these aggressive Cushites was not without merit. For what Satan dreaded were the "**F**" Factors of the Cushite Africans. Their *Favored* relation, their *Fierce* nature, their *Fighting* prowess, and their *Formidable* reputation.

The combination of Nimrod's warrior legacy and the aggressive nature of the Cushite Africans could pose a threat to him if that militant nature were turned against him. He feared that there could be generations of Cushite warriors and fighters for God to challenge his diabolical agenda and to thwart his evil schemes.

So through deception he sought to sabotage their effect early, undermine their impact, and neutralize their strengths, but unfortunately for him he became *headed* toward what he *dreaded*—his defeat. As evidenced in the remaining words of this prophecy in Isaiah 18:7

> **How?** – "be brought" [yabal /yaw•bal/] *meaning to flow, be led, direct or guide the movement of an object in a direction. There is God-directed, spirit-led flow of our destiny. It is a fluid movement like a mighty river that is powerful and unstoppable. Our destiny is not a pond – stagnant and unmoving – but a river forcefully flowing and pulling us forward to God's assignment.*

> **Why?** – "Unto lord of hosts" [tsâba'ah /tsaw•baw/] *army, war, warfare, battle, host of organized army, a military large fighting unit. The Lord of Hosts is God's military name, the one He uses when He is about to engage in combat, and spiritual warfare. The fact that God is using this designation indicates that he has war on his mind, and victory in his sights. The fact that he uses this title with Cushite people indicates he is ready to fight for them, with them—but not against them.*

Where? – "come unto Mount Zion" *We learn that in the New Testament the church is referred to as the Mount Zion of the present age in Hebrews 12:22-23, NIV.*

"But you have come to Mount Zion, to the city of the living God, the heavenly Jerusalem. You have come to thousands upon thousands of angels in joyful assembly, to the church of the firstborn, whose names are written in heaven. ..."

The church is not only the flock of God, the body Christ—it is a *spiritual* army (1 Timothy 6:12, 2 Timothy 2:4, Ephesians 6:13, Romans 8:36-37) a Spiritual warfare—Mount Zion (Church). The name Mount Zion is synonymous with *city of God*, and is a place that God loves.

Mount Zion is the high hill on which David built a citadel. *Zion* occurs over 150 times in the Bible - It essentially means *"fortification,"* the church is a *spiritual citadel* and *fortification*. It is a stronghold against Satan from which assaults on the armies of Darkness are launched.

Cushite people of African descent given their warrior nature will be at the forefront of the battle employing their expert *archer* skills plus their aggressiveness.

Interpretive conclusion: out from the smooth-skinned Cushitic people of African descent who were feared with reverence from the beginning (that is from the time of Nimrod in Genesis). The Lord of hosts, the God of armies, warfare and military troops is going to bring to himself a Cushitic black people to a standing place, a prominent place in the Church, and in his army. He is about to do battle against the enemy, and the people with a *skin of darkness* will *lead* the challenge against the *forces* of *darkness*.

Discussion Questions

1. How have the words of Isaiah 18:1-7 been misrepresented to distort the destiny of Cushites?
2. How do the essential questions of the prophecy of Isaiah 18:1-7 relate to the destiny of black people?

CHAPTER 8

An Oppressed Christ and Oppressed Cushites

꙰

"The ultimate tragedy is not the oppression
and cruelty by the bad people
but the silence over that by the good people"
~ MARTIN LUTHER KING, JR.

The oppression of people of African descent has affected them socially, economically, and physically and impacted their psychological well-being. Just as the chronic pressure soldiers face in military conflict can pursue them to their domestic residences in the form of debilitating stress, African-Americans and other people of color who deal with constant exposure to racial discrimination may have a raised likelihood of experiencing a race-based *battle* fatigue, according to Penn State researchers.

According to Jose Soto, assistant professor, of psychology, African-Americans who reported in a survey that they experienced more instances of racial discrimination had *significantly higher* levels of suffering generalized anxiety disorder (GAD) sometime during their lives.[78]

Comparatively, Jesus lived the suffering and oppression of Cushitic people throughout the world. Which is why as a Savior he relates so well *to them*; he was one *of them*.

He is one of them *emotionally* because like people of African descent he was a man of *sorrows* and acquainted with suffering experiencing both physical and mental anguish:

> *Isaiah 53:3, CEV:* "He was hated *and* rejected; *his life was* filled *with* sorrow *and terrible suffering. No one wanted to look at him. We* despised *him and said,* "He is a nobody!"

He is one of them *socially* because he *himself* was *oppressed*, treated harshly and according to Isaiah 53:7-8, NRSV.

> *He was* oppressed, *and he was* afflicted, *yet he did not open his mouth; like a lamb that is led to the* slaughter, *and like a sheep that before its shearers is silent, so he did not open his mouth. By a* perversion *of justice he was taken away. Who could have imagined his future? For he was* cut off *from the land of the living,* stricken *for the transgression of my people.*

Lastly, he is one of them *genetically* for he not only had Shemitic blood flowing through his veins, but also the blood of Hamites via the blood lines of the Hamitic Canaanites like *Tamar*, *Rahab*, and possibly *Bathsheba* who are all mentioned in Christ's genealogy. Matthew 1:1-16, AMP

---

78   Matt Swayne and Andrea Messer, "Discrimination creates racial battle fatigue for African-Americans," Penn State News, 11 March 2011, http://news.psu.edu/story/160177/2011/03/11/campus-life/discrimination-creates-racial-battle-fatigue-african-americans.

> *The record of the genealogy of [a]Jesus the [b]Messiah, the son
> (descendant) of [c]David, the son (descendant) of Abraham:
> Abraham [d]was the father of Isaac, Isaac the father of Jacob, and
> Jacob the father of [e]Judah and his brothers [who became the
> twelve tribes of Israel]. Judah was the father of Perez and Zerah
> by Tamar, Perez was the father of Hezron, and Hezron the father
> of Ram. Ram was the father of Aminadab, Aminadab the father
> of Nahshon, and Nahshon the father of Salmon. Salmon was the
> father of Boaz by [f]Rahab, Boaz was the father of Obed by Ruth,
> and Obed the father of Jesse. 6 Jesse was the father of [g]David the
> king. David was the father of Solomon by [h]Bathsheba who had
> been the wife of Uriah.*

Thus, as mentioned earlier, at least two of possibly three of Jesus' female ancestors came from the patriarch Ham from which Cushites, and African and people of color descended. This is why we maintain that Christ relates to the socially, economically, physically, and mentally *oppressed* of society, which Cushites of African descent have been.

Contrary to the real image of Christ, many evangelicals and religious conservatives have devised a Euro-Americanized Christ with white skin, long hair, and blue eyes.

He is a Republican draped in the American flag, or worst, a white supremacist member wrapped in the Confederate flag, He is not only a Christ created in their ethnic image, but a Christ projected to other ethnic groups as *THE* image.

This is a far cry from the biblical, historical Christ who was a dark-complexioned Jew who came from a poor family—who associated as well as ministered to the oppressed poor masses of his day.

Therefore, many black evangelicals though similar in orthodox Christian beliefs have divergent views from white evangelicals on matters of justice and social fairness.

Sociologists Michael Emerson and Christian Smith state that only one thing separates white and black evangelicals, but it makes all the *difference* in the world: vastly *different* experiences of structural and systemic oppression.

Black evangelicals have a long historical legacy of interaction with oppressive systems and social structures. African Americans see more than 2,000 passages of Scripture about God's *abhorrence* for poverty and oppression. They see God's concern for systems and structures to be favorable to all of humanity — not partial to some.[79]

They see Jesus' own stated agenda to preach good news to the *poor*, his reference to *poor*, is decidedly *not* a reference to only the "spiritually impoverished." Jesus meant that he had come to preach good news (of *liberation*, *freedom* and *new life*) to people trapped in both spiritual and *material* poverty. Poor here is the Greek word *potochos* which means *beggarly*, of little value, *destitute* of *wealth*, *influence*, *position*, *honor*, *lowly*, and *afflicted*.

These words have characterized the social and economic status of people of African descent as well as other people of color in America and other nations. White evangelicals generally do not experience such systemic oppression.

According to Emerson and Smith, as mentioned, most white evangelicals don't prioritize or even see the thousands of references in the Hebrew Scriptures and New Testament about structural and systemic injustice.

---

79   Michael O Emerson and Christian Smith, Divided by Faith: Evangelical Religion and the Problem of Race in America (New York: Oxford UP, 2001).

In fact, they have been conditioned by evangelical instruction and training *not* to see or to ignore these Scriptures.[80]

Albeit, our *oppression* resulted in *intercession* it caused us to cry out to God for help and Psalm 146:5-7, NLT, states:

> "*He gives* justice *to the* oppressed, *and food to the hungry. The* LORD *frees the* prisoners"

The original language Hebrew word for *oppressed is* [`ashaq /*aw•shak/*] meaning to press upon, violate, crush, defraud, do violence, to get deceitfully, to wrong, extort, mistreat, treat a *disadvantaged* member of society *unjustly* with the effect of causing one to suffer ill treatment, steal from disadvantaged persons in a financial transaction that has unjust leverage in favor of rich over the poor, and so creating suffering of the poor or disadvantaged. The original Hebrew word here translated *judgment* in KJV is [*mishpat /mish•pawt/*] meaning *"justice."*

As stated above part of Christ's agenda by his own admission was releasing the *oppressed* according to Luke 4:18: The ESV, GNT, HCSB, ISV, NET, NCV, NIV, NKJV, NLT, NRSV, RSV, and TNIV, all translate the word *bruised* in the KJV as *oppressed.*

> "*The Spirit of the LORD is on me, because he has anointed me to preach good news to the* poor. *He has sent me to proclaim freedom for the prisoners and recovery of sight for the blind, to set the* oppressed free." *NIV*

> "*The Lord has put his Spirit in me, because he appointed me to tell the Good News to the* poor. *He has sent me to tell the captives they*

---

80 Lisa Sharon Harper, "Black Evangelicals, White Evangelicals and Franklin Graham's Repentance," Sojourners, 1 March 2012, https://sojo.net/articles/black-evangelicals-white-evangelicals-and-franklin-grahams-repentance.

are free and to tell the blind that they can see again. God sent me to free those who have been treated unfairly." *NCV*

The original Greek word for *oppressed* that is translated *bruised* in the KJV translation is *thrauo* [throwo]. Religious researcher Reza Aslan says the "historical Jesus was a day laborer, a peasant from the countryside of Galilee who hung closely with the *most oppressed, dispossessed, poor, weak, outcasts* of *his society*— people whom the temple *rejected.*"

Today Jesus would not hang out with Wall Street types or Donald Trumps that have a penchant for flaunting their wealth before the poor. He would have associated himself with the societal downtrodden which black people in America and people of color in general have been.

Thus, he related to the *oppressed* people of his time, and was a card-carrying member; as stated, he was *one* of them.[81]

Aslan says of Christ: "He would have been what is referred to as a *Palestinian Jew*. He would look the way that the average Palestinian would look today. So that would mean *dark* features, *hairy*, probably a *longer nose*, black hair."[82]

Furthermore, James H. Charlesworth professor of New Testament language and director of the Dead Sea Scrolls Project,

---

81 Paul Brandeis Raushenbush, "Reza Aslan Introduces Jesus The Zealot... And Revolutionary To HuffPost Live (VIDEO)," The Huffington Post, 17 July 2013, http://www.huffingtonpost.com/2013/07/17/reza-aslan-zealot-_n_3611504.html.

82 Max Fisher, "Reza Aslan on Jesus's skin color: 'Megyn Kelly is right. Her Christ is white,'" The Washington Post, 12 December 2013, https://www.washingtonpost.com/news/worldviews/wp/2013/12/12/reza-aslan-on-jesuss-skin-color-megyn-kelly-is-right-her-christ-is-white/?utm_term=.e7eaba2424d2.

says Jesus' face was "*most* likely *dark* brown, so in appearance he would have looked like oppressed people of *color*.[83]

There are also other people of Scripture to which people of color can relate, and who personify their destiny. A review of such persons is our next discussion.

Discussion Questions

1. Cushite people of color have been an oppressed people. What does the Bible say about the oppressed?
2. How do black evangelicals and white evangelicals often differ and why?
3. How does Christ relate to people of color by appearance and condition?

---

83 Wikipedia contributors, "Jesus," Wikipedia, The Free Encyclopedia, Wikipedia, The Free Encyclopedia, https://en.wikipedia.org/wiki/Jesus.

CHAPTER 9

Cushites of Scripture Who Personify our Destiny

༈

"When deeds speak words are nothing"
~ **AFRICAN PROVERB**

There are Cushities and other people of African descent in Scripture that are prophetic symbols that personify God's destiny for black people. The following is a list of such persons:

Tirhakah

Scholars have identified Taharqa with Tirhakah, a Cushite African king who waged war against Sennacherib during the reign of King Hezekiah of Judah (2 Kings 19:9; Isaiah 37:9). Tirhakah was a Cushite African pharaoh of the Ancient Egyptian 25th dynasty and king of the Kingdom of Kush, which was located in Northern Sudan.

He was the son of Piye, the Cushite African king of Napata who had first conquered Egypt. The successful campaigns of Piye and Shabaka paved the way for a *prosperous* reign by Tirhakah which can be dated from 690 BC to 664 BC this would give Tirhakah a reign of 26 years.

He was described by the ancient Greek historian Strabo as having "advanced as far as Europe" and (citing Megasthenes), even as far as the Pillars of Hercules in Spain.[84]

The name of this ruler of Egypt and his native realm appears in hieroglyphics as Taharqa, his prenomen being Nefer-atmu-Ra-chu, "Nefer-atmu-Ra protects." The Assyrian form of Tirhakah is Tarqu or Tarqu'u (inscriptions of Assur-bani-pal).[85]

> 2 Kings 19:8-10, NIV: "When the field commander heard that the king of Assyria had left Lachish, he withdrew and found the king fighting against Libnah. Now Sennacherib received a report that Tirhakah, the king of Cush, was marching out to fight against him. So he again sent messengers to Hezekiah with this word. Say to Hezekiah king of Judah: Do not let the God you depend on deceive you when he says, 'Jerusalem will not be given into the hands of the king of Assyria.'"[86] In the Bible, Tirhakah is the savior of the Hebrew people, as they are being besieged by Sennacherib (Isaiah 37:8-9, & 2 Kings 19:8-9).

He is a significant prophetic symbol, first of all, because the events of the hallmark prophecy of this writing of Isaiah 18:1-7 are historically related to him as mentioned earlier. Historically, the passage probably refers to the time right before the great invasion of Sennacherib (about B.C. 700), when Tirhakah was the ruler of Egypt reigning at Napata the Capital of Cushitic Africa.

---

84 Wikipedia contributors, "Taharqa," Wikipedia, The Free Encyclopedia, Wikipedia, The Free Encyclopedia, https://en.wikipedia.org/wiki/Taharqa.

85 James Orr, "Definition for 'TIRHAKAH'," International Standard Bible Encyclopedia, http://www.bible-history.com/isbe/T/TIRHAKAH/.

86 Wikipedia contributers, "Taharqa"

However, as stated earlier, it also has a prophetic meaning.[87] For He is important because he symbolizes the warrior role of the people of African descent in the last days that will come to the aid of God's people and join forces cross-culturally to fight a common spiritual enemy.

Simon (Worshipper from Cyrene of North Africa)

Another prophetic symbol is Simon of Cyrene; the people of Cyrene were Africans who inhabited what is now Libya. Located on the Mediterranean coast of Northern Africa, it was the major city of the region known then as Cyrenaica, the nation that bordered Egypt on the west. Cyrene itself was about 450 miles west of Alexandria, Egypt.

Even though Northern Africa is often considered Arab today, there were no Arab peoples in northern Africa in Bible times (Old Testament or New Testament), only Africans. Arab peoples did not move into Africa until the 7th–11th centuries A.D., about 600–1,000 years after the Bible was completed.[88]

I have stated that Ethiopian is the term Greeks used for black Africans. Herodotus writes about the Ethiopians (black Africans) that lived in parts of Libya, which was the Greek name for ancient Phut, one of the four sons of Ham who resided in North Africa and was related to Cush.

---

87 "Matthew Henry's Commentary"

88 Robert Ash, "People of Color In the Bible (Part 1 – Egypt)," Black and Christian.com, January 2001, http://blackandchristian.com/articles/pulpit/ash-01-01.shtml.

Libya to the Egyptians and Greeks meant all North Africa.[89] Many researchers and archeologist are now purporting that the ancient Phutite Libya of North Africa consisted of the tribes designated by the ancient people as the *"Temehu,"* or at other times called the *"Tehenu"* who were *more closely* related to the Cushite Africans than previously expected.

Many excavations into southern Libya have proven that the Cushites of Lower Nubia had relations with the Temahu or Tehenu themselves and were often *synonymous* with the *Ta- Nehesy Cushites* of *Nubia.* Pre-dynastic early material culture of the Southern portion of the Northwest Wadi fragments shows Cushite Nubian and Phutite Libyan culture *intertwined.*[90]

Cyrene is the African country where Simon of Cyrene came from. It had been colonized by the Greeks, but also had a Jewish community where 100,000 Judean Jews had been forced to settle during the reign of Ptolemy Soter (323–285 BC) and was an early center of Christianity.[91]

He and his people were descendants of the Phutite North African region of people ethnically related to Cushites. He was probably an African proselyte of Judaism.

Proselytes were Jews by profession of religion. Though they were born Gentiles in other places, they embraced the Jewish religion. There was such a people in Cyrene. According to Acts 2:10 (GW) there were converts from:

---

89 "The ancient North Africans," Mathilda's Anthropology Blog, 17 July 2008, https://mathildasanthropologyblog.wordpress.com/2008/07/17/the-ancient-libyans/.

90 AksumVanguard, "Temehu and Tehenu," World Historia, 22 April 2010, http://www.worldhistoria.com/temehu-and-tehenu_topic125561.html.

91 Wikipedia contributors, "Simon of Cyrene," Wikipedia, The Free Encyclopedia, Wikipedia, The Free Encyclopedia, https://en.wikipedia.org/wiki/Simon_of_Cyrene.

> *"Phrygia, Pamphylia, Egypt, and the country near Cyrene in Libya. We're Jewish people, converts to Judaism, and visitors from Rome."*

Simon was forced by the Romans, but chosen by God to support our Savior by carrying his cross to Calvary.[92] Of Simon we read in the gospel of Matthew 27:32 (Mark 15:21, and Luke 23:26)

> *"As they were going out, they met a man from Cyrene, named Simon, and they forced him to carry the cross." NIV*

Simon is a significant prophetic symbol for people of African descent because:

1. He was an African worshipper

> *Zephaniah 3:10 "From beyond the rivers of Cush my worshipers, my scattered people ..."*

2. Like the people of African descent who experienced the journey of slavery, he was forced by Europeans (Romans) against his will to carry a burden.

3. He carried the cross of Christ and the cross represented the suffering of Christ, a suffering that resulted in the salvation of men. Those sufferings where prophetically exclaimed in the words of Isaiah 53:3-9:

> *"He was despised and rejected by men, a man of sorrows, and familiar with pain. Like one from whom men hide their faces he was despised, and we held him in low esteem. Surely he took up our pain and bore our suffering, yet we considered him punished*

by God, smitten by him, and afflicted. *But he was pierced for our transgressions, he was* crushed *for our iniquities; the punishment that brought us peace was upon him, and by his wounds we are healed. We all, like sheep, have gone astray, each of us has turned to our own way; and the LORD has laid on him the iniquity of us all. He was* oppressed *and* afflicted, *yet he did not open his mouth; he was led like a lamb to the slaughter, and as a sheep before her shearers is silent, so he did not open his mouth. By* oppression *and* judgment *he was taken away. Yet who of his generation protested? For he was* cut off *from the land of the living; for the transgression of my people he was* punished" NIV

In these passages are words spoken of Christ our Lord, but they are words that could have been easily used to describe the suffering experience of people of African descent at the hands of Europeans, Euro-Americans, and others. Words like *despised, rejected, sorrows, stricken, smitten, crushed, oppressed, slaughter, afflicted, pierced* and *wounds.*

It is not by coincidence that an African man carried the cross of Christ, not a European man. Simon is more than a Bible character of history; he is an Afroistic type of Christ, a prophetic symbol representing the journey of suffering, prophecy, and destiny of the people of African descent.

He relieved the weariness of the savior, but he had to be forced into service by Roman Europeans. Christ's body was drained, tired, and wounded; this African came along and helped to bear his burden.

Simon was instrumental in relieving Christ weary *physical* body. People of African descent will also be instrumental in relieving the *spiritual* body of Christ; they will also be forced into service but by European-Americans.

God has used the coercion from European oppressors of the people of African descent to press them into their assignment of supporting a weary, wounded Body of Christ.

Simon represents a journey of an African man typifying an African people who carry a cross of suffering for Christ as a group, but whose actions would ultimately result in Christ using that cross to bring salvation to people around the globe.

Ebed Melech (Cushite African servant of the king)

> Jeremiah 39:16-18 "Go and tell Ebed-Melech the Cushite, 'This is what the LORD Almighty, the God of Israel, says: I am about to fulfill my words against this city—words concerning disaster, not prosperity. At that time they will be fulfilled before your eyes. But I will rescue you on that day, declares the LORD; you will not be handed over to those you fear. I will save you; you will not fall by the sword but will escape with your life, because you trust in me, declares the LORD" NIV

Ebed Melech was a Cushite African mentioned in the Book of Jeremiah, he was probably a high-ranking military attache and an official at the palace of king Zedekiah of Judah during the Siege of Jerusalem.

Some Euro-American Bible commentators like to make him a slave or a castrated eunuch, but the events of the text bring us to a different conclusion. Several translations of Jeremiah 38:7 confirm his status as an *official*.

> "But Ebed-Melek, a Cushite, an official *in the royal palace, heard that they had put Jeremiah into the cistern.*

While the king was sitting in the Benjamin Gate." NIV

"But Ebed-melech the Ethiopian, an important court official,
*heard that Jeremiah was in the cistern. At that time the king was
holding court at the Benjamin Gate." NLT*

"But Ebed-melech, a Cushite court official *employed in the king's
palace, heard Jeremiah had been put into the cistern. While the
king was sitting at the Benjamin Gate." HCSB*

His name is translated as *"Servant of the King"* and as such may not be his proper name but a hereditary title (Jeremiah 38:7). In verse 7 he is called a eunuch in the KJV. The Hebrew word *saris* used originally meant an *official.*

According to the *Bible scholar* J. Daniel Hays, writing in the August 1998 issue of the scholarly magazine *Bible Review,* the term *saris* is *never* used in Jeremiah in a way to mean eunuch, but implies a *high-ranking official.*[93]

This title name speaks to God's agenda for Cushite people of African descent in the present times, for they will also be servants of the king Jesus Christ and given a *significant role in His kingdom.*

Ebed Melech is notable for rescuing the prophet Jeremiah from the cistern where he was imprisoned (Jeremiah 38:7-13). Later, the prophet informed him that he would be spared after the fall of Jerusalem to the Babylonians (Jeremiah 39:15-18).

He can be seen as a precursor to the faith of the New Testament believers, since he is saved because he trusted in God.

---

93 Ian Boyne, "Ebedmelech, an African, saved Jeremiah," Jamaica Gleaner, 2001, http://old.jamaica-gleaner.com/gleaner/20020324/relig/relig2.html.

Moreover, he rescued God's prophet from the pit—a down place, a dark place, and a captive place. God is positioning people of African descent in the end times to be rescuers and deliverers.

As we demonstrate confidence, boldness, and security in the God of Armies, we will help to pull up the church out of its own lowly, spiritual pit, and lift it to a higher position of liberty in the spirit. As African people accept this fate—like Ebed Melech— as servants of the king God will cause their own deliverance to spring forth. We will revisit the discussion of Cushite official in the chapter called "Mercy Suits Our Case."

Makeda the (Cushitic African Queen of Sheba)

The Cushite African queen who visited Solomon adopted Yahweh religion, and is alleged to have borne his son, Menelek. She received a strong note of endorsement from Christ himself in the gospels (Matthew 12:42, Luke 11:31).[94]

> 1 Kings 10:1-7 "When the queen of Sheba heard about the fame of Solomon and his relation to the name of the LORD, she came to test him with hard questions. Arriving at Jerusalem with a very great caravan—with camels carrying spices large quantities of gold, and precious stones—she came to Solomon and talked with him about all that she had on her mind. Solomon answered all her questions; nothing was too hard for the king to explain to her. When the queen of Sheba saw all the Wisdom of Solomon and the palace he had built the food on his table, the seating of his officials, the attending servants in their robes, his cupbearers, and the burnt offerings he made at the temple of the Lord, she was

---

94 Legrand H. Clegg, "Queen of Sheba (960 B.C.)," Geni.com, https://www.geni.com/people/Bilquis-Queen-of-Sheba/6000000000961704280.

overwhelmed. She said to the king, 'The report I heard in my own country about your achievements and your wisdom is true. But I did not believe these things until I came and saw with my own eyes. Indeed, not even half was told me; in wisdom and wealth you have far exceeded the report I heard.'" NIV

Matthew 12:42 "The Queen of the South will rise at the judgment with this generation and condemn it; for she came from the ends of the earth to listen to Solomon's wisdom, and now one greater than Solomon is here." NIV

Luke 11:31 "The Queen of the South will rise at the judgment with the men of this generation and condemn them, for she came from the ends of the earth to listen to Solomon's wisdom; and now one greater than Solomon is here." NIV

The phrase Shall *Rise Up*: *egeiromai,* means to cause to stand up, rise, arise; cause to wake up; raise to life; restore, raise up what is torn down, to arouse from sleep.

Christ himself prophesied that a queenly African woman would stand up at the judgment with authority, and render a verdict of condemnation against the men of Christ generation for their rejection of the Savior.

For Christ to mention an African woman in this context, and acknowledge that she would be given such an important role makes her a very significant symbol for black women in this time. They are also African queens with a message.

An African woman whose descendants would be rejected would rise up to condemn Christ's generation for their rejection of Christ of the Savior.

Shulamith (Solomon's black spouse)

The name Shulamith's origin and use are both in the Hebrew language. The name means *peacefulness*. It is derived from the word *shalom*, meaning *peace*. The name is featured in the Song of Solomon.[95]

The black-complexioned woman Solomon loved in Song of Solomon. The Shulamite woman married King Solomon. She was alleged to be a young virgin, probably about sixteen years old, whom Solomon found when he was out in the country touring his vineyards.

Although some scholars maintain that this is allusion to the Queen of Sheba many Bible scholars have said that the Song of Solomon is a type of Christ love for the church.

Ironically then Christ chose a *black* woman to symbolize his bride the church, Song of Solomon 1:5

> "I am so black; but [you are] lovely and pleasant [the ladies assured her]. O you daughters of Jerusalem, [I am as dark] as the tents of [the Bedouin tribe] Kedar, like the [beautiful] curtains of Solomon!" AMPC.

> "I am black and beautiful, O daughters of Jerusalem, like the tents of Kedar, like the curtains of Solomon." NRSV

The term *shachor* is a word pertaining to the color *black* meaning not simply *swarthy* or *tan* as some Euro-American biblical translators allege.

Euro-American Bible translators like to hide the color and implied ethnic implications of Shulamith by suggesting that *black*

---

95 "Song of Solomon – Introduction," Bible Study Tools.Com, http://www.biblestudytools.com/commentaries/scofield-reference-notes/song-of-solomon/song-of-solomon-introduction.html.

here refers to a tan from the sun, but if you are white you don't get *black* from being out in the sun you become sun-burned red.

You can go from *dark brown* to *black* but you sure can't go from *white* or *tan* to black. If you are already *dark brown*, then staying out in the sun working could darken your already dark skin to the point where you look black.

In addition, we have another measure of the extent of her dark pigmentation that is compared to the *tents* of *Kedar*. These Bedouin tents were made out of *black* goat's hair, *not* tan goat's hair or white goat's hair.

She had a *black*-colored body and a name that meant *peace;* she stands as a prophetic symbol for the destiny of the church and the role that black people will play in this destiny; for God is going to use the *blackness* of the body (that is people of African descent) to bring a *Shulamith* experience that is a *peaceful perfecting* to the unity of the body of Christ.

Bachos (the Cushite African treasurer under African Queen Candace)

Philip the Evangelist was directed by an angel to go to the road from Jerusalem to Gaza, and there he encountered the Cushite African treasurer of Queen Candace. In Ethiopian Orthodox Tewahedo tradition he was referred to as Bachos. The treasurer was sitting in his chariot reading the Book of Isaiah and had come to Isaiah 53:7-8.

> *KJV Isaiah 53:7-8 "He was* oppressed, *and he was* afflicted, *yet he opened not his mouth: He is brought as a lamb to the slaughter, and as a sheep before her shearers is dumb, so he openeth not his*

> *mouth. He was taken from prison and from judgment: And who shall declare his generation? For he was cut off out of the land of the living: For the transgression of my people was he stricken."*

Philip inquired whether he understood what he was reading. He said he did not ("How can I understand unless I have a teacher to teach me?") and asked Philip to explain the text to him.

How ironic that this black man asked Philip to explain this passage concerning the *oppression* of Christ. An oppression with sufferings that in time his own African people would simulate. Philip shared the Gospel of Jesus, and the treasurer asked to be baptized. They went down into some water and Philip baptized him.

This encounter is real racial reconciliation of two men of different ethnicities, and a genuine example of cross-cultural evangelism. Philip, a Jew, moved toward a man of African ancestry who invited him into his chariot—that is, into his space.

White evangelicals must learn what Philip learned and that is Cushite African people have a chariot, a journey, and a space that they must respect. Philip had to leave his broader cultural world to enter the minority context of the Cushite's chariot. He entered this African's sphere humbly without force. He demonstrated cultural pliability. This is what Paul meant when he said in 1 Corinthians 9:19-23:

> *"Yes, I try to find common ground with everyone, doing everything I can to save some. I do everything to spread the Good News and share in its blessings."*

If authentic reconciliation is to occur, white evangelicals and conservatives will need to move toward people of African descent and enter into their space at their invitation with no political agenda, and be immersed in the water of genuine cross-cultural relations together.[96]

We will say more about this Cushite in the chapter entitled "Riding the Cushites Chariot."

Simeon called Niger

We witness the remarkable racial diversity in the early church, which included full African participation. One of two African leaders mentioned in Acts 13 was Simeon called Niger, which is Latin for the *"black man."* Some Bible scholars equate him with Simon of Cyrene, who carried Christ's cross, since Simeon was a form of Simon.[97]

He was fully accepted as an equal among the leadership, and was part of those who laid hands on and commissioned Paul and Barnabas. He symbolizes what the church looks like when there is multi-ethnic equity.

He is a prophetic symbol for persons of African descent being fully equal in the church body. He is the standard for God's intent for a multiracial church at the end.

African Americans, Native Africans, Africans from the Caribbean, and those of African heritage globally are being positioned by God to fulfill prophecy. There are factors that make us ripe for the fulfillment, part of which is the often unknown African legacy of faith.

---

96 Wikipedia contributors, "Ethiopian eunuch," Wikipedia, The Free Encyclopedia. Wikipedia, The Free Encyclopedia, https://en.wikipedia.org/wiki/Ethiopian_eunuch.

97 Felder, The Original African Heritage Study Bible, 1594

Discussion Questions

1. What are the names of Cushitic Africans in this section and what do they symbolize about the fate of black people?
2. Which of the aforementioned biblical black characters stands out for you and why?

CHAPTER 10

Rediscovering the African Origin of the Faith

꣢

The creature is not greater than its Creator
~ AFRICAN PROVERB

In 1885, the brilliant German classicist Theodor Mommsen wrote: "In the development of Christianity, Africa plays the first part; if it arose in Syria, it was in and through Africa that it became the religion of the world."[98]

Thomas C. Oden, Ph.D., from Yale and professor of theology at Drew, in his book *How Africa Shaped the Christian Mind* states that Westerners have turned away from entertaining Africa's ancient Christian heritage because of seated *prejudices* concerning the non-significance of Africa to world history. As a result, theology has been taught from a *European* perspective.[99]

Oden relates that classical Christian theology was heavily shaped by *Africans*. The language we use to worship, the Trini-

---

98 quicksiva, "Ancient African Christianity: From the Pyramid Texts to Augustine," Library Thing, 9 December 2011, https://www.librarything.com/topic/128340.

99 Thomas C. Oden, How Africa Shaped the Christian Mind: Rediscovering the African Seedbed of Western Christianity, (Downers Grove: Intervarsity, 2010).

ty, the received definitions of the Christ's two natures, the early church's methods for restoring repentant sinners, our fundamental approach to biblical interpretation, the church's devotion to its martyrs—all of these things have their roots in African theological debate, African prayer, and African biblical study.[100]

Oden says Africa shaped the Christian mind of the Western church in the very earliest centuries after Christ by being the seedbed of western Christianity. More specifically, He details seven ways Africa influenced Christian Thought:

1. How the birth of the European university was anticipated within African Christianity.
2. How Christian historical and spiritual exegesis of Scripture first matured in Africa.
3. How African thinkers shaped the very core of the most basic early Christian doctrine.
4. How early ecumenical decisions followed African conciliar patterns.
5. How Africa shaped Western forms of spiritual formation through monastic discipline.
6. How Neo-platonic philosophy of late antiquity moved from Africa to Europe.
7. How influential literary and dialectical skills were refined in Africa.[101]

Many people who purport to know a lot about the Bible often lack knowledge about what happened right after the time of the Bible, after Jesus and His apostles. This is the period of time from A.D. 100 to A.D. 500. Few Christians are aware that the *most*

---

100 Oden

101 Oden, 42-61.

eminent of all thinkers, and scholars, of this time were found on the continent of *Africa*.

These theologians all lived in North Africa. They were great African theologians such as Augustine, Origen, Clement, Tertullian, Cyprian and Athanasius as well as others.

These Christian leaders and saints emerged out of a distinctly African experience on African soil. They were born as Africans, struggled in the African setting, socialized within generations of indigenous African cultures.

They were *not* European imports. They encountered the sweat and knew the thirst of African deserts and mountains. They understood the resistance of local religious practices and customs to the transformative.[102]

These African theologians and writers played a decisive role in the formation of Christian culture from its earliest beginnings. They unquestionably influenced world Christianity and were instrumental in the formulation of some of the most decisive intellectual achievements of faith.

Contrary to common perception, the intellectual leadership of Christianity largely moved from Africa to Europe—south to north. Oden says inattention of Eurocentric scholars to this south to north movement has been unhelpful (even hurtful) to the African sense of intellectual self-worth.

Lack of attention given to this distinguished literary and intellectual history has helped to propagate the false claim that Christianity is a late development in African religious history

---

102 "Summary," The Center for Early African Christianity, 2012, http://www.earlyafricanchristianity.com/about/aboutceac.html.

and therefore should not be considered an indigenous or traditional African religion.[103]

In light of this, we see that Africa played an integral part in the formation of Christian theology, but not just theology. It impacted Christian worship as well, which will culminate in the last days with a restoring of the African mother tongue in worship that initiated at Pentecost.

Discussion Questions

1. How did Africa affect the development and the spread of the early Christian faith?
2. Who were some of the early African Christian fathers who shaped Christianity?

---

103 Oden, 42-61

CHAPTER 11

Restoration of the African Mother Tongue in Worship

꧁

"God conceals himself from the mind of man,
but reveals himself to His heart"
~ AFRICAN PROVERB

As has been previously stated scientists have concluded that the original language from which all other languages originated was an African mother tongue. It was the language of the whole earth up until the confounding of language at the Tower of Babel.

At the tower of Babel in Genesis 11:1-9 the African mother tongue, the one language and the original language that the whole earth spoke was confounded. The original word translated confound [*balal /baw•lal/*], which means to mix, mingle, confuse, and cause difficulty for understanding.

Pentecost was a reversal of Babel. The Scripture says there were men of *every nation* who when they heard of this event were confounded. This scenario was a revisiting of Babel. The original Greek word for confounded is *sugcheo, sugchuno,* which means to pour together, commingle, baffle, confuse so it is synonymous with the meaning of Babel.

However, the confusion of the Pentecost incident was different. They were not confounded because they did not understand, but rather because they did.

The Scripture says that they heard them speak in their own language.

Those at Pentecost were all speaking at the same time, but the men of other nations heard them speak their unique language, so although each man had a different language; they heard one message.

This diversity of tongues spoken culminated in a oneness of language in worship and Yadah praise extolling the wonderful works of God.

> Acts 2:7-11, KJV "And they were all amazed and marveled, saying one to another, Behold, are not all these which speak Galilaeans? And how hear we every man in our own tongue,
>
> Wherein we were born? Parthians, and Medes, and Elamites, and the dwellers in Mesopotamia, and in Judaea, and Cappadocia, in Pontus, and Asia, Phrygia, and Pamphlet, in Egypt, and in the parts of Libya about Cyrene, and strangers of Rome, Jews and proselytes, Cretes and Arabians, we do hear them speak in our tongues the wonderful works of God."

Dr. Craig Keener, scholar and professor of the New Testament, says "some commentators have thought that this list of nations corresponds to ancient astrological lists, but the parallels are not very close. More likely it is the proposal that Luke has simply updated the names of nations in the Table of Nations (Genesis 10). Those nations were scattered at the tower of Babel, where God judged them by making them unintelligible to each other (Genesis 11); here at Pentecost God *reverses* the judgment in a miracle that transcends the language barrier."[104]

I concur with Keener that Pentecost was a reversal of the Tower of Babel judgment, but we must remember what was reversed. Genesis 11:1-4 NIV says:

> *Now the whole world had* one language *and a* common speech. *As people moved eastward, they found a plain in Shinar and settled there. They said to each other, "Come, let's make bricks and bake them thoroughly." They used brick instead of stone, and tar for mortar. Then they said, "Come, let us build ourselves a city, with a* tower that *reaches* to the heavens, *so that we may make a name for ourselves; otherwise we will be scattered over the face of the whole earth."*

Their unity of language would enable them to come together to build a city and a *tower* (probably a high ziggurat) which was an ancient temple that was common in Mesopotamia during the civilizations of Sumer, Babylon, and Assyria.

Ziggurats were pyramidal in shape. They had mystical purposes as shrines, with the top of the ziggurat as the most sacred spot.

The purpose of building a tower that reached into the heavens was to make a name for themselves, to become famous, and to extol their own greatness. This was not worship of the true God, but rather worship of oneself as God.

The same idolatry sin was committed by Lucifer, Adam and Eve, and Nimrod. That is manmade and the consequence of hu-

---

104 Craig Keener, "Dr. Craig Keener on the Historicity of the Book of Acts," Seedbed, 23 January 2013, http://www.seedbed.com/dr-craig-keener-on-the-historicity-of-the-book-of-acts/.

man-built religion; in the end it is the human builders of the religion who are deified. The end of such efforts is confusion.

If Pentecost was a reversal of Babel of confused language, then it means a return to the original language—a restoring of the oneness of language and oneness of speech. Scientifically we have established that this original one language was an African mother tongue the purpose of which was unity among humanity.

God surmised that with *oneness* of language nothing would be restrained from them at Babel; this was a negative thing. It becomes a positive factor at Pentecost for this unity of language returns in Christ, and because of it there is nothing that the body of Christ cannot accomplish as they are united in purpose and praise to the true God.

Therefore, Pentecost was a reversal of confounded language of the African mother tongue and a restoring back to the original language so everyone could understand each other, and ethnic oneness could be established.

It signaled that the Holy Spirit was restoring an African mother language of unity among the different races, but through the body of Christ.

Since the Holy Spirit is essentially the mother heart of the Trinity that is easily grieved (Ephesians 4:30), and the one responsible for our spiritual birth (John 3:6), who better to restore the mother tongue than the Mother Heart of the Godhead.

I am not suggesting that everyone will start speaking an African dialect. I am saying that there is a spiritual language that will be a precedent, and that it will be African not so much in dialect, but in *essence*, *nature*, and *culture*—an African spiritual language by the Holy Spirit with Afroistic features :

African language is a language of *diversity*; there is a high linguistic diversity of many African countries. Africa is the *most* linguistically *diverse* continent in the world.[105]

There is no continent more favored with varied beauty from this physical and genetic diversity that permitted Africans to birth the rest of humankind. Indigenous Africa is testimony to the full range of skin tones, hair textures, and rich religious and cultural practices.

All this diversity has a destiny that converges into one African family. There are at least 3,000 different ethnic groups on the continent.[106]

Therefore, the Holy Spirit is restoring a language to the church that will eliminate Euro-centrism and embrace ethnic diversity. The new African mother language will cause us to speak in *tongues* in terms of *diversity*, but speak in *one* tongue in terms of our *unity*.

African language is a language of *community*; the sense of community is one of the highly cherished values of basic African life. For traditional Africans, the community is viewed as sacred rather than secular.

A visitor to Africa is soon struck by the frequent use of the first person plural "*we*," and "*ours*" in everyday speech.[107]

---

105 "Are indigenous languages dead?" BBC, 6 January 2006, http://news.bbc.co.uk/2/hi/africa/4536450. stm.

106 timdrluv, "PEOPLE OF AFRICA (Beautiful and Diverse People of Africa)," AfricaWe, 5 March 2012, https://africawe.wordpress.com/2012/03/05/people-of-africabeautiful-and-diverse-people-of-africa/.

107 Ejizu, Christopher I. "African Traditional Religions and the Promotion of Community-Living in Africa." African Encyclopedia, http://traditions-afripedia.wikia.com/wiki/AFRICAN_ TRADITIONAL_RELIGIONS_AND_THE_PROMOTION_OF_COMMUNITY-LIVING_IN_ AFRICA.

The Holy Spirit is restoring the African mother tongue to the church that will be a language of *community* and communalism and not individualism. It will be a language of *"we"* of community instead of the *"I"* individualism, and that emphasizes the whole body as opposed to just a certain ethnic portion, a language that embraces community.

African language is a language of *vitality*. African culture and languages, in their many expressions, are not static, but throughout history have been dynamic.[108] The Holy Spirit is restoring the African mother tongue to the church; that will be a language of *vitality*. That is a life-giving, life-changing, and life-restoring language, especially in worship and the declaring of the Gospel.

Thus, the returning to this tongue means returning to a spiritual language that emulates the elements of the African language of *diversity*, *community*, and *vitality*, not a singular European language of Euro-ethnicity, individuality, and rigidity.

The reversal of Babel and return to the original language of the African mother tongue at Pentecost is a clue to the last day move of God, and destiny of Cushitic people of African descent. It is a clue to how God will use a people who spoke in an African mother language to bring unity in Christ—to the nations of the world through the last day outpouring of the Holy Spirit.

Kwame Gyekye, African scholar, says in the African ethics all human beings are brothers by reason of our common humanity, and that this is an African moral ideal that must be cherished and made a vital feature of global ethics in our modern world. It is a

---

108 "Introduction to Module Eight: Culture and Society in Africa," Exploring Africa, Michigan State U, 2017, http://exploringafrica.matrix.msu.edu/curriculum/unit-two/module-eight/.

major defense against bigoted attitudes toward peoples of different cultures or skin colors.[109]

The church returning to an African spiritual language that includes the features of *diversity*, *community*, and *vitality* is the key to making this happen. For it will only happen in Christ.

The language of the church must change and the voice of the ethnically excluded parts of the Body must increase. This decrease is manifesting in a Euro-American religious decline.

Discussion Questions

1. What is the change in spiritual language that people of African descent have?
2. What is the relation between Cushites, the tower of Babel, and Pentecost?

---

109 "African Ethics." Stanford Encyclopedia of Philosophy. Stanford U, 9 Sept 2010, https://plato. stanford.edu/entries/african-ethics/.

CHAPTER 12

A Eurocentric Religious Decline

🙋

God conceals himself from the mind of man,
but reveals himself to his heart.
~ **AFRICAN PROVERB**

The Cushites lost their power, wealth, and achievements because of false worship which led to them being victimized by the enemy and those he used as oppressors, but the conditions for fulfillment of Isaiah 18:1-7 are ripe for the positioning of people of African descent to a place of spiritual and economic prominence.

One such condition is the spiritual decline among Europe and Euro-Americans. The influence of traditional Christianity on people's lives has significantly *declined*, even among those who call themselves "Christian." The self-reported Christian population of America fell from 92% to 78%, and the nonreligious population rose from two percent to between thirteen and fifteen percent.

Although the U.S. is more evangelical than before depending on how you define evangelical and there are some indicators that it has remained stable, the Landscape Survey suggests that the United States is on the verge of becoming a *minority* Protestant country; the number of Americans who report that they are members of Protestant denominations now stands at barely 51 percent.[110]

Another study reports only 56 percent of Americans say they are religious people.[111] A major survey of more than 35,000 Americans by the Pew Research Center finds that the percentage of adults (ages 18 and older) who identify themselves as Christians has *decreased* by nearly eight percentage points in seven years, from 78.4 percent in an equally very large Pew Research survey in 2007 to 70.6 percent in 2014.

Over the same period, the percentage of Americans who are religiously unaffiliated—describing themselves as atheist, agnostic or "nothing in particular"—has *increased* more than six points, from 16.1 percent to 22.8 percent. And the share of Americans who identify with non-Christian faiths also has inched up, rising 1.2 percentage points, from 4.7 percent in 2007 to 5.9 percent in 2014.[112]

Researcher David Kinnaman, president of the California-based Barna Group, calculates that when he adds "the *unchurched*, the *never-churched* and the *skeptics*" to the "*nones*" it amounts to 38 percent. This is based on 15 measures of identity, belief, and practice in more than 23,000 interviews in 20 surveys.

110 "Religious Landscape Study." Pew Research Center, 2014, http://www.pewforum.org/religious-landscape-study/.

111 Giordano, Morgan. "The world's most and least religious countries." AOL News.com, 14 April 2015, https://www.aol.com/article/2015/04/14/the-world-s-most-and-least-religious-countries/21171934/.

112 Felder, The Original African Heritage Study Bible

By his count, roughly four in 10 people living in the continental United States are actually "post-Christian" and "essentially secular" in belief and practice.[113]

In addition, nonbelievers have mostly come from the ranks of Christian defectors. As a whole, American Christians lose about six thousand members a day, more than two million a year, while the population increases by 1.2 percent; currently 3.3 million people a year.[114]

For evangelicalism, the facts are that about a thousand evangelicals walk away from their churches every day and most *don't* return. Although smaller in number they wield considerable political clout. Thanks to their so-called prolife, pro-corporate politics. Racial politics.[115]

Furthermore, the Barna Group, in association with the American Bible Society, measured how frequently residents of 100 U.S. cities read the Bible and how fervently they believed in the book's accuracy. The organization considered respondents to be Bible-minded if they had read the Bible in the past seven days and believed strongly in its accuracy. The survey found, however, that only 27 percent of the American population qualified as being Bible-minded.

In a book entitled *The Next Evangelicalism: Freeing the Church from Western Cultural Captivity*, Professor Soong-Chan Rah presents research that suggests the rapid decline of *mainline* and *evangelical* Christianity in America is *mostly* among *whites*. He ar-

---

113 Grossman, Cathy Lynn. "Secularism grows as more U.S. Christians turn 'churchless'." Religion News Service, 24 October 2014, http://religionnews.com/2014/10/24/secularism-is-on-the-rise-as-more-u-s-christians-turn-churchless/.

114 Christine Wicker, The Fall of the Evangelical Nation: The Surprising Crisis Inside the Church (San Francisco: Harper One, 2008), ix.

115 Wicker, ix

gues that by contrast among immigrants and ethnic minorities, Christianity is *not* declining; it is actually exploding![116]

Sociologist R. Stephen Warner points out that the *immigrant* and *minority* population have caused a revised *de-Europeaniza-tion* of American Christianity. It is alive and well among the ethnic minority communities, and not among the majority white churches in the United States. We are actually seeing the *revival* of American Christianity in a vastly different form.[117]

There is a new era for Christianity in America. A Next Evangelicalism, an evangelicalism that crosses racial and ethnic lines with a shared value system rather than a political agenda.[118]

The anti-immigration *moves*—the xenophobic racist posture against Latinos and racism against people of African descent—is nothing more than Satan using the race divide to attempt sabotage, and halt the spiritual revival to America that these minorities will bring.

Philip Jenkins, 2010 Golden Canon Book winner, has chronicled how the next Christian movement has shifted away from the Western church toward the global South and East. It has exploded in sub-Saharan *Africa, Latin America, Asia,* and *India.*

Likewise, changing demographics mean that North American society will accelerate its diversity in terms of race, ethnicity, and culture.

116 Greg Boyd, "More Good News: Only WHITE American Christianity Is Dying!," ReKnew, 18 April 2009, http://reknew.org/2009/04/more-good-news-only-white-american-christianity-is-dying/.

117 Soong-Chan Rah, "The End of Christianity in America?" Patheos, 06 August 2010, http://www.patheos.com/Resources/Additional-Resources/End-of-Christianity-in-America.

118 Rah

He further relates that evangelicalism has been held captive by its *predominantly* white cultural identity and history.[119]

Europe, which used to be the center of Christianity, has also experienced a *major* decline among developed nations, a median of only 38 percent of European people say that religion is important in their daily lives; eight of the eleven least religious countries in the world were located in Europe.

According to the Gallup Millennium Survey of Religious Attitudes" barely 20 percent of Western Europeans attend services at least once a week, compared to a majority 82 percent of West Africans who attend weekly.

Less than half of Western Europeans say God is a "very important" part of their lives, but virtually all of West Africans say that God is "very important."[120]

These statistics represent a spiritual decline in American and European Christian faith that sets the stage for what God will do with people of African descent, and other people of color in the end times.

The pendulum has swung away from European/Euro-American domination of Christianity to an African/Latino/ Asian domination in this season. The way has been made for people of African descent. They will regain power, wealth and prominence, but for this to occur will require believers of African descent operating in the threefold anointing of *priest, prophet,* and *prince.*

---

119 Peter Wagner, "Where are the Apostles and Prophets?" Charisma Magazine, 25 June 2014, http://www.charismamag.com/spirit/church-ministry/15676-where-are-the-apostles-and-prophets.

120 Jerold Aust and John Ross Schroeder, "The tragic decline of European Christianity," The Good News Magazine, 2 October 2005, United Church of God, https://www.ucg.org/the-good-news/world-news-and-trends-the-tragic-decline-of-european-christianity.

Discussion Questions

1. What are the changes in worship that people of African descent have brought?
2. What does the decline in Euro-American and European Christianity mean to the fate of people of African descent?

CHAPTER 13

Rise Up Black Priests, Prophets and Princes!

꩜

A leader who does not take advice is not a leader.
~ AFRICAN PROVERB (KENYAN)

In this session I will be referring to the threefold anointing of *priest, prophet,* and *prince.* By anointing I mean the three main ministry tendencies and scope of abilities that proceed from the Holy Spirit to members of the body of Christ.

I will speak of this threefold anointing contextually as they relate to Christian believers of African descent. As we embrace our destiny all three of these anointings will be operative among the people of African heritage.

Christ exemplified all three of these anointings for he was *priest, prophet,* and *prince* (king). We, on the other hand, will need to exercise this threefold anointing through the corporate body, since no one man or woman possesses all three despite what some may claim.

First of all, we will need *priests.* They are those called of God to minister in the tabernacle (the church) to serve people of African heritage and, bring spiritual healing to the people, and represent them to God.

This anointing has been the one exercised primarily among our people, and seen through the vocation of pastors and clergy.

From a Cushite African standpoint it was modeled by Jethro, father-in-law of Moses and Cushitic priest of Midian. (Exodus 2:16; 3:1; 18:1).

The Kenites, Jethro's people, may have been the original worshipers of God by the name of the LORD that is Yahweh. Jethro was the person who also instructed Moses in the governance of the newly liberated Israelites (Exodus 8:13-27).[121]

Another priest in Scripture was related to Hamitic people of color, namely, Melchizedek the Edenic/African priest.

I find it fascinating that Christ did not derive his priesthood from Aaron because he did not come from the tribe of Levi, but rather he received it from Melchizedek, an Edenic/African priest of pre-Jerusalem Canaan.

This means that Christ's priesthood was a royal priesthood combining the positions of both king and priest.[122]

What we black people don't need are priests like Phinehas, the grandson of Aaron the High Priest and a part of the priestly class (Exodus 6:25). The name *Phinehas* is Egyptian (therefore African) and we have said means literally *"The Nubian,"* the *Negro,* or "The *Dark-skinned One.*"

---

121 Dr. Cain Hope Felder, "Blacks in Biblical Antiquity," African American Jubilee Bible (Philadelphia: American Bible Society, 1999), http://bibleresources.americanbible.org/resource/blacks-in-biblical-antiquity.

122 Felder, The Original African Heritage Study Bible

He and his brother Hophni were considered scoundrels who didn't know the Lord.[123] In 1 Samuel 2:12 he and brother Hophni were guilty of taking portions of the people's sacrifices for themselves, and demanding it of them even before the fat was offered to the Lord.

Moreover, they also committed adultery, so like some in clergy today he and his sibling engaged in both material and sexual indiscretions- for which destruction came on the house of Eli.

He consequently died in battle with the Philistines (1 Samuel 4:41 Samuel 4:11); and his wife, on hearing of his death, gave birth to a son, whom she called "*Ichabod*," and then she died (19-22).

There are Phinehas-like priests in God's house, that are self-aggrandizing, motivated by greed, taking the people's financial sacrifices for themselves, also taking advantage of vulnerable females, and with such actions they are disrespecting God's house.

Some of them are leading megachurches and going through the motions of worship, but they have brought destruction on their own family, and have fostered an "*Ichabod*" spiritual environment in which the true glory of God is absent. The meaning of Ichabod is *inglorious*, the *glory is gone, there is no glory*, or *the glory is departed*.

To fulfill our destiny necessitates a Jethro-type priestly anointing from black men and women of moral integrity.

The *second* anointing that must be operative among those of African heritage is the *prophets*. These are the ones called of God to receive revelation from God and to speak to African-blooded people, and to morally challenge the injustices of leaders, na-

---

123 Felder, "Blacks in Biblical Antiquity"

tions, political establishments, economical systems, and the church.

They are the genuine social advocates for the oppressed. Heretofore, the prophetic voices have come mostly from mainstream denominations such as Baptists, Methodists, AMEs, some Pentecostals and other denominations.

However, this prophetic voice has been muted among some Black evangelicals, particularly among many African American members of my party—the Republican Party.

Regrettably, many Black evangelical conservatives have often honed the craft of placating to the religiously conservatives and the evangelical power establishment. This has left a great void in the prophetic message needed in this hour in light of the racial injustices going on in our nation and globally.

Eddie Glaude, Jr., Ph.D., professor of religion and chair of the Center for African American Studies at Princeton University, maintains that, "We see organization and protests against same-sex marriage and abortion, even billboards to make the anti-abortion case. But where are the press conferences and impassioned efforts around black children living in poverty?"

He goes on to say that Black churches and preachers must find their *prophetic* voices in this momentous present.[124] Glaude notes that Black evangelicals are speaking out on issues like same-sex marriage and abortion but many have given racists a pass and racism the silent treatment.

They can be very incensed about the killing of fetuses in the womb only to be quiet about the dying of black children and youth born outside the womb. The challenge then is that racist

124 Glaude, Eddie, Jr. "The Black Church Is Dead." The Huffington Post, 24 Feb. 2010, http://www.huffingtonpost.com/eddie-glaude-jr-phd/the-black-church-is-dead_b_473815.html.

conservatives can ignore those with prophetic voices from mainstream denominations, and be dismissive of their truth concerning racism.

Therefore, many black evangelicals have been complicit in reinforcing the defense mechanism of denial used by many conservative racists. Sad to say, but many of these black evangelicals have been seduced by money and notoriety offered by white conservative evangelicals, and the wealthy conservative political establishment.

Still others have behaved like Stephen (portrayed by Samuel L. Jackson in *Django Unchained*), the spiteful Uncle Tom-like character who participated in the oppression of his own people. (Many blacks in America have relegated Clarence Thomas and Ben Carson to that position) in that they have also endorsed policies, sanctioned, and participated in racist practices counter-productive to black people.

What people of African descent need are prophets like Zephaniah, whose father was Cushi. It is a Hebrew term generally used to refer to a *dark*-skinned person usually of African heritage.

This term was recently interpreted as being similar to the English word *Negro*,[125] meaning also the *black*, the *Nubian*, the *Cushite*, and the Ethiopian.

We conclude that if Zephaniah's father was a black man, then the prophet was a black man.[126]

He was active about 630 B.C. and sparked a religious revival in Judah. When Zephaniah-like prophets are active from those

---

125 Wikipedia contributors, "Cushi," Wikipedia, The Free Encyclopedia, Wikipedia, The Free Encyclopedia, https://en.wikipedia.org/wiki/Cushi.

126 Felder, "Blacks in Biblical Antiquity"

of African descent they too will be used by God to help bring spiritual revival.

The teaching of the book of Zephaniah is that those who seek *justice* and walk humbly before their God may be hidden and protected in the Day of the Lord.

The genuine prophetic voices need not fear reprisal from the racists or the "Stephen"-like black conservatives, for God has their back.[127]

The challenge of being a prophet is that there are not the same kinds of financial support for their calling that are available to priests and princes. Priests get support from the tabernacles that they serve and princes get financial support from the governments and businesses they serve, but, where do the prophets get their support? They often have to resort to taking a job as a priest (pastor) and in doing so function in a position they were not called to, or they take on a secular job and are often not able to exercise the passion of their true calling.

The people of African descent suffer since they don't get the maximum benefit of the prophetic anointing needed to fulfill their destiny. Support for the prophets should come from the community at large they serve, for if they get their money from the priests and princes unless it is no strings attached it can become a form of bribery, and they become like Balaam (2 Peter 2:15, Jude11) Assuming the role of *profiteer* instead of *prophet*.

Those with a prophetic anointing have to be free to be the ethical voices they were called to be without compromise. Prophets have to first and foremost remember who their provider is and really rely on Him. He is Jehovah Jireh.

---

127 Felder, The Original African Heritage Study Bible, 1331

An example who comes to mind is Elijah who was directed by God to hide out by the brook Cherith (1 Kings 17:1-2). There, he survived by drinking from the waters of this brook and being fed bread and meat brought by the ravens morning and evening (1 Kings 17:4-6).

The ravens symbolize resources God supernaturally targets to his prophets to support their livelihood—resources that would not normally be available to them. It is a miraculous provision from God via situations he sends.

The reality of the prophetic anointing is that in all likelihood prophets are not going to become wealthy; some will, but most won't. So they cannot be motivated by money, yet God will meet all their basic needs and then some.

Notwithstanding, if the truth be told, there will be seasons where it appears the brook is drying up.

The good news is that in those seasons God will prepare a second means of livelihood support, that of a widow of Zarephath. Her kindness permitted Elijah to move forward into his calling of challenging the political model of Jezebel/Ahab and the prophets of Baal on their payroll.

These widows are persons who have endured a great loss—the death of something they were wedded to. God then strategically places them in the paths of prophets to support the prophets.

They aren't necessarily wealthy individuals, but their investment in the prophet plus exposure to the prophetic anointing causes them to become prosperous so that they can continue to bless the prophet.

This is why African Americans and Africans must reroute giving away from tele-evangelists that support political positions that hurt African blooded people socially, but then solicit funds from them to support their mega ministries. The rechanneling of funds away from such ministries helps to free up financial resources to support people of African descent with a prophetic call.

Prophetic pursuits by Elijah on the political establishment of Ahab/Jezebel resulted in threats against the prophet that made him take flight, and go into a state of depression (this often happens with prophets).

His melancholy worsened to the point that he requested that God take his life. He became too depressed to care for himself so God intervened and sent an angel to care for his livelihood while he recovered.

Now the angels are messengers sent by God to touch the lives of prophets in their despondent state, to uplift them by providing for them. Prophets will encounter angels in their down seasons not so much spirit being messengers coming from heaven, but rather spiritually minded human messengers sent by heaven—to edify and resource God's spokespeople.

Prophets must be cautious in dealing with people in their down times, which are seasons that put them at risk for being rude, because they don't always know who an angel is, and if they mistreat one they could miss out on the deposit that angel brings. Hebrews 13:2 says:

> *"Forget not to show* love *unto* strangers: *for thereby some have* entertained *angels unawares"* ASV

I recognize that in writing this book I am operating in the prophetic, it is not my intent to soothe egos, cater to cowardice, placate racists or pacify prejudice, but to speak the truth, for the destiny of my people is at stake, and their prophetic purpose is on the line in this historic season.

The *third* anointing is that of *princely* anointing, those of African descent who are called by God to achieve great wealth, power, affluence, influence, lead nations, states serve in high government offices or strategic business positions.

They are called with an anointing to use their status for the benefit of people of African descent, and to enable them to fulfill their destiny.

There are several black examples of this anointing in Scripture. The Cushite treasurer under the African queen Candace as mentioned previously.

The other examples of the princely anointing of a person of African heritage is Ebed-Melech, a government official, Pharaoh Tirhakah, the Queen of Sheba, and Candace herself in Acts 8. When these three anointings are activated they contribute significantly to the change that is coming to the destiny of people of African descent.

Therefore, it will mean they discover their place in the body, and function out of the three anointings. As people of color assuming these anointed roles it will bring change and change is coming.

Discussion Questions

1. What are the three anointings and how do they relate to God's purpose for people of African descent?
2. What anointings do Jethro and Candace typify for the destiny of black people?

CHAPTER 14

A Change a Comin'

ﷺ

"You must change to survive"
~ PEARL BAILEY

"If the rhythm of the drumbeat changes, the dance step must adapt."
~ AFRICAN PROVERB

The prophecy of Isaiah 18 signals that there is a change coming for people of African descent in the world, a redemptive and restorative change.

Spiritual Change of African Americans

Today religion plays a significant role in the lives of millions of African Americans. Black men and women serve in positions of leadership in a variety of denominations and churches. They are a potent force for unity and progress in the black community. They have served as the origin of leadership and uplift from the time of slavery, through the trials of Jim Crow and the struggle for civil rights up to the present day. They have served by helping to support education, to engender economic growth and urban renewal, and to fight for equal rights in a society that can be unfair and cruel.

Black churches remain a critical factor of the African American experience as well as the national American experience. Consider the effects of one movement.[128]

The Azusa Street Revival was a historic revival meeting that took place in Los Angeles California, and is the origin of the Pentecostal movement. It was led by William J. Seymour, an *African American* preacher.

It began with a meeting on April 9, 1906, and continued until roughly 1915. The revival was characterized by ecstatic spiritual experiences accompanied by miracles, dramatic worship services, speaking in tongues, and *interracial* fellowship.

This revival spurred by an African-American man brought *interracial* fellowship and the next major revival that comes to America will also bring *interracial reconciliation* and be led by people of *African descent* and other people of color.

Today, the Azuza revival is considered by historians to be the primary catalyst for the spread of Pentecostalism in the 20th century. By the end of 1906, most leaders from Azusa Street had spun off to form other congregations, such as the 51st Street Apostolic Faith Mission, the *Spanish* AFM, and the *Italian* Pentecostal Mission. These missions were largely composed of *immigrant* or *ethnic* groups.

The Southeast United States was a particularly prolific area of growth for the movement, since Seymour's approach gave a useful explanation for a charismatic spiritual climate that had

---

128 "Black Churches in America," Oxford African American Studies Center, http://www.oxfordaasc.com/public/features/archive/0707/index.jsp.

already been taking root in those areas. Nearly all of these new churches were founded among *immigrants* and the *poor*.

Many existing Wesleyan-holiness denominations adopted the Pentecostal message, such as the Church of God (Cleveland, Tennessee), the Church of God in Christ, and the Pentecostal Holiness Church. The formation of new denominations also occurred, such as the Assemblies of God formed in 1914, Pentecostal Assemblies of the World in 1916, and the Pentecostal Church of God, formed in 1919.

As a product of this movement initiated by this *black* man, today, there are more than 500 million Pentecostal and charismatic believers across the globe and they are the *fastest-growing* form of Christianity today.

The Azusa Street Revival is commonly regarded as the *beginning* of the modern-day Pentecostal Movement and a precursor influence of the white charismatic movement—a movement that a black man of African descent started.[129]

In general, today's statistics indicate that African Americans are the *most spiritually devout* racial demographic in the United States.

- When African American adolescent girls were asked how important religion is to their life, **89.22%** of the sample reported that religion was *very* important.

---

129 Wikipedia contributors, "Azusa Street Revival," Wikipedia, The Free Encyclopedia. Wikipedia, The Free Encyclopedia, 29 September 2013, https://en.wikipedia.org/wiki/Azusa_Street_Revival.

- **90%** of the most represented age group in the sample, the 14-year-old teens also responded that religion was very important.[130]
- In general, nearly **8 in 10** African-Americans, **79%**, say religion is very important in their lives, compared with **56%** of the U.S. population as a whole.
- Of 30 million, **26 million** are involved with church. That amounts to about 65,000 congregations.
- **87%** of African-Americans belong to one religious group or another **Just 3%** of blacks say they have no religion.
- By wide margin, African Americans are the *most* Protestant racial and ethnic group in the U.S.
- **78%** of blacks are protestant compared to 51% of U.S. as a whole.
- **66%** of blacks describe themselves as evangelical-born-again Christians, *double* the share of whites. Of the black Protestants, **89%** attend evangelical churches.
- **77%** of African Americans pray daily. **55%** of them interpret the Bible as the literal word of God compared to **33%** for U.S. as whole.
- **77%** of African Americans pray before bed every day compared to **45%** of Hispanics. **32** % of whites and **18** % of Asians.[131]
- A *nationwide* survey conducted by The Washington Post and the Kaiser Family Foundation - the *most* extensive look at black women's lives in decades, reveals that as a group nearly **nine in 10** African American women turn to faith in a crisis.

130 Williams, Olivia A. "Effects of Faith and Church on African American Adolescents." Michigan Family Review, vol. 8, no. 1, 2003, pp. 19-27, https://quod.lib.umich.edu/m/mfr/4919087.0008.103/--effects-of-faith-church-involvement-on-african-american?rgn=main;view=fulltext.

131 Heimlich, Russell. "Blacks Are The Most Religious Americans." Pew Research Center, 03 Nov. 2008, http://www.pewresearch.org/fact-tank/2008/11/03/blacks-are-the-most-religious-americans/.

- Black women are among the *most* religious people in the nation. Although black men are almost as religious as their female counterparts, there is a clear divide along *racial* lines.
- The study found that **74 percent** of *black women* and **70** percent of *black men* said that *"living a religious life"* is very important to them. Contra wise, with that same question, the number falls to **57 percent** of *white women* and **43 percent** of white men.
- In times of turmoil, about **87 percent** of black women — *much more* than *any* other group — report that they resort to their faith to get through.
- Black women, across the spectrum of education and income levels, say living a religious life is *more* important than being married or having children, and this call to faith either surpasses or is even with having a career as a life goal.[132]
- Albeit, this deep devout spirituality does not cease with African Americans, but extends to the Africans of Africa.

Discussion Questions

1. What religious statistics and measures demonstrate that a change has come to African Americans?
2. Which of these change statistics do you relate to?

✤ ✤ ✤

---

132 Theola Labbé-DeBose, "Black women are among country's most religious groups," The Washington Post, 6 July 2012, https://www.washingtonpost.com/local/black-women-are-among-countrys-most-religious-groups/2012/07/06/gJQAoBksSW_story.html?utm_term=.60d45ffbaf9f.

Africans

Geoff Waugh who has historically studied spiritual revivals over the globe states that the church in Africa has increased from nearly 10 million in 1900 to about 400 million now, half the population. In the early 1900s one out of every 13,000 were Christians; now *one* out of *three* are reported as being Christians.

The killing and persecution of African Christians in places like the Belgian Congo, Zaire, Uganda and the crusade work of men and women evangelists called to Africa, has resulted in powerful revival outpourings. Many African revivals experienced supernatural manifestations, visions, prophecies, and healings. For 40 years there has been an ongoing revival in East Africa. Revivals include a powerful move of God in Ethiopia in 1978.

Revived Christians survived the Mau massacres in Kenya and the church continued to grow. For example, 700 new churches began in Kenya in 1980 alone, a rate of about two a day.

Nigeria experienced revivals in 1983–1984, accelerating church growth there.

Moreover, South Africa has experienced a great revival. Today we see prayers being answered as revival that started in the late 1800's is moving across South Africa today.[133]

Christianity has *grown substantially* in Africa according to research by the Pew foundation. Conrad Hackett, lead researcher on the "Global Christianity" reports that the Christian faith has grown *exponentially* in sub-Saharan Africa, from just 9% of the population in 1910 to 63% today.

---

133 Waugh, Geoff. "20th Century Revivals." The Revival Library, 2015, http://www.revival-library.org/index.php/catalogues-menu/20th-century/20th-century-revival

Nigeria, home to more than 80 million Christians, has *more* Protestants than Germany, where the Protestant Reformation began. To reiterate, 82% of West Africans attend service regularly.

Furthermore, according to Philip Jenkins, an expert in religious history at Baylor University in Texas, there has been a *phenomenal* growth of Christianity in Africa. He says the number of African Christians in 2050 will be almost *twice* as large as the total figure for all Christians alive anywhere in the globe back in 1900.

The Center for the Study of Global Christianity at Gordon-Conwell Theological Seminary has released a report: "*Christianity in its Global Context, 1970–2020 Society.*" In an article it is noted that the Mission Neo-Pentecostal mega-churches are *booming* in Africa, particularly in West Africa. "As a result of historic missionary activity and indigenous Christian movements by Africans, there has been this *change* from about one in 10 sub-Saharan Africans identifying with Christianity in 1910 to about **six in 10** doing so today" Hackett said:

"Christianity is *growing faster* in Africa than *anywhere* else in the world. There are over 390 million Christians in sub-Saharan Africa today, up from 117 million in 1970 according to the Center for the Study of Global Christianity in South Hamilton, Massachusetts.

It is most Africans' life situations that make Christianity very attractive to the people," observed Jonathan Bonk, the editor of the International Bulletin of Missionary Research in New Haven, Connecticut. He says that "It's a faith of *hope* for *poor* people. Which is what Jesus said was part of his mission and reason for coming

Luke 4:18 (NIV) "The Spirit of the Lord is on me, because he has anointed me to proclaim good news to the poor. He has sent me to proclaim freedom for the prisoners and recovery of sight for the blind, to set the oppressed free"

One prominent prophetic voice states that *"Revival, renewal, awakening"* — none of these words seem big enough to describe what is currently taking place in Africa. Entire regions are being impacted by the gospel, and whole cities are falling to their knees confessing Jesus as Lord.

Looking at the numbers, there is *nothing* in history to compare with the present move of God in Africa. One African newspaper reported that "Africa is being saved."

In Aba, Nigeria, in a six-day crusade, 1,400,000 new believers professed faith in Christ. Prior to that 1,100,000 came to the Lord in Calabar, Nigeria during a six-day meeting. To put this in historical context, during the great Welsh revival of 1904, 100,000 people were saved in six months.

Truly, our traditional religious vocabulary does not have a word *big* enough to capture this move.[134]

In an article entitled Africa's Azusa Street in Christianity today by Timothy C. Morgan says East Africa has experienced revival continually for nearly 80 years. Revival in East Africa is a familiar story that shows few signs of slowing down, despite entering its eighth decade.

About 85 million Pentecostal and charismatic Christians can be found in Africa today. A hundred years ago, there were only a handful. African Pentecostals and Charismatics are growing at

---

134 Rick Joyner, "Report on Revival in Africa," MorningStar Ministries, https://www.morningstarministries.org/resources/prophetic-bulletins/2000/report-revival-africa#. WUPYmhPytE4.

about 4.5 percent annually, nearly *double* the continent's overall rate of population growth.[135]

These developments highlight another prophetic reference to Cushite Africans in the last day namely Psalms 68:31:

> *"Ambassadors will come from Egypt;* Cush *will* stretch out *its* hands *to* God"

Today people of color such as *Africans, Latinos,* and *Asians,* are more typical representatives of Christianity than Euro-Americans or Europeans. This trend suggests a transition in the centrality of global influence of the faith away from United States and Europe and toward more third world nations.

Nineteen of the top twenty countries where the Christian faith is *growing* are in Asia and *Africa,* 11 countries on the top 20 list are *Muslim* majority countries. *Not a single country* from *Europe* or *Northern America* makes the top 20 list.

The highest Christian growth rates are found among all major non-Christian religious groups: Hindus, Non-Religious, Buddhists, Muslims and Ethno-religionists (Benin and South *Sudan*). The majority of the top 20 countries are clustered in three areas: Eastern Asia, *Western Africa* and the Arabian Peninsula-in other words, people of color.

This may partly explain the step up terrorist attacks against black Churches in the US by white Supremacist or the Islamic murders of black Christians in Africa by groups like ISIS and Boka Haram.[136]

---

135 Morgan, Timothy C. "Africa's Azusa." Christianity Today, 28 March 2006, http://www. christianitytoday.com/ct/2006/marchweb-only/113-23.0.html.

136 Mitchell, Russ. "The Top 20 Countries where Christianity is Growing the Fastest." Disciple All Nations, 25 August 2013, https://discipleallnations.wordpress.com/2013/08/25/the-top-20-countries-where-christianity-is-growing-the-fastest/

It also could explain the rise of Islamphobia against the muslims of the US from white Supremacists and hate groups. God wants the church to reach out to this community they are ripe for the gospel but the hatred toward them coming from these groups has turned them off to Christianity.

There are socio-economic factors that account for one's spiritual affiliations in these nations. *Wealthier* and more educated individuals in these places reported *lower* levels of religious identity.[137] These nations have been some of the *poorest* and *most oppressed* on the globe which has caused a turning to Christ and a crying out to God. A crying out which has been responded to in this time: so says Psalm 12:5:

> *"Now will I arise, says the Lord, because the* poor *are oppressed, because of the groans of the needy; I will set him in safety and in the salvation for which he pants" AMP.*

Cushites of Caribbean and Latin Americans

A study examined distinctions in religious involvement and spirituality among African Americans, Caribbean Blacks, and non-Hispanic Whites. Data was taken from the National Survey of American Life, a nationally representative study of African Americans, Black Caribbean's and non-Hispanic Whites.

Selected measures of organizational, non-organizational and subjective religious participation were reviewed. African American and Caribbean Blacks were *very similar* in their reports of re-

---

137 Giordano, Morgan. "The world's most and least religious countries." AOL News.com, 14 April 2015, https://www.aol.com/article/2015/04/14/the-world-s-most-and-least-religious-countries/21171934/.

ligious involvement; both groups generally showed *higher* levels of religious participation than Whites.

They reported reading religious materials *more* frequently than even African Americans.[138]

The religion of the Caribbean is dominated by Christianity where many blacks of the Diaspora and slavery find their home. One of the distinctive elements of Caribbean Christianity is the racial and ethnic diversity of its adherents. A large portion of the people of the region is either black or African American (mixed African and non-African descent).

Christianity has continued to spread *widely* in the region.[139]

Evangelical churches have made inroads in Latin America and the Caribbean. Relatively obscure decades ago, evangelicals including Pentecostals, Baptists and others now count roughly for 97.5 million followers in the region, according to data provided by a coalition of evangelical churches.

The Pew Forum on Religion and Public Life's 2011 report on Christianity found 94 million Protestants in Latin America and the Caribbean. The growth of the evangelical movement has come as the number of Catholics has fallen.[140]

Caribbean Blacks had *significantly higher* levels of spirituality than did whites. There were *no* significant differences in spirituality between African Americans and Caribbean Blacks.[141]

---

138 Chatters, Linda M. et al. "Race and Ethnic Differences in Religious Involvement: African Americans, Caribbean Blacks and Non-Hispanic Whites." Ethnic and racial studies 32.7 (2009): 1143–1163. PMC, https://www.ncbi.nlm.nih.gov/pmc/articles/PMC2962581/.

139 "Christianity in the Caribbean Region." Encyclopedia of Religion, 2nd ed., March 2005.

140 Fieser, Ezra and Lise Alves. "Latin Evangelicals' Explosive Growth." Catholic San Francisco, 11 May 2012.

141 Chatters

God is bringing Cushitic Africans from Africa, from North America, South America, the Caribbean, and from all over the world to lead a global revival and a spiritual war against the enemy. They are qualified because they were feared far and wide, they were a conquering people. They know how to *war* and they know how to *win*. They will once again be a conquering people, they will once again be feared by the enemy, but their enemy will be the spiritual forces of darkness, and will not be made of flesh and blood although he may use those made of flesh and blood. Their weapons won't be carnal but mighty through God to the pulling down of strongholds.

As the Cushitic people of African heritage turn to Jesus Christ, worship the true God Yahweh, and embrace their divinely ordained destiny, a spiritual awakening is breaking forth, and the spiritual revival is causing other changes.

The conditions of Cushites of Africa, North and South America, and the Caribbean are going to be turned around, the yoke of poverty and oppression is going to be broken. This is our time and this is our destiny. The spiritual change will prompt other changes as well.

Discussion Questions

1. What religious and spiritual changes have come to people of African descent in Africa, Latin America, and Caribbean?
2. What do all of these changes mean to God's agenda for black people?

❧ ❧ ❧

Socio-demographical Change

A change is coming in racial attitudes about Cushites and people of African descent, not so much from the established older white generation of evangelicals and political conservatives because for most of them their racism is too entrenched and political positions too fixated for any substantive transformation to occur, but it lies with an emerging younger generation of conservatives and evangelicals who understand that today we live in a different world and at a different time. They understand that America has changed in terms of racial diversity.

Today's young millennials are *more* ethnically diverse than their older generation. They are the *most* racially *diverse* generation in American history, because of a large influx of people of color like Hispanic and Asian immigrants who have been coming to the U.S. for the past half century, and whose U.S.-born offspring are now maturing into adulthood.

Consequently, millennials are a transitional generation—a 2009 survey found that they are *more racially tolerant* than their elders and more open to interracial dating. 93% agreed it was acceptable for black and white people to date and they are also more accepting of interracial marriage.

Large majorities of 18-to-29-year-olds express support for interracial marriage within their families, and the level of acceptance in this generation is *greater* than in other generations.

A Pew Research Center's report concerning racial attitudes in the U.S., revealed that an overwhelming majority of millennials, regardless of race, say they would be supportive of a family member's marriage to a person of a different race or ethnicity.

Roughly nine in ten say they would be fine with a family member's marriage to an African American (88%), a Hispanic American (91%), White American (92%) and an Asian American (93%); they were also more receptive to immigrants.[142]

Six in 10 millennials are non-whites; some 43% of millennial adults are non-white, the *highest* share of *any* generation. About half of newborns in America today are non-white, and the Census Bureau projects that the full U.S. population will be *majority* non-white sometime around 2043.[143]

Ethnic minorities will also become a *majority* among millennial adults 18–29.[144]

Moreover, another factor contributing to the diversifying of America is the increased immigrant population of students, especially students of color from China and India who are coming to America to study.

According to new federal data, the number of international students studying at U.S. colleges increased by 10 percent last year, marking the *largest* single-year gain in 35 years.

---

142 Fry, Richard. "Millennials overtake Baby Boomers as America's largest generation." Pew Research Center, 25 April 2016, http://www.pewresearch.org/fact-tank/2016/04/25/millennials-overtake-baby-boomers/.

143 Fry

144 "Whites no longer a majority in U.S. by 2043." CBS News/AP, 12 December 2012, http://www.cbsnews.com/news/census-whites-no-longer-a-majority-in-us-by-2043/.

Of the almost 1 million students who came to the U.S. in the 2014–15 school year, about a *third* came from China, the *most* from any country. But much of last year's growth was due to a surge in the number of students who came from *India*, drawn by strong research programs, experts say.

In all, the number of Indian students in the U.S. grew by 30 percent to more than 130,000, the *largest* jump since the nonprofit started collecting data in 1954. Many of these students are not only studying in America but remaining, working, and permanently residing in the U.S. after graduation.[145]

However, underlying the major demographic changes is the rapid growth of minority groups compared with whites. The nation's racial and ethnic minority groups are increasing *more* rapidly than the white population, caused by both immigration and birthrates.

The Pew Foundation reported that more than 16 million Mexican immigrants have migrated to the United States in the last 50 years, *more* than from *any* other country.[146]

The results from the 2010 Census indicated that racial and ethnic minorities accounted for 91.7% of the nation's growth since 2000, but white, accounted for only 8.3% of growth over the decade.

---

145 Colin Binkley, "More students come to US colleges from China, India, but relatively few Americans study abroad," US News/AP, 16 November 2015, https://www.usnews.com/news/us/articles/2015/11/16/us-adds-foreign-students-but-few-americans-study-abroad.

146 Gonzales, Suzannah. "More Mexican immigrants leaving U.S. than entering: Pew." Reuters, 19 November 2015, http://www.reuters.com/article/us-usa-immigration-mexico-idUSKCN0T82F220151119.

Minorities accounted for 93.3% of the nation's population growth from April 1, 2010, to July 1, 2011, according to Census Bureau data.[147]

Moreover, the death rates among whites is also a contributing factor to the change in demographics. A study by Anne Case and Angus Deaton of Princeton University reported the death rates for other races have continued to *fall*, but death rates for *whites* 35 to 44 have been *going up*—the rates for whites 55 to 64, and —most *strikingly*—death rates for whites ages 45 to 54 have *risen* by *half* a percent *every year* since 1998. White Americans have been dying more frequently in middle age over the past 15 years, and the causes are mostly *self-inflicted*.

Federal researchers have reported—repeatedly—on *worrisome* increases in deaths from *suicides*, substance abuse, alcoholic liver disease, and overdoses of heroin and prescription opioids.

In 2011, deaths from drug or alcohol overdoses exceeded lung cancer as a *major* cause of death among this group. Suicide follows closely behind.

Addiction and suicide have fueled a 15-year uptick in mortality rates for Caucasians between 45 and 54 years old in the United States. White Americans have been dying more often in middle age over the past 15 years, per a new study. This signals a reverse of a long-term trend of declining death rates among this age group in the United States.

"Accidental poisonings are the largest part of the increase," study author Angus Deaton, Ph.D., a professor at Princeton University, wrote in an email to Healthline. "But that is both

---

147 Passel, Jeffrey S., Gretchen Livingston, and D'Vera Cohn. "Explaining Why Minority Births Now Outnumber White Births." Pew Research Center, 17 May 2012, http://www.pewsocialtrends. org/2012/05/17/explaining-why-minority-births-now-outnumber-white-births/.

(legal) opioids and (illegal) opiates, as well as alcohol. And suicides and liver disease are also important."

Middle-age whites are dying at a *startling* rate and as death rates went up among Caucasians in the United States. The death rates among middle-aged *Hispanics* and *African Americans* continued to *go down*.

Those with lowest education were most likely to die between 1999 and 2013, middle-aged whites with less than a high school degree had the *largest* rise in overall death rates,[148] and unlike their counterparts in other rich countries, death rates in this group have been *rising*, not falling.

The Case and Deaton findings aren't exactly surprising, said Robert Anderson, who oversees the Centers for Disease Control and Prevention branch that monitors death statistics.

This crisis of whites dying is the nation's best-kept secret, going unnoticed by millions of people and being all but ignored by the media;[149] but it is a *serious* issue that is having a profound effect on American demographics. I find it interesting that this is the same demographic in age and race that is also the most racist and xenophobic in this nation.

Furthermore, the other reality concerning the changing face of demographics is that interracial marriages in the U.S. have climbed to 4.8 million—a record 1 in 12.

---

148 Radcliffe on November 2, Shawn. "More White People Are Dying at Middle Age." Healthline, 2 November 2015, http://www.healthline.com/health-news/more-white-people-are-dying-at-middle-age-110215.

149 Mike Stobbe, "More Middle-Aged White People Are Dying, Study Says," US News/AP, 2 November 2015, http://health.usnews.com/health-news/news/articles/2015/11/02/study-deaths-rates-rising-in-middle-aged-whites?offset=2800.

In another report researcher at the Pew Research Center reported that nearly 1 out of 7 new marriages in the U.S. are interracial or interethnic. The report interviewed couples married for less than a year and discovered that *racial* lines are *blurring* as more people choose to marry outside their race as the rise of new Asian and Hispanic immigrants expands the pool of prospective mates.[150]

Blacks are now considerably *more* likely than before to marry whites. A Pew Research Center study reveals a *diversifying* America where interracial unions and the mixed-race children they produce are challenging traditional views of race.[151]

By 2060, multiracial people are predicted to multiply more than *three* times from 7.5 million to 26.7 million, rising *even faster* and rendering notions of race labels increasingly irrelevant. Apparently, race is mattering *less* these days, especially among millennials.

Ironically, a Pew Foundation study found the largest *multiracial* group in America are whites with *Native American* ancestry. They constitute a full half of the current population of mixed-race Americans, but are often the *least* likely to admit that they are multiracial.

This ignorance of or denial by Euro-Americans of their Native American ancestry is unfortunate to say the least.

Many of these whites cannot deal with the fact that they are carrying the blood of a *people* of *color*. Whose blood was of-

---

150 Chen, Stephanie. "Interracial Marriages at an All-time High, Study Says." CNN, 04 June 2010, http://www.cnn.com/2010/LIVING/06/04/pew.interracial.marriage/index.html.

151 Hope Yen, "Interracial marriage in US hits new high: 1 in 12," Yahoo News/AP, 16 February 2012, https://www.yahoo.com/news/interracial-marriage-us-hits-high-1-12-051151085.html.

ten spilled by Euro-Americans, and who, like African Americans, were persecuted.

They also may not be able to deal with how the white and Native American genes became intermingled since much of it was not the product of marriage.

In the past, Native American women living under a white colonial rule experienced sexual violence against them. Even today, Native American women are more than *twice* as likely as White women, Asian American women, and Black women to experience sexual violence. 78% of the *perpetrators* are *White men*.[152]

Thus, mixed-race whites cannot come to grips with the reality that their biracial nature makes them a walking contradiction, and their own racism often contributes to their avoidance in accepting a part of themselves.

If they could embrace their Native American side perhaps they would be more empathic to the plight of other people of color, and become more whole as people in the process.[153]

However, soon even they will be eclipsed by other multiracial Americans, with many of the mixed-race babies born in 2013 being either biracial *white* and *black* or biracial *white* and *Asian*.

A report from the Center for Immigration Studies analyzed new figures from the U.S. Census and found by 2023 fifty-one million legal and illegal immigrants will be residing in the country. That's one in seven U.S. residents who were born in anoth-

152 Wikipedia contributors, "Sexual victimization of native American women," Wikipedia, The Free Encyclopedia. Wikipedia, The Free Encyclopedia, https://en.wikipedia.org/wiki/Sexual_victimization_of_native_American_women.

153 Holland, Jesse J. "Pew study: Whites with Native American ancestry largest multiracial group in United States." US News/AP, 11 June 2015, https://www.usnews.com/news/politics/articles/2015/06/11/pew-white-native-american-adults-largest-multiracial-group

er country. They will be the *highest* immigrant population since 1910.[154]

Moving forward, the U.S. will become the *first* major post-industrial society in the world where *minorities* will be the *majority*.[155] Whites will not only become the minority in the U.S.; they will also become the minority on the *entire* globe as a percentage of world inhabitants.

They will plunge to a single digit (9.76%) by 2060 from a high point of 27.98% in 1950. Of the seven population groups studied *only* whites are predicted to undergo a probable *decline* in numbers.

By 2060 the number of *immigrants* will increase to 78 million—or about one in five residents. The Center of Immigration Studies' report forecasts that the *surge* in immigrants will have a vast impact on the nation.[156]

Immigrants and racial minorities, especially those who are people of color, are changing the American demographic landscape. In 1950 whites and blacks were respectively 27.98% and 8.97% of the world population. By 2060 these numbers will almost reverse as blacks increase to 25.38% and whites decrease to 9.76%.

From 2010 the white population will *decline* while blacks will *expand* their numbers by a billion.[157] The changing national and global demographics are a reality that is both present and

---

154 Whitaker, Morgan. "Census data reveals US immigrant population to top 51 million in 2023." AOL.com, 24 April 2015, https://www.aol.com/article/2015/04/24/census-data-reveals-us-immigrant-population-to-top-51-million-in/21175968/

155 CBS

156 Whitaker

157 Whitaker

coming; they speak to a younger, racially *diverse* generation of *millennials*.

Unfortunately, this demographic shift has been met with extreme xenophobia and racism, primarily from political ultra-conservatives and *white supremacy* groups.

According to a count by the *New America Foundation, more* people have been *killed* on American soil by *white extremists* than by *Muslim jihadists* in the years since 9/11.[158]

This year, the millennial generation is projected to *surpass* the Baby Boom generation as the nation's *largest* living generation, according to the population projections released by the U.S. Census Bureau last month. Millennials (whom we define as between ages 18 to 34 in 2015) are projected to number 75.3 million, *surpassing* the projected 74.9 million Boomers (ages 51 to 69).

The Gen X population (ages 35 to 50 in 2015) is projected to outnumber the Boomers by 2028. The Millennial generation continues to grow as young *immigrants* expand their ranks. Boomers—a generation defined by the boom in U.S. births following World War II—are older and *shrinking* in size as the number of deaths exceeds the number of immigrants arriving in the country. Some of whom are young evangelicals and conservatives.

In addition, to the socio-demographic change, people of color are poised for other changes in the political and economic sphere.[159]

---

158 "FBI: Two Virginia men planned to incite a 'race war' by bombing black churches," AOL, 10 November 2015, https://www.aol.com/article/2015/11/10/fbi-two-virginia-men-planned-to-incite-a-race-war-by-bombing/21262511/.

159 Fry

Discussion Questions

1. What do the socio-demographic changes mean to people of African descent in the last days?
2. What is the role of millennials in God's destiny for people of African descent in the end times?

❧ ❧ ❧

The Political Change

The socio-demographical change and a younger more diverse population are causing a shift in the political landscape. To that point Jonathan Merritt, of *The Atlantic* said:

"As I survey the rising generation of Christians in America, I see many who recognize the ways in which the thirst for power has corrupted the faith. They're eschewing *partisan politics* to coerce and control the country, and they are finding ways to work with others they may disagree with. They are looking for new ways to live their faith in our rapidly changing world, and they give me hope that American Christians may be on the cusp of a healthier engagement with the public square."[160]

The winds of political change have already begun to blow. The evidence for this change can be seen by the election of two political figures in the twenty-first century who have become iconic internationally.

---

160 Merritt

Namely, Nelson Mandela and Barack Obama. When you think about it, each of their ascendances to office was nothing short of astonishing and God-orchestrated. That is the only explanation that makes any sense given the racist history of the two countries to which they were elected.

Both men were elected in convincing landslide victories and Obama was elected *twice*—reflect on that, an African American was elected twice in a majority white culture with a rather unflattering past as to race relations.

When Obama was elected, he promised change. He brought that change not so much by what he *did*, but by what he *was*—a black man who was elected to two terms in the White House.

Like it or not, his precedence is sealed in history as was Mandela who, like Joseph in Genesis of the Old Testament, went from being a *prisoner* of his country to *prime minister* over his country.

The world mourns the loss of this icon, arguably one of the greatest justice leaders of the twenty-first century, and certainly one of the most notable freedom fighters.

Nelson Mandela passed on the 5th of December 2013 at his home in Houghton, Johannesburg, South Africa, after an extended illness. He was a remarkable 95 years old—just five years short of living for a century.

He exemplifies the notion that African Americans and African political leaders must make integrity a virtue they passionately seek and display. They must place the love of God and people above themselves—be willing to coalesce with other men and women of integrity—sacrifice personal egos—lay aside individual agendas and to put what is good for those of African descent front and center. In the words of Mandela:

"Those who conduct themselves with morality, integrity and
consistency need not fear the forces of inhumanity and cruelty."

Discussion Questions

1. What socio-demographic changes are setting the stage for God's purpose for people of African descent?

2. What political changes national and internationally are preparing black people for God's last day purpose?

❧ ❧ ❧

ECONOMICAL CHANGE

Africans of the United States of America

There is discrimination against black college grads. A study released by the Center for Economic and Policy Research highlights that black college graduates have *twice* as hard a time finding employment than their white peers.

According to the data, in 2013, 12.4% of black graduates between the ages of 22 and 27 were unemployed, compared to a 5.6% general population unemployment rate for college grads.[161]

---

161 Courtney Connley, "Study Shows Employment Discrimination Against Black College Grads," Black Enterprise, 22 May 2014, http://www.blackenterprise.com/career/employment-discminination-black-college-grads/.

In addition, like many other students today, they often face very burdening student debt. The numbers are *staggering*: more than $1.2 trillion in outstanding student loan debt, 40 million borrowers, who owe an average balance of $29,000.[162]

Congressman Elijah Cummings says Black students are especially *vulnerable* to crushing student debt. They face unique challenges because of entrenched racial disparities in wealth.

The result is African-American students are more likely to take on education debt than their white, Latino, or Asian-American peers."[163]

Notwithstanding, education remains one of the best ways for African Americans to have a viable chance at economic progress. Since economics is often related to education there must be progress in closing these gaps.

The *positive* news is there have been important strides made in that arena. New data show positive signs to that effect. Between 2010-11 and 2012-13, the graduation rates for American Indian, *black*, and Hispanic students increased by nearly four percentage points over two years, compared with just 2.6 percentage points for white students, and *outpacing* the growth for *all* students.

This demonstrates that the gap between minority and white students is modestly closing.[164]

---

162 Kelley Holland, "Looking for the next crisis? Try student debt," CNBC, 15 ÐJuneÐ Ð2015, USA Today, https://www.usatoday.com/story/money/markets/2015/06/24/cnbc-student-debt-crisis/29168475/.

163 Long, Richard. "Black Students Feeling Especially Crushed By Student Debt." Our Future.org, 29 April 2015, https://ourfuture.org/20150429/black-students-feeling-especially-crushed-by-student-debt.

164 "New Grad Rate Data Show Gap between Minority and White Students is Closing." Homeroom, 16 March 2015, The US Department of Education, https://blog.ed.gov/2015/03/new-grad-rate-data-show-gap-between-minority-and-white-students-is-closing/

Nearly *every racial* and *ethnic* subgroup has seen a growth in graduation rates that *outpaces* that of white students – a sign that the achievement gap is incrementally closing.

In addition, across the US, African-American enrollments in higher education have *increased* to an all-time *high*. Combining both bachelor's and graduate degree programs and enrollments in two-year community colleges, there are now more than 2 million African Americans enrolled in higher education in the United States. But a more important statistical measure of the performance of blacks in higher education is not simply the number of black students entering college but how many are earning a college degree.

The economic benefits that follow from a four-year college degree are clearly seen. Census Bureau data show that African-American students who achieve a four-year college degree have incomes that are substantially higher than blacks who have only some college experience but have not earned a degree.

Blacks who complete a four-year college education have a median income that is now nearly *equal* with similarly educated whites.[165] Even though black students have lower rates of college completions there is even positive news on that front. Over the past four years, the black student graduation rate has improved by five percentage points.

Furthermore, the economic potential can be seen in the fact that there are 43 million African Americans in the United States, about 13 percent of the total population, the second largest racial minority in the country. The median age is 32, and 47 percent

---

165 "Here Is Good News on Black Student College Graduation Rates but a Huge Racial Gap Persists," *The Journal of Blacks in Higher Education,* no. 58, 2007, http://www.jbhe.com/features/58_gradratesracialgap.html.

are under 35 years of age.[166] And despite the elevated unemployment rate and ongoing issues with poverty for some segments, a report commissioned by the Nielsen Company entitled *"African-American Consumers: Still Vital, Still Growing"* reported that the African-American population is an *economic force* to be reckoned with—they will have a projected buying power of $1.1 trillion by 2015.[167]

The population of African-American consumer's growth *outpaces* the rest of the population by 30 percent. As indicated by previously stated statistics, the demographic is younger, more educated, and has *higher* incomes than commonly believed. This means African Americans wield tremendous consumer power.

There were other significant observations from the report. With a buying power of about $1 trillion annually, if African-Americans were a country; they'd be the 16th largest country in the world. Considering that there are about 196 countries this would place them in the top 20 in rank.

The number of African-American households earning $75,000 or higher grew by almost 64%, a rate close to 12% *greater* than the change in the overall population's earning between 2000 and 2009.

This continued growth in social influence and household income will continue to impact the community's economic power.[168] The economic progress was not limited to African people but also includes the continent of Africa.

---

166 Black Demographics, http://blackdemographics.com/.

167 "African- American Consumers: Still Vital, Still Growing: 2012 Report." The Nielsen Company. 21 September 2012, http://www.nielsen.com/content/dam/corporate/us/en/microsites/publicaffairs/StateOfTheAfricanAmericanConsumer2012.pdf.

168 "African- American Consumers: Still Vital, Still Growing: 2012 Report."

Africans of Africa

Like African Americans, Africa, especially the sub-Saharan region, is becoming an economic power. Consider that there are many possible opportunities in Africa among the continent's 54 nations, particularly in Nigeria, an oil-rich region and the most populated of African nations.

Institutional investment into Africa could be set for a boost due in part to a task force that was expected to work to develop capital flows into infrastructure projects in the region. Connected to former President Barack Obama's Power Africa initiative, the task force was set to identify opportunities, tackle risk and establish structures connecting investors with new projects.[169]

As Africa's economies progress, opportunities are opening in areas such as retailing, telecommunications, banking, infrastructure-related industries, resource-related businesses, and all along the agricultural value chain.

Population trends suggest that Africa is poised to become a formidable business market. Africa's middle class is already numbering about 300 million people, but will continue to grow into the prime spending years.

Consumer expenditures in sub-Saharan Africa are predicted to soar, increasing 65% to nearly $1 trillion by the end of this decade. Working in Africa's favor is its abundance of natural resources such as oil, natural gas, copper, iron ore, and gold.

Also, factoring in the coming boom is the rapid growth of Africa's population; it has a relative abundance of arable land, rapid urbanization, and growing domestic markets, making it an attractive economic market.

---

169 Sophie Baker, "New effort puts focus on Africa," Pensions and Investments, 18 August 2014, http://www.pionline.com/article/20140818/PRINT/308189977/new-effort-puts-focus-on-africa.

The International Monetary Fund predicts that sub-Saharan Africa will *exceed* Asia as the world's *fastest*-growing region over the next decade. African countries such as Botswana have a *leading* economy. The *diamond-rich* country in southern Africa posted a relatively *high* per capita Gross Domestic Product (GDP) of $15,176.

The country also fared well in terms of governance, education and personal freedom. As the nation spent 8% of its GDP on education, it is among the *biggest* proportional spenders in the world per the World Bank.

South Africa, the *second most*-prosperous nation, has developed a rather *successful* economy.[170] Through investment in financial services, oil and gas, alternative and renewable energy, chemicals, communications, infrastructure, tourism, software and IT services, South Africa is directly involved in *driving* the continental growth of Africa.

The outlook for Africa, and specifically for sub-Saharan Africa, is a positive one.

In recent years, there have been *substantial* growth, improving governance, regulation and reforms, better fiscal policies, and diversification of economies, while attracting an increasing volume of FDI.

Sub-Saharan Africa will grow 4.5% this year (according to the IMF) and 5.1% next year, which compares favorably with forecast growth for the world economy of 3.5% and 3.8% respectively.[171]

---

170 Alex Court, "Top 10: Africa's most prosperous countries," CNN, 10 August 2015, http://www.cnn.com/2014/12/18/business/africa-prosperity-rankings-2014/index.html.

171 Menell, Richard. "How South Africa is helping deliver prosperity to all Africans." World Economic Forum, 4 June 2015, https://www.weforum.org/agenda/2015/06/how-south-africa-is-helping-deliver-prosperity-to-all/.

Over the past decade, Africa's real GDP grew by 4.7% a year, on average, *double* the pace of its growth in the 1980's and 1990's. The *surging increase* was across nations and sectors.

By 2009, Africa's national GDP of $1.6 trillion was about equal to Brazil's or Russia's. The continent is among the *fastest-expanding* economic regions. It was one of only two continents that grew during the global recession.

Their growth rate grew to nearly 5% in 2010; the prospects for consumer-facing companies are *bright*. They spent $860 billion on goods and services as of 2008—35% *more* than the $635 billion that Indians spent, and slightly more than the $821 billion of consumer expenditures in Russia.

Africa offers a *higher return* on investment than *any* other emerging market. Competition is less intense; few foreign companies are present, and consumer demand is *vibrant*. Companies that desire profits can no longer ignore Africa.

By some estimates, by 2050 or sooner, Nigeria will be *more* of a *significant* player in the world economy than even Russia.[172]

Africa will continue to meet its social and political challenges such as poverty, tribalism, political corruption, and the terrorism of groups like *ISIS* and *Boko Haram*.[173]

Like African Americans, Africans of the continent, the Africans of Latin America and the Caribbean will be impacted economically.

---

172 Baker

173 Freeman, Colin. "Nigeria hired South African mercenaries to wage a secret war on Africa's deadliest jihadist group." Business Insider, 15 May 2015, http://www.businessinsider.com/south-african-mercenaries-waged-secret-war-on-boko-haram-2015-5.

Africans of Brazil, Latin America and Caribbean

Brazil is beginning to emerge from its economic downturn in 2016 and is slowly making a recovery. Africans in Brazil, the Caribbean and the rest of Latin America benefit from the economic growth that was set to increase to about 3Ð percent in 2013. This region will continue to benefit from favorable external financing conditions and relatively high commodity prices.[174]

The world economic crisis did not dramatically impact the continent, as the region maintained a certain *resilience* to external shocks throughout the year." The continuously buoyant internal demand in many of the region's economies will result from improved labor indicators, increased bank credit to the private sector and rising commodity prices that will not fall significantly despite high external uncertainty.[175]

Furthermore, investments in Brazil and throughout the region are up, as is consumer demand. The prices of raw materials remain high, and Latin America's agricultural industry is strong, two positive indicators for the region's exports.

The region's technology ecosystem has gained *significant* momentum. Brazil's telecommunications market is expanding at a compound annual rate of 5.3% and is set to reach almost $100 billion by 2017.

Latin America's e-commerce sector was expected to grow 11 times over the 10-year period from 2005 to 2015, and Brazilian e-commerce was predicted to expand by twenty-five percent.[176]

---

174 Western Hemisphere Time to Rebuild Policy Space, (Washington D.C.: International Monetary Fund, May 2013), https://www.imf.org/external/pubs/ft/reo/2013/whd/eng/pdf/wreo0513.pdf.

175 "ECLAC predicts economic growth for Caribbean in 2013," Caribbean 360, 26 August 2013.

176 "ECLAC predicts"

However, African-blooded leaders must be vigilant in dealing with European and Euro-American businesses. While they can welcome them as investors, they cannot permit them to economically *control*, *dominate*, or *manipulate* the *African*, *Caribbean*, or *Latin American* economies.

African-blooded leaders should maintain the majority advantages of their countries, and avoid business transactions that don't benefit their economy or the people of African descent in their countries.

This is where integrity becomes critical. Unethical, illegal, or unscrupulous business dealings, and corruption must cease, because such activities will have a boomerang effect and come back to harm the perpetrators. Economics plays a major role in our destiny as a people, and progress will necessitate communal action.

However, we must also maintain and in some measure, regain our sense of family. There is a wealth of family relations necessary for the achieving of our destiny that cannot merely be measured in dollars.

Discussion Questions

1. What economic and financial changes are setting the stage for God's purpose for people of African Americans?
2. What economic and financial changes are setting the stage for God's purpose for African Americans?
3. What economic and financial changes are setting the stage for God's purpose for Africans?
4. What economic and financial changes are setting the stage for God's purpose for people of African descent in Latin America and the Caribbean?

CHAPTER 15

Pro-Family is Pro-Destiny

꙲

*"In every conceivable manner,
the family is link to our past, bridge to our future."*
~ ALEX HALEY

"Because I relate therefore I am"
~ AFRICAN PHILOSOPHY

We have spent the bulk of this book focused on our identity as a people in both history and prophecy. We must remember that for people of African descent identity was very much tied to family, for without family one virtually had no identity.

They shared common experiences and perceptions of which kinship was paramount. Kinship is about sharing common values. One was cultured to show generosity to the whole world because being a relative ingrained a belief in Africans that one was part of a *common* agenda.

Africa and the West are *fundamentally different*, in that Africa depends on *communalism*. What is important to Africans is "a sense of belonging." I am who I am today because I know I count not necessarily to the whole world, but to my relatives and the villages around me.[177]

I feel proud to be blood related to someone. Unlike the European notion of *"I think therefore I am,"* African identity can be summed up in the words of the African philosophy, *"Because I relate therefore I am."*[178] If people of African descent are going to fulfill their prophetic destiny it will require serious attention being given to family relations.

e

"A man without a wife is like a vase without a flower."
~AFRICAN PROVERB

Marriage is sacred in Africa and beyond, because it solidifies relationships that enrich communities and nations by bringing forth new life and new hope.

Our destiny is very much tied to family and the treatment of our women. Men of African descent must be taught the biblical truth about how God honors black women, and that to dishonor them is to dishonor God. 1 Peter 3:7 says:

> *"Husbands, in the same way be considerate as you live with your wives, and treat them with respect as the weaker partner and as heirs with you of the gracious gift of life, so that nothing will hinder your prayers." NIV*

---

177 de Ngor, Mading. "Globalization and The African Kinship Network System: Will It Sustain?" Sudan Tribune, 27 July 2006, http://www.sudantribune.com/Globalization-and-the-African,16826.

178 de Ngor, Mading.

Ephesians 5:25 "Husbands, love your wives, just as Christ loved the church and gave himself up for her" NIV

Colossians 3:19 "Husbands, love your wives and do not be harsh with them." NIV

Proverbs 18:22 "He who finds a wife finds what is good and receives favor from the LORD." NIV

The word that characterizes how God views the black woman is *"mother."* She is the ultimate maternal nurturer on the earth. If I were to make an acronym out of the word '**MOTHER**' it would be **M**atriarch **O**riginating **T**he **H**uman's **E**ntire **R**ace.

Black women in Scripture exemplify the *mother* honor that all black women should be given. They should be honored because of:

1. *Eve (**The Mother of Humanity**)*: the first woman from Africa who became the mother of humanity from whom all the people of the generations, and nations owe their origin. Genesis 3:20

    "Adam named his wife Eve, because she would become the mother of all the living." NIV (We have devoted a significant portion of the beginning of this book to Eve)

2. *Keturah (**The Mother of Nuptial Spice**)*: the Cushite black woman who was Abraham's wife after Sarah. Her name means *"incense spice"* and judging from the six sons she bore him she should be called the *mother* of *spice*, for that is how she influenced Abraham's virility.[179] Genesis 25:1–2:

---

179 Olitzky, Rabbi Kerry M. "Was Abraham's Second Wife Really Hagar?" My Jewish Learning, http://www.myjewishlearning.com/article/abrahams-second-marriage/.

> *"Abraham had taken another wife, whose name was Keturah.*
> *She bore him Zimran, Jokshan, Medan, Midian, Ishbak and*
> *Shuah." NIV*

3. **Bithiah/Thermuthis/Hatshepsut (The Mother of Adoptee Moses):** There are at least three possible name identities for this woman. According to Hebrew beliefs; *Bithiah* or in Modern Hebrew *Bitmap* (literally *"daughter of God"*) was the Egyptian princess, and a daughter of Pharaoh in the Exodus story.

In Jewish tradition, she was exiled by the Pharaoh for bringing Moses the Levite into the house of Pharaoh and claiming him as her own child. She left Egypt with Moses during the mass Exodus of the children of Israel. She is mentioned in 1 Chronicles 4:18 by name.

> *"His wife from the tribe of Judah gave birth to Jered*
> *the father of Gedor, Heber the father of Soko,*
> *and Jekuthiel the father of Zanoah.) These were the*
> *children of Pharaoh's daughter* Bithiah, *whom*
> *Mered had married." NIV*

The Midrash identifies the two as the same person, and says she received her name, literally *"daughter of Yah,"* rendered in English as LORD, because of her compassion and pity in saving the baby Moses.

In the Midrash (Leviticus Rabbah 1:3), God says to her that because she took in a child not her own, and called him her son (Moses can mean *"child"* in Egyptian), God will take her in and call her YHWH's daughter (which is what Bithiah means). The Midrash portrays her as a pious and devoted woman to Yahweh.[180]

Another view is Jewish historian Josephus, who says her name was *Thermuthis (Pharaoh's daughter)*, the African princess from Egypt who became Moses' adopted mother, and taught him how to be a prince.[181]

Some think that this Egyptian princess was Hatshepsut, daughter of Pharaoh Thutmose I. Her husband was Pharaoh Thutmose II. Since she could not have children. Some have suggested the childless Hatshepsut may have seen a baby as a gift from one of her gods. By adopting Moses, she would have a son of her own who would be the legal heir to the throne.[182]

> 4. *Zipporah (The Mother of timely Intervention)*, the Cushite black woman whose mother instincts saved the life of Moses, Israel's greatest prophet, and probably saved her son. She was *mother* of *timely intervention*.
>
> *Exodus 4:24-26 "At a lodging place on the way, the Lord met Moses and was about to kill him. But Zipporah took a flint knife, cut off her son's foreskin and touched Moses' feet with it. "Surely you are a bridegroom of blood to me," she said. So the Lord let him alone. (At that time she said, "bridegroom of blood," referring to circumcision) NIV*

---

180 Wikipedia contributors, "Bithiah," Wikipedia, The Free Encyclopedia, Wikipedia, The Free Encyclopedia, https://en.wikipedia.org/wiki/Bithiah.

181 Paul L. Maier, translator, Josephus The Essential Writings, by Flavius Josephus (Grand Rapids: Kregel, 1988).

182 Lynne Chapman, "Pharaoh's Daughter - Moses' Other Mother," BellaOnline, Christian Living, http://www.bellaonline.com/articles/art59375.asp.

5. *Makeda* (*The Mother of a Hebrew/Cushitic Royalty*)
   Cushite African queen who visited, with Solomon,
   adopted Yahweh religion, and allegedly bore his son
   Menelek. She became the mother of a Hebrew/Cushitic
   royalty in Africa.

She also received a strong note of endorsement from Christ
himself in the gospels.[183] 1 Kings 10:1–7:

> "When the queen of Sheba heard about the fame of Solomon
> and his relation to the name of the Lord, she came to test him
> with hard questions. Arriving at Jerusalem with a very great
> caravan—with camels carrying spices, large quantities of gold,
> and precious stones—she came to Solomon and talked with
> him about all that she had on her mind. Solomon answered all
> her questions; nothing was too hard for the king to explain to
> her. When the queen of Sheba saw all the Wisdom of Solomon
> and the palace he had built, the food on his table, the seating
> of his officials, the attending servants in their robes, his
> cupbearers, and the burnt offerings he made at the temple of
> the LORD, she was overwhelmed. She said to the king, "The
> report I heard in my own country about your achievements
> and your wisdom is true. But I did not believe these things
> until I came and saw with my own eyes. Indeed, not even half
> was told me; in wisdom and wealth you have far exceeded the
> report I heard." NIV

> Matthew 12:42 "The Queen of the South will rise at the
> judgment with this generation and condemn it; for she came
> from the ends of the earth to listen to Solomon's wisdom, and
> now one greater than Solomon is here" NIV (Luke 11:31)

---

183 Legrand

6. *Amanitore ("Mother Queen" Candace of Kush):*
The African Queen of Kush and Meroe who succeeded
her mother and co-ruled with her husband. She is
mentioned in Acts 8:27 (in a line of other African queens
with the same title). There are three translations
that we will cite that use the names *Candace, Kandake,*
and *Kush.*

"... *he arose and went: and, behold, a man of Ethiopia, a eunuch
of great authority under* Candace *queen of the Ethiopians,
who had the charge of all her treasure, and had come to
Jerusalem for to worship." KJV*

"*So he started out, and on his way he met an Ethiopian eunuch,
an important official in charge of all the treasury of the*
Kandake (*which means* "queen *of the* Ethiopians"). *This
man had gone to Jerusalem to worship." NIV*

"... *he arose to go and met a certain Eunuch who had come from*
Kush, *an official of Qandiqe, Queen of the* Kushites, *and he
was authorized over all her treasury and had come to worship
in Jerusalem." (Aramaic Bible in Plain English)*

The name Candace or Kandace means *Queen mother*; so, she
was the royal mother to her people of Cush.[184]

Africa was the *first* continent in which women became sover-
eign. The continent gave rise to a royal line of females called Ken-
takes and later *Candace.*[185]

The Aramaic Bible in Plain English seems to suggest that she
along with her husband presided over a Meroitic *Golden* Age, as

---

184 Wikipedia contributors, "Amanitore," Wikipedia, The Free Encyclopedia, Wikipedia,
The Free Encyclopedia, accessed 28 December 2008, https://en.wikipedia.org/wiki/Amanitore.

185 Louis Rushmore, "Candace, Queen of the Ethiopians," Gospel Gazette, vol.3 no.12,
2 December 2001, 2, http://www.gospelgazette.com/gazette/2001/dec/page2.htm.

the remains of numerous buildings bear their names. In the decorative scheme of this temple the figure of the queen appears just as prominently as that of her husband, providing validating evidence of the very *high* status accorded women in the Cushite Meroitic Monarchy.[186]

> 7. ***The Cyrenian Mother (The Spiritual Mother of Paul):***
> The Northern African wife of Simon of Cyrene who was the nurturing spiritual mother of the Apostle Paul. She was also probably likely a person of color who would have appeared as dark brown or blackish in color given what the people of that time and region look like.
>
> *Romans 16:13 "Greet Rufus, chosen in the Lord, and his* mother, *who has been a* mother *to me, too." NIV*

Rufus was one of the sons of Simon of Cyrene. He went on to become a well-honored saint by the early church. His biological mother served the role of mother figure to Paul.

She and the other maternal examples we have cited are just a few examples of the natural and spiritual maternity of black women,[187]

> 8. *Canaanite Woman (**The Mother of Great Faith**):*
> *Matthew 15:21-28 "Jesus having come forth thence, withdrew to the parts of Tyre and Sidon, and lo, a woman, a Canaanitess, from those borders having come forth, did call to him, saying, `Deal kindly with me, Sir—Son of David; my daughter is miserably demonized.' And he did not answer her a word; and his disciples having come to him, were asking him, saying—*

---

186 Queen Amanitore (10 AD - 40 AD).

187 A Spiritual Parent: The Mother of the Apostle Paul.

`Let her away, because she crieth after us, and he answering said, `I was not sent except to the lost sheep of the House of Israel.' And having come, she was bowing to him, saying, `Sir, help me;' and he answering said, `It is not good to take the children's bread, and to cast to the little dogs.' And she said, `Yes, sir, for even the little dogs do eat of the crumbs that are falling from their lords' table;' then answering, Jesus said to her, `O woman, great [is] thy faith, let it be to thee as thou wilt;' and her daughter was healed from that hour. YLT

Mark 7:24-30 "Jesus left that place and went to the territory of Tyre and Sidon. He went into a house, not wanting anyone to know he was there. However, it couldn't be kept a secret. In fact, a woman whose little daughter had an unclean spirit immediately heard about him and came and fell down at his feet. Now the woman happened to be a Greek, born in Phoenicia in Syria. She kept asking him to drive the demon out of her daughter. But he kept telling her, "First let the children be filled. It is not right to take the children's bread and throw it to the puppies." But she answered him, "Yes, Lord. Yet even the puppies under the table eat some of the children's crumbs." Then he told her, "Because you have said this, go! The demon has left your daughter."

We have two different gospel accounts of this woman Jesus encountered that came out of Tyre and Sidon. Matthew is targeting the Jews; his heavy reliance upon the Old Testament Scriptures indicates this. He is writing for those who accept the Old Testament Scriptures as authoritative. He calls her a "Canaanite" woman.

The pagan inhabitants of the land that Israel conquered under Joshua were known as Canaanites, being descended from Canaan, the son of Ham and younger brother of Cush. Many

Canaanites had migrated northward into Phoenicia when the Hebrews invaded the territory. This woman was designated as a Canaanite—her ancestry came from Ham and they were the despised enemies of Israel.

Mark, on the other hand, is writing to Romans, who controlled the Mediterranean world of the first century. This woman lived in Phoenicia (which, politically speaking, belonged to Syria). She was the Lord's puppy love that displayed determined dog like faith.

Hence, she is identified as a Syro-Phoenician. While Canaanite was her ancestry she was Syro-Phoenician "Greek" by culture.[188]

Furthermore, the ancient Canaanites and the people who are called Phoenicians were essentially one and the same *Afro*-Asiatic people.

Recent genetic research in the Middle East and North *Africa* seems to confirm the indigenous *African* origin of the ancient "Cushitic"-related Phoenicians.

In the year 2004 the national Geographic reported that two or more *"African"* chromosome groups (*M89 & M172*) had been found in the populations of today's *"Phoenicians."*

Today Sidon is called Sayda or Saida. This name has a North *African* as well as maritime connection, which may help to throw more light on Phoenician origins.[189]

Historian Paul Fenton shows that, from the Middle Ages onward, several Arab historians came to identify certain North *Af-*

---

188 Wayne Jackson, "The Canaanite Woman: A Conflict between Matthew and Mark?" ChristianCourier.com, https://www.christiancourier.com/articles/468-canaanite-woman-a-conflict-between-matthew-and-the.

189 Dr. Anu Mauro, "Black Africans of Ancient Mediterranean Part 1 (Across the River)," Rasta LiveWire, 9 July 2009, http://www.africaresource.com/rasta/sesostris-the-great-the-egyptian-hercules/black-africans-of-ancient-mediterranean-part-1-across-the-river-by-dr-anu-mauro/.

ricans with the Middle Eastern *Canaanites*.[190] This Canaanite woman was for all intent and purposes a Hamitic black woman connected to both Canaanites and Cushites.

⚜

"The beauty of a woman becomes useless if there is no one to admire it."
~ AFRICAN PROVERB

The above African proverb has been true when it comes to the beauty of black women. We of African descent have been aware of the comeliness of black women in the world, but that beauty seemed to be invisible to others.

However, for the last several decades in America and the world, that beauty has been acknowledged and rewarded.

Today we see God elevating women of African descent to a prominent visible status. We have witnessed several African *firsts* as it relates to their beauty.

Consider that there have been eight black Miss Americas and at least nine black Miss USAs. The latest was newly crowned 2016 Miss USA, Deshauna Barber.

Four black women have won Miss *Universe*.[191]

Moreover, Halle Berry at age 46 was ranked among the ten most beautiful women over 40 and ranked No. 1 on People's "50

---

190 Paul Fenton, "The Origins of the Berbers according to Medieval Muslim and Jewish Authors," The Gift of the Land and the Fate of the Canaanites in Jewish Thought, edited by Katell Berthelot, Joseph E. David, and Marc Hirshman (London: Oxford UP, 2014).

191 Sanskrit Sinha,"The Four Black Women Who Won Miss Universe," International Business Times, 13September 2011, http://www.ibtimes.com/four-black-women-who-won-miss-universe-title-photos-552628.

Most Beautiful People in The World" list in 2003 after making the top ten list *seven* times.[192]

Another such beauty *first* is Yityish Aynaw, the *first* woman of Ethiopic *African* descent to win the Miss *Israel* pageant. Stop and ponder, that a black woman of Cushitic African blood became the winner of one of Israel's most important beauty pageants.

Within a matter of weeks, her name and image were spread across print media and websites, both in Israel and around the globe. As the *first* ever *black* Miss Israel.

Aynaw is seen by some as a beacon of hope that racial prejudice is decreasing in the country.[193]

On March 8, 2015, Ariana Miyamoto made *history* by becoming the *first African-Asian* to be crowned Miss Japan. And she represented the country in the Miss Universe pageant, with a Japanese mother and an *African American* father. With some controversy she is breaking racial barriers.[194]

Furthermore, People Magazine named actress Lupita Nyong'o, a woman of Kenyan *African* ancestry, as the *"World's Most Beautiful Woman"* for 2014. The 31-year-old won a best supporting actress *Oscar* for her role in "12 Years a Slave."[195]

---

192 Wikipedia contributors, "Halle Berry," Wikipedia, The Free Encyclopedia, Wikipedia, The Free Encyclopedia, https://en.wikipedia.org/wiki/Halle_Berry .

193 Sara Sidner and Earl Nurse, "Yityish Aynaw: The firstblack Miss Israel," CNN, 12 June 2013, http://www.cnn.com/2013/06/12/world/africa/yityish-aynaw-miss-israel-ethiopia/index.html.

194 Veronica Wells, "Do People Have A Right To Be Mad At A Half-Black Woman Representing Japan At Miss Universe?" Madame Noire, 20 March 2015, http://madamenoire.com/520151/do-people-have-a-right-to-be-mad-at-a-half-black-woman-representing-japan-at-miss-universe/.

195 "'12 Years a Slave' StarLupita Nyong'o Named People Magazine 'Most Beautiful Woman' Of 2014," The Huffington Post UK, 24 April 2014, http://www.huffingtonpost.co.uk/2014/04/24/lupita-nyongo-most-beautiful-woman-2014-people-magazine_n_5203462.html.

In another form of beauty combining physical beauty with creative arts, 32-year-old Misty Copeland became the *first* African-American female principal ballerina in American Ballet Theatre's *seventy-five-year* history.

Lastly, as one who has been married to a beautiful black woman with beauty both inside and out, I have been favored by God to have known this beauty for 40 years with my wife Ja'Ola.

These are just some examples of the prominent place God is assigning black women of African descent or mixed African heritage. This discussion about black mothers and black women leads to our discourse about our children and youth of African descent as well as black fatherhood.

Discussion Questions

1. How is marriage related to the destiny of people of African descent?
2. How is the treatment of women of African descent important to our destiny?
3. What black women in Scripture symbolize the mother nature of black women?

❧ ❧ ❧

PRO-CHILDREN PRO-DESTINY

You cannot abort the pregnancy of a born child.
~AFRICAN PROVERB

We must protect the life of the unborn and the born children of African descent. This focus is critical to our prophecy, and achieving our destiny. We can't achieve our *destiny* by destroying our *progeny*. For our *progeny* are key to our *prophecy*. Consider that:

Biblically, abortion is anti-Scripture because:

> *Unborn not killed in the womb by God Jeremiah 20:17* "He didn't kill me *in the* womb, *with my mother as my* grave."

> *Amos 1:13 and God vowed to punish those who ...* ripped open *the women* with child

> *Unborn child is the heritage from God; Psalm 127:3 ESV* "Behold, *children are* a heritage *from the* LORD, *the* fruit *of the* womb *a* reward."

> *Unborn child especially created by God: Psalm 139:13-14 ESV* "For *you formed my inward parts; you* knitted me together in my mother's womb. *I praise you, for I am fearfully and wonderfully made. Wonderful are your works; my soul knows it well.*"

Unborn child purposed by God: Isaiah 49:5 ESV, "now the LORD says, he who formed me from the womb to be his servant, to bring Jacob back to him; and that Israel might be gathered to him—for I am honored in the eyes of the LORD, and my God has become my strength—"

Unborn child personally known by God Jeremiah. 1:4-5 ESV, "Now the word of the LORD came to me, saying, Before I formed you in the womb I knew you, and before you were born I consecrated you; I appointed you a prophet to the nations."

Unborn can respond to God: Luke 1:39-41 ESV, "In those days Mary arose and went with   haste into the hill country, to a town in Judah, and she entered the house of Zechariah and greeted Elizabeth. And when Elizabeth heard the greeting of Mary, the baby leaped in her womb. And Elizabeth was filled with the Holy Spirit."196

Culturally Abortion is Anti-African Ethos

African cultures celebrate the coming of the rains, the first harvest, and the *birth* of a child.[197] Concerning abortion in Africa, Emil Hagamu of Human Life International (HLI) states that:

"In African communities, the death of a child is no small matter. We have never 'accepted' abortion in African culture. Expanded legalization of abortion is being forced upon us by the traditional colonizing powers of the West, who are using their money and power to destroy innocent lives. I went to the university, where I specialized in languages and African literature. Together with my studies in sociology, my perspective broadened

---

196 African Anti-Abortion Coalition No Place for Abortion in Traditional African Life.

197 African Marriage: Most Important Ceremony in African Culture.

greatly as I learned about African cultures through various literary works, and as I learned how the culture of people is embodied in its language. While investigating whether or not any African language has any word or phrase that would correspond to the English word "*abortion*," I have yet to find a *single* example."[198]

We call this endeavor the Genocide Awareness Project (GAP) because Webster's New World Encyclopedia defines "*genocide*" as "the deliberate and systematic destruction of a national, racial, religious, political, cultural, ethnic, or other group defined by the exterminators as undesirable." That definition readily applies to abortion. The national group" is the American "unwanted" unborn children, and in particular, African American children.

Sociologically Abortion is Anti-demographic

The U.S. Centers for Disease Control and Prevention has provided the tragic statistics. According to the CDC, since 1973, the year of the Supreme Court Decision Roe vs. Wade, 13 million (13,000,000) *African American* lives have been lost to abortion.

The CDC reports that of the approximately 4,000 abortions that are performed daily in the United States, 1,452 of them are performed on African American women and their pre-born children.

This means that although African Americans represent only 13% of the population of the United States, they account for 35% of the abortions performed; it has taken away 1/3 of our present black population. They are now being destroyed at the rate

---

198 Emil Hagamu, "Inside View 'Abortion is foreign to Africa,'" Lifesite News, 10 October 2012, https://www.lifesitenews.com/opinion/an-inside-view-abortion-is-foreign-to-africa.

of nearly 1 out of every 3 conceived.[199] This kind of genocide also leads to an anti-demographic effect.

Margaret Sanger, a eugenicist and her precursor to Planned Parenthood, the Birth Control Federation of America, decided to turn their attention to *black* people. They devised a plan for an "experimental" clinic that Sanger said would "reduce the birth rate among elements unable to provide for themselves, and the burden of which we are all forced to carry," writes Tanya L. Green, author of *"The Negro Project: Margaret Sanger's Eugenic Plan for Black Americans."*[200]

Dr. Ben Carson, a black neurosurgeon and U.S. HUD secretary under President Donald Trump, asserted that Planned Parenthood founder Margaret Sanger used abortions as a population control measure to try and *destroy* the *black* population.

He says that Sanger was a strong advocate of eugenics. "She wrote articles about eugenics and believed that certain members of the population weakened the population and she was *not* enamored of black people," he explained.[201]

Political liberals who are pro-choice support a position that contributes to the aborting of black children *in* the womb, but it could be also be argued that evangelicals and conservatives support a political position that contributes to the aborting of black children born *outside* the womb, with economic and social policies reducing their quality of life.

Therefore, the authentic "pro-life" definition must include the lives of children *after* birth. The term as it is used by most

---

199 John Chester Miller, The Wolf by the Ears, (Charlottesville: U of Virginia Press, 1991).

200 "Silent No More: A Major Crisis in the African-American Community."

201 Ben Carson, "Abortion Is the No. 1 Killer of Black People," Mother Jones, 14 August 2015, http://www.motherjones.com/politics/2015/08/ben-carson-abortions-are-main-cause-black-deaths/.

evangelicals and religious conservatives is much too narrow. My problem with my fellow evangelicals and religious conservatives is that even though they claim to be pro-life they are *only* pro *unborn* life. They have a very limited concept of the term *abort*. The word means the act of *terminating* a project or procedure *before* it is *completed*, to cease development, to die, to abort something is to end it.[202]

Abortion can occur at any of the early stages of a child or youth's life in the womb or outside of it. If a child is born and dies or is killed, it did not complete its life journey, or finish its destiny—it was aborted, it does not matter if it was aborted by animal, vegetable, mineral, human, or some other force, its life ended or was stopped before it completed the life cycle.

Therefore, I am pro-*life*, pro *unborn* life, pro *born* life, pro-*infant* life, pro *toddler* life, pro-*tweener* life, pro-*teen* life, in other words *pro-life*. The concept of pro-life should encompass all of a child's early stages of development and not just in-the-womb development.

Evangelicals and conservatives forget life starts in the womb, but does not end there (unless of course that life is aborted in the womb).

What is needed is an *expanded* view of abortion and pro-life by evangelicals and conservatives as opposed to a limited view that essentially assigns life as only the events of the womb, but nothing beyond.

---

202 "Abort," Vocabulary.com, https://www.vocabulary.com/dictionary/abort.

An Expanded View of Abortion and Pro-Life

Birth is the only remedy against death.
~ AFRICAN PROVERB (NIGERIAN)

Evangelicals and religious conservatives claim they are pro-life and want babies to have life. This belief seems commendable at first until you compare it to the Christ agenda for life. That agenda is found in John 10:10 which will be cited in four different Translations:

> *"The thief does not come except to steal, and kill, and destroy. I have come that they may* have life, *and that they may have it* more abundantly." (*NKJV*)

> *"The thief comes only to steal and kill and destroy; I have come that they may* have life, *and* have it to the full." (*NIV*)

> *"The thief's purpose is to steal and kill and destroy. My purpose is to give them a* rich *and* satisfying life." (*NLT*)

> *"The thief comes only to steal and kill and destroy. I have come so they can* have life. *I want them to* have it in *the* fullest possible way." (*NIRV*)

Jesus says here in John 10:10 that the threefold agenda of the thief is *steal, kill,* and *destroy.* Abortion is a form of medical *thievery* for it steals the life of innocent children. It *kills* a baby's right to live, and it *destroys* a pre-born child's chance of becoming.

Christ goes on to say his agenda is counter to these three satanic purposes. His desire is both life and life more *abundantly.*

The abundant life Christ discusses here is not only the eternal life we receive when we accept Christ. It is a fuller and *wholesome* life lived out on earth. If these translations are any indication of the Christ life agenda for babies, then the pro-life agenda proposed by evangelicals falls woefully short of the mark. What He is proposing is a *life plus* agenda, and not just so that babies experience natural life.

Religious conservatives and evangelicals seem obsessed with abortion; the termination of a fetal child *inside* the womb, but the real issue may be *infanticide*—the killing of an infant child *outside* the womb.

Virtually all the references to the killing of children in the Bible were more about infanticide than pre-birth abortion. They were talking about children who were *already* born who had survived the health challenges and medical complications of the ancient birthing process.

Children who then became victims of infanticide activity such as the alleged killings of first-born male children by Pharaoh of the Old Testament and King Herod in the New Testament, or pagan child sacrifice. As indicated in the following scriptural passages:

> *Exodus 1:22 HCSB "Pharaoh then commanded all his people: "You must throw every son born to the Hebrews into the Nile, but let every daughter live."*

> *Matthew 2:16 ESV "Then Herod, when he saw that he had been tricked by the wise men, became furious, and he sent and killed all the male children in Bethlehem and in all that region who were two years old or under, according to the time that he had ascertained from the wise men."*

God had a clear prohibition against child sacrifice and infanticide.

Deuteronomy 12:31 (GWT) "Never worship the LORD your God in the way they worship their gods, because everything they do for their gods is disgusting to the LORD. He hates it! They even burn their sons and daughters as sacrifices to their gods."

Our nation is engaging in a form of infanticide and child sacrifice with the proliferation of guns. Television host Trevor Noah wondered why politicians who label themselves as *pro-life* don't focus their efforts on another potentially life-saving measure: *gun control.*

There is hard evidence that guns are deadly. "Imagine if we could bring some of that pro-life passion into being more, well, *pro-life*," he said. "But right now, they're more like comic book collectors. Human life only matters until you take it out of the package, and then it's worth nothing." They need to deal with the facts concerning the death of children by guns:

- Firearm homicide is the *second-leading* cause of death (after motor vehicle crashes) for young people ages 1-19 in the U.S.
- More preschool-age children were killed by guns than police officers killed in the line of duty.[203]
- In 2013, 1,670 children (age 0 to 18 years) died by gunshot and an additional 9,718 were injured.[204]

Therefore, the life Christ wants for babies encompasses more than just the *humanity* of life; it is inclusive of the *quality* of life,

---

203 "About Gun Violence," Brady Campaign, http://www.bradycampaign.org/about-gun-violence.

204 Marian Wright Edelman, "Who Put the NRA in Charge of Our National Security?" The Huffington Post 4 December 2015, http://www.huffingtonpost.com/marian-wright-edelman/who-put-the-nra-in-charge_b_8724912.html.

the *prosperity* of life, the *security* of life, the *dignity* of life and the *identity* of life.

His life agenda is not just for white children, but for all children, and that means children of African descent, especially if they are born to believers.

What Christ states in John 10:10 is the authentic pro-life agenda. He demonstrated how important children were to him in the following passages

> *Children are the reward of life.*
> **~ AFRICAN PROVERB**

> *In Matthew 19:14 GOD'S WORD Translation, Jesus said, "Don't stop children from coming to me! Children like these are part of God's kingdom."*

> *In the New Living Translation "Jesus said, "Let the children come to me. Don't stop them! For the Kingdom of Heaven belongs to those who are like these children"*

Marian Wright Edelman, child Advocate and president of Children's Defense Fund, says when Jesus Christ asked little children to come to him, he didn't say *only* rich children, or white children, or children with two-parent families, or children who didn't have a mental or physical handicap. He said, let *all* children come unto me.[205]

> *Matthew 18:1-6, King James Version (KJV): "At the same time came the disciples unto Jesus, saying, who is the greatest in the kingdom of heaven? And Jesus called a little child unto him, and set him in the midst of them, And said, Verily I say unto*

---

205 African American quotes: God and Religion.

you, Except ye be converted, and become as little children, ye shall not enter into the kingdom of heaven. Whosoever therefore shall humble himself as this little child, the same is greatest in the kingdom of heaven. And whoso shall receive one such little child *in my name* receiveth me. *But whoso shall* offend *one of these* little ones *which believe in me, it were better for him that a millstone were hanged about his neck, and that he were drowned in the depth of the sea."*

The word *"offend"* is the Greek word *"scandalidzo,"* which means to put a stumbling block or impediment in the way, upon which another may trip and fall, to entice to sin, to cause a person to begin to *distrust* and desert one whom he ought to trust and obey, to *cause* to *fall away*, to be *offended* in one, to see in another what I disapprove of and what hinders me from acknowledging his authority, to cause one to judge unfavorably or unjustly, to *cause one displeasure* at a thing, and to make one indignant.

This word has multiple meanings and ways that a child can be offended and they apply to the plight of children of African descent and children of color more than any other group.

Most children believe in God. Research shows that 62 percent of children say religion is important to them; 26% say it's somewhat important.

Thus, 88 percent of those surveyed view religion as important,[206] and to reiterate, African American children and youth are *particularly* religious.

Research revealed 89.2% African American girls reported religion was very important to their life, of the sample reported, 90%

206 Wikipedia contributors, "Religion and children," Wikipedia, The Free Encyclopedia, Wikipedia, The Free Encyclopedia, https://en.wikipedia.org/wiki/Religion_and_children.

of the most represented age group the 14-year-old teens also responded that religion was *very* important.[207]

Another study demonstrated that African-American children and youth both male and female are very religious.[208]

In addition, a study done in 2004 of children who attended religious services at least once a month reported *African American* children attended such religious services *more* than *any* other racial group.

The percentages were 72.0 for African Americans; 64.3 for whites; 62.0 for Hispanics; 59.2 for Asians; and 58.5 for other.[209]

This makes the warning that Jesus gave to those who offend them even more serious. He would not be very happy with the treatment accorded black and brown children in the U.S. Such as the killing of unarmed black youth—or the rejection of Latino children trying to flee violence in their own country.[210]

Which is why the notion of Donald Trump being the president of the United States has *children* of *color* frightened for their very lives.

A new report from the Southern Poverty Law Center reports he's *scaring* our children, and turning some into *racists*. Between March and April, SPLC surveyed more than 2,000 K-12 school

---

207 Williams

208 ChristianSmith, Lisa Pearce, Melinda Lundquist Denton, "Religion and Spirituality on the Path Through Adolescence," National Study of Youth and Religion, 2008, https://youthandreligion. nd.edu/assets/102568/religion_and_spirituality_on_the_path_through_adolescence.pdf.

209 Jane Lawlor, "Children's Religious and Child Well Being by findings from 2004 SIPP," American Sociological Association Annual Meeting, Boston, MA, 1-4 August 2008, https://www.census.gov/ population/www/socdemo/files/religious_poster.ppt, https://www.census.gov/population/www/ socdemo/files/religious_poster.ppt.

210 Pamela Constable, "Immigrant parents urge U.S. officials to help their children flee Central American Violence," The Washington Post,12 June 2014, https://www.washingtonpost.com/ national/immigrant-parents-urge-us-officials-to-help-their-children-flee-central-american-violence/2014/06/12/dc751266-f0b4-11e3-914c-1fbd0614e2d4_story.html?utm_term=.2f971587e25f.

teachers who either subscribe to the organization's email list or visit its website. They found that a substantial number of children from racial minority groups were *frightened* about what would happen to them under a Trump presidency.

Respondents, who gave their replies anonymously, reported that *black*, *Hispanic* and *Muslim* children especially had given voice to concerns that they would be deported — a fear related to Trump's *racist*, *anti-immigrant* and *Islamophobic* rhetoric as well as his vow to deport the country's estimated 12 million undocumented immigrants.

The discussion of African American children brings us to our discussion of black fatherhood.[211]

Discussion Questions

1. Why is abortion a challenge to the generational destiny of God's purpose for people of African descent?
2. What is an expanded view of abortion and what elements does it entail?

---

211 Zak Cheney-Rice, "Trump is scaring the hell out of America's children, study finds," Mic, 15 April 2016, https://mic.com/articles/140936/donald-trump-is-scaring-the-hell-out-of-america-s-children-study-finds#.kkXlRLBBa.

❧ ❧ ❧

Fatherhood is not a falsehood

*"A father never resembles his son.
It's the son that resembles the father."*
~AFRICAN PROVERB

Last but by no means least is the role and responsibility of black men in general and black fathers more specifically. 2011 U.S. Census Bureau data says nearly 2 in 3 (64%) of African-American children live in father-absent homes.

Children who live absent their biological fathers are, on average, at least two to three times more likely to be poor, to use drugs, to experience educational, health, emotional and behavioral problems, to be victims of child abuse, and to engage in criminal behavior than their peers who live with their married, biological (or adoptive) parents.[212]

There is positive news concerning black fatherhood, The Centers for Disease Control and Prevention (CDC) released new data on the role that American fathers play in parenting their children that was inclusive of African-American fathers.

In fact, in its coverage of the study, the Los Angeles Times states that the results *defy* stereotypes about black fatherhood" because the CDC found that *black dads* are *more* involved with their kids daily than dads from *other* racial groups.

---

212 "Father Absence + Involvement | Statistics," National Fatherhood Initiative, http://www. fatherhood.org/fatherhood-data-statistics.

The fact that there's no dramatic drop-off for African-American fathers is still a *surprising* revelation for some people. The *new* data builds upon *years* of research that concluded hands-on parenting is *similar* among fathers of *all* races.[213]

It is still important that black fathers maintain their paternal African roots and responsibilities, in West African culture. Fathers are considered the head of the family. In many African societies, elderly fathers are viewed as the village judge. The authority of the father to judge within the limits of the family and the village level enables them to settle conflicts of any kind.

The concept of a father as one with ultimate power and responsibility was central to the deciding of the role of men in African family and society. This concept sees the father as a patriarch, ruler of the family, founder of a colony, religion, business or tribe like the founders of the ancient Hebrew families.

African society reveres the father or the eldest male as the head of the family or tribe, descent and kinship.[214]

What makes fatherhood challenging today is societal changes that create different types of fathers. The modern-day father comes in various forms. Today's father is no longer always the traditional married breadwinner and disciplinarian in the family.

One thing is consistent: Psychological research across families from all ethnic backgrounds suggests that the fathers' affection and increased family involvement help promote children's social and emotional development.[215]

---

213 Tara Culp-Ressler, "The Myth of the Absent Black Father," Think Progress, 16 January 2014, https://thinkprogress.org/the-myth-of-the-absent-black-father-ecc4e961c2e8?gi=93916e243828.

214 Gerald Chijioke Ogbuja, "Fatherhood from African Perspective," 19 June 2008, http://articles.onlinenigeria.com/articles/3984-fatherhood-from-african-perspective.html.

215 "The Changing Role of the Modern Day," American Psychological Association, http://www.apa.org/pi/families/resources/changing-father.aspx.

In addition, for black male believers, we must not only return to our African roots but back to the Bible. The following translation of Ephesians 6:4 captures our duties.

> *New Century Version (NCV): "Fathers, do not make your children angry, but raise them with the training and teaching of the Lord,"*

This passage clearly states that fathers are to avoid performing actions that cause anger in children. Such actions as verbal or physical abuse, harsh discipline, criticism, emotional and financial neglect, absenteeism, addictive lifestyles, criminal or unethical activity, and the mistreatment of the children's mother are some examples.

The alternative is becoming intentional regarding your obligation of ethical training and Christian teaching. This verse makes it the duty of the father, not the mother, to perform this instruction.

> *Proverbs 17:6, Holman Christian Standard Bible, says* "*Grandchildren are the crown of the elderly, and the pride of sons is their fathers.*"

Obviously, the role of black fathers is primal in our quest to fulfill our purpose as a people and to the fulfilling of the prophetic destiny.

Part of which must coincide with our last day movement. The Cushites in latter times have a journey to complete. They are on both a historical and prophetical chariot ride—a trip in which they will meet a Philip.

Discussion Questions

1. What is the misrepresentation of men of African descent concerning fatherhood?

2. How does the role of black fathers relate to the destiny of people of African Descent?

CHAPTER 16

Riding the Cushite's Chariot
Our Movement

꙳

"Despise not a snail for its slow and struggling movement;
it has a destination and with time it shall arrive."

~AFRICAN PROVERB

Acts 8:26–39 NRS "Then an angel of the Lord said to Philip, "Get up and go toward the south[a] to the road that goes down from Jerusalem to Gaza." (This is a wilderness road.) So he got up and went. Now there was an Ethiopian eunuch, a court official of the Candace, queen of the Ethiopians, in charge of her entire treasury. He had come to Jerusalem to worship and was returning home; seated in his chariot, he was reading the prophet Isaiah. Then the Spirit said to Philip, "*Go over* to this *chariot* and *join* it." So Philip ran up to it and heard him reading the prophet Isaiah. He asked, "Do you understand what you are reading?" He replied, "How can I, unless someone guides me?" And *he invited* Philip to get in and sit beside him. Now the passage of the scripture that he was reading was this: "Like a sheep he was led to the slaughter, and like a lamb silent before its shearer, so he does not open his mouth. In his humiliation justice was denied him. Who can describe his generation? For his life is taken away from the earth." The eunuch asked Philip, "About whom, May I ask you, does the prophet say this, about himself or about someone else?" Then Philip began to speak, and starting with this scripture, he proclaimed to him the good news about Jesus. As they were going along the road, they came to some water; and the eunuch said, "Look, here is water! What is to prevent me from being baptized?" He commanded the chariot to stop, and both of them, Philip and the eunuch, went down into the water, and Philip baptized him. When they came up out of the water, the Spirit of the Lord snatched Philip away; the eunuch saw him no more, and went on his way rejoicing."

People of African descent are part of a divinely orchestrated movement, on a path to their destiny. There is a very important role that a God select group of non-African people will play in the fulfillment of that destiny.

That role will be a *loving discipleship,* and *reconciling relationship* role—a *Philip* role, which we will review from Acts 8:26-39. There are several principles that this passage reveals concerning this group's responses to Cushite Africans in the latter times.

> The Receiving for the Cushite *vs. 26 "Then an angel of the Lord said to Philip, "Get up and go toward the south*[a]* to the road that goes down from Jerusalem to Gaza." (This is a* wilderness *road.)*

In the biblical times of Acts 8:26-39 the Philip of this episode was a Jew, but in this season of our destiny the *Philips* will be primarily Euro-Americans, Europeans, and some will be Jews.

If Philips were an acronym the letters could represent (**Pro**claimers **H**eading **I**nto **L**oving **I**nterracial **P**ersonal **S**ervice). In these end times, God is raising up *"Philips"*—non-African righteous people who will *receive* a *Rhema* message from the angel of the Lord. That is, an angel in the sense of the book of Revelation.

For angel is from the Greek word *angelos,* which means *messenger* of *God* – In this sense, pastoral messengers who speak the truth, and challenge the "Phillips" of their congregations to *not* be isolated from people of African descent, but to go to where they are—go to the wilderness road. For people of African descent their journey in this country and abroad has been like a *wilderness* road—a dry, dismal pilgrimage with pests, wild beasts, challenges, struggles, and hazards.

However, the wilderness is also deeply valued for cultural, spiritual, moral, and aesthetic reasons.[216] In a spiritual sense, the wilderness is a place God leads you to be tested and proved for ministry. It was in the wilderness where Jesus encountered and overcame Satan:

> *Matthew 4:1 NIV "Then Jesus was led by the Spirit into the wilderness to be tempted by the devil."*

It is a place of wandering as in the case of Israelites:

> *Psalm 107:4 NLT "Some wandered in the wilderness, lost and homeless."*

In the last days "Philips" will *receive* the word from their *pastoral* angel, and with the courage of their obedient conviction will respond to that word.

---

216 Wikipedia contributors, "Wilderness," Wikipedia, The Free Encyclopedia, Wikipedia, The Free Encyclopedia, https://en.wikipedia.org/wiki/Wilderness.

The Revering of the Cushite: *vs. 27 "So he got up and went. Now here was an* Ethiopian *eunuch, a* court official *of the* Candace, *queen of the Ethiopians, in charge of her entire treasury. He had* come *to Jerusalem to* worship."

As mentioned in a previous chapter, *Ethiopian* is the Greek word for the ancient term *Cushite* which meant *"black* or *burnt face,"* referring to African people of color.

As also mentioned earlier, according to the Ethiopian Orthodox Tewahedo tradition, this Cushite official was referred to as *Bachos*, and in Eastern Orthodox tradition he is known as an Ethiopian Jew:[217]

The Cushite in this passage was a *dark*-complexioned African. Although *Ethiopian* was used generally for anyone with this physical appearance, here it refers to an inhabitant of the ancient kingdom of Meroe, which encompassed what is now northern Sudan south of Aswan in Africa.

Therefore, He was a African from the Sudan. This man was powerful, the chief treasurer of a kingdom wealthy from its iron smelting, gold mining, and trading position. It had been a channel for goods from the rest of the continent. He had such integrity that Candace queen of the Cushite Africans had entrusted her entire treasury to him.

More importantly, he was a God-fearing man who had come to Jerusalem to worship—a devout man of *reverence*. Once again here we have another example of the deep God consciousness of the people of African descent. That consciousness will be integral to their restoration as a people, and the fulfilling of their divine destiny.

---

217 "Ethiopian eunuch"

This official was returning to Meroe after traveling to Jerusalem for one of the feasts, and he is *sitting in his chariot* reading Scripture, probably moving slowly enough to allow for reading, and for Philip to approach it on foot.

Reading aloud was the common practice in ancient times, and was necessary when words were strung together on a manuscript without spacing or punctuation.

He is referred to as a *eunuch,* a word that Euro-American scholars are quick to designate as meaning a *castrated* male, when applying the label to blacks in Scripture. European and Euro-American translators are often guilty of literary castration when applying certain terms to black men in Scripture.

However, the Greek word for Eunuch in Acts 8:27 is *eunouchos,* the equivalent of the Old Testament word *Saris,* which means a *high official.* It is a word that is of ancient Semitic origin, related to the concepts of *"trained, reliable,* and *experienced,"* but *no* direct connection with castration, unlike the Greek words *ektomias, spadon* and *apokopai,* which can be directly related to eunuch and castration.[218]

> The Riding of the Cushite: *vs. 28 "and was returning home; seated in his* chariot, *he was reading the prophet Isaiah."*

The Cushite official rode a physical chariot in the past, Cushite people of African descent ride a symbolic **CHARIOT** in the present, and it is a transport through trials—a journey of perseverance individually and corporately.

---

218 FP Retief, "EUNUCHS IN THE BIBLE," Acta Theologica Supplementum 7, 2005, https://www.ajol.info/index.php/actat/article/viewFile/52578/41183Vulgate.EUNUCHS IN THE BIBLE ABSTRACT 7 20051968). Hug (1918:449-50) indicated that eunouchos, like saris, may have a primary meaning of "official". Spadon refers to both congenital and man-made eunuchism (Hug 1918:449-50).

If the word **CHARIOT** were an acronym, the letters could stand for (**C**ushite **H**istorical **A**frican **R**ide **I**ncluding **O**ur **T**imes). As a people we have been on a historical ride, a journey of adverse challenges, pain, mountains and valleys.

It is a chariot that has rode throughout our history. The vehicle is our *destiny* on the move, and our *purpose* as a people going forward.

> "*Nobles shall come from Egypt; Cush shall hasten to* stretch out her hands *to God.*"

> The Returning of the Cushite: *vs. 28* "(*He*) *was* returning home; seated in his chariot, he was reading the prophet Isaiah."

The Cushite African official was returning home when he encountered Philip. Home to his place of *standing*. Home to his place of *prosperity* and *respect*. Home to his place of *community* and *affinity*. The chariot he was riding was traveling *forward* to his destination, and yet it was journeying *back* to his *original* place of origin from whence he started.

In the same manner, people of African descent are riding their symbolic chariot *forward* to their destiny, but *back* to their *original* place of honor. It is a ride that will encounter ups and downs, jostling movements, shakes and bumps. It is a journey replete with predators and road hazards, grueling at times, but ultimately the chariot and its passenger will arrive safely to its destination.

> The Relating to the Cushite: *vs. 29* "*Then the* Spirit *said to* Philip, 'Go over *to this* chariot *and* join *it.*'"

Like Philip certain Euro-Americans will *go over* to people of African descent. Prompted by Spirit they will simply *go over* but they will not try to *rule over* Cushites. God will raise up people in this season, Euro-Americans who will exemplify the name Philip, for they will be *"lovers of horses."*

That is the symbolic horses pulling Cushite Africans toward their destiny. They will love the *strength* of the destiny of black people, and will recognize God's purpose for them in this time.

Today's "Philips" are not just non-African righteous people who respond to the message of their angelic messengers, but they will also be people who will respond to the Holy Spirit to join with the chariot.

They will engage and interact with black people directly. They will do so with *no* political agenda, but simply out of their love for God, their fellow Cushite African brothers, and their recognition of God's purpose for them in this season.

They will not avoid contact with them, engage in anti-minority rhetoric, espouse xenophobic language, or make racist remarks. They will not show the kind of racial prejudice toward Cushite Africans that Miriam and Aaron showed in Numbers 12:9-10, and therefore received severe chastening from Yahweh God:

> *Numbers 12:1, 10-11 "While they were at Hazeroth,* Miriam and Aaron *chastised Moses for marrying a* foreign *woman—a* Cushite *and it was true that he did indeed marry such an* African). ... *When the cloud lifted from the congregation tent, you could see that Miriam had been* stricken *with a disfiguring skin condition. Her skin looked white, like snow. Aaron looked at her, saw this, and immediately turned to Moses. ..." The Voice*

It is ironic that God's judgment on Miriam involved skin disfigurement and skin *discoloration and* apparently, the *loss* of *melanin pigmentation.*

Unfortunately, many whites will not initiate this kind of closer relating due to their racial bias. They will remain segregated from minorities, will continue in their cultural ignorance. Jesus said in John 8:32:

> *"You will know the truth, and the truth will make you free."*
> *—NASB*

Racism is spiritual captivity, a mental shackle. It is a pervasive form of social bondage especially for Euro-Americans and their attitudes toward other racial minorities. They are not trying to move closer to Cushite Africans, but would rather separate themselves in both their residential and their religious communities.

Therefore, you get the phenomenon known as *"white flight,"* when blacks attempt to move toward whites. Quiet as it is kept, there are a lot of Euro-Americans who prefer segregation (and some blacks as well). Although they openly express belief in equality, they privately shun it.

This is also symptomatic of certain white male paranoia. That is why Frank Schaeffer, an ex-evangelical, says, "The American political process is being hijacked by a reckless, whining dangerous gang of psychologically damaged white men who are far-right ideologues."

He says he used to be one of them and says It's time to tell the truth about our white male problem."[219]

Thus, to expect major change concerning racism is unrealistic, but there will be the *"Philips,"* a God-selected group of whites who will be obedient to the Spirit, and actively seek to make connections with black people, and run *toward* them, not *away* from them.

These people will be key to racial reconciliation, and the facilitating of the destiny of Cushitic people of African descent in the last days.

The Reading of Cushite: *vs.30 "So Philip* ran *up to it and* heard him *reading the prophet Isaiah. He asked, "Do you understand what you are reading?"*

The "Philips" will be inquisitive, and will show their willingness to assist people of African descent. They will give that assistance and not abandon that agenda, but will be committed to the end. They will be people who will *listen* to them, and be receptive to hear what is coming from their mouths.

They will be listening to hear how Cushite Africans *understand* things, and how they *read* a situation. They will not attempt to control or dominate the conversation, but in the words of James they will be quick to *hear* and *slow* to speak. They will not shut down, go into a state of denial, or attempt to divert the conversation as so many conservative evangelicals do.

When people of African descent speak, they will be all ears, and will give them their undivided attention. They will not be

219 Frank Schaeffer, "America's White Male Problem," World News Daily, Information Clearing House, 7 January 2013, http://www.informationclearinghouse.info/article33545.htm.

tone death to what they are thinking and saying in this hour and will be *attentive* to their voices and responsive to their petitions for help.

> The Replying of the Cushite *vs.31* "*He* replied, "*How can I, unless someone guides me?*" *And* he invited *Philip to* get in *and* sit *beside him.*"

When Cushite people of African descent encounter genuine Philip-like people, they will respond with openness; will put down their barriers; and will be open. They will invite them into their world, and into their space.

They will allow them to be part of their community, and embrace them as brothers.

Cushite Africans will invite the Philips to sit beside them as *equals* not above them as *superiors* or beneath them as *subordinates*. The love coming from these Philips, will dispel the mistrust by African-blooded people toward Euro-Americans.

In the story, Philip was very honoring of the Cushite's chariot. Before he rode it he had to first move *alongside* of it, and enter by *invitation*, not by *intrusion*. He showed deference to the Cushite official, and respect for his chariot. He did not attempt to *take over* the reins, *control* the chariot, *determine* or *change* the direction in which it was headed. He understood that this was *not* his chariot.

Therefore, he approached it humbly, ran beside it long enough to gain the African's *trust*, and at the right time the Cushite invited him to come up into it to bond with him. He discerned Philip's noble intention.

The Reaching of the Cushite: *vs. 34 "The eunuch asked Philip, "About whom, May I ask you, does the prophet say this, about himself or about someone else? Then Philip began to* speak, *and starting with* this *scripture, he proclaimed to him the* good news *about Jesus"*

Philips will be accommodating to Cushite Africans, and they will *start* where they are, and address their confusion and misunderstandings. Their interventions will play an important role in the spiritual destiny of black folks. They will be purpose driven to reach out to them.

On the other hand, people of African descent will also feel free to ask questions and request support. They will be a key to the destiny of people of African descent, by helping to make disciples of them, which is why *authentic* relations with them will be so crucial.

Philip taught the Cushite about Jesus. It is interesting that this African got stuck on that part of Isaiah which chronicled the oppressive suffering of Christ—a suffering that in time his own black people would socially emulate corporately.

More significantly, Philip showed the *love* of Jesus to him before hearing his words the African saw his *heart*. Philips must first enter the *"road"* of the Cushite before understanding the *"read"* of the Cushite.

The Refreshing of the Cushite: *vs. 36 "As they were going along the* road, *they came to some* water; *and the eunuch said, "Look, here is water! What is to prevent me from being baptized?"*

The Cushite desired to be baptized into water. After a time of *riding* the chariot with Philip the trust and comfort level grew, so that he desired not only a faith *conversion* to Christ, but water *immersion* for Christ.

When Philips have ridden the Cushite's chariot for a while, the trust level will be such that they will be able to move from verbal *communication* with the Cushite Africans to *ritual* participation with them.

> The Reconciling of the Cushite: *vs.38 "He commanded the chariot to stop, and both of them, Philip and the eunuch, went down into the water, and Philip baptized him."*

Verse thirty-eight is not only about baptism, and cross-cultural evangelism, it is a picture of racial reconciliation. Genuine reconciliation between blacks and whites happens as Cushite people of African descent slow down their chariot so Philips can go down *together* in the cleansing and refreshing waters of love.

Cushites can't be so committed to the chariot destination that they don't take time to stop and go down together in the river of forgiveness and racial reconciliation. Not only Christ's forgiveness of us, but Christ forgiveness *through* us.

It will be the love of the Philips that immerses the African Cushites into these waters of love and forgiveness, and they will emerge from those waters refreshed and healed of racial wounds. On our chariot ride to our destiny we must pause to pick up Philips.

> The Rejoicing of the Cushite: *vs. 39 "When they came up out of the water, the Spirit of the Lord snatched Philip away; the eunuch saw him no more, and went on his way rejoicing."*

The result of this baptism was that Philip experienced a supernatural high, and was caught away. Likewise, the same for today's Philip like Euro-Americans for their relationships with the Cushite Africans will be strategic and time-limited. They will be timed to accomplish the purpose of God—delivering the deposit they must to the destiny of Cushites.

The African resumed his chariot ride, but this time he went toward his destination *rejoicing*. His ride was no longer one of *confusion* and *misunderstanding*, it was now a ride of *joy*.

As African Cushites come together with the Philips—get baptized into forgiveness—they will discover the joy of their journey, they will move on toward their destiny, with the joy of the Lord as their strength, and the pull of the horses of their destiny as their momentum.

The chariot the official rode would have rolled along on *four* wheels. In the same manner, our destiny will ride forward on four aspects; they are our *message*, our *mission*, our *munitions*, and our *mercies*.

We will fulfill our destiny, and it will be because we are riding it on all four of these *wheels*. They are the subject of my discussion in the succeeding chapters.

Discussion Questions

1. Who are the Philips and what will be their relationship with Cushite Africans?
2. What is the Cushite's chariot?
3. What is the other meaning of baptism in this story?
4. Overall how does this story relate to the destiny of black people?

CHAPTER 17

Step Aside and Let the Cushite Tell It — Our Message

꙰

"The words you say to tell the truth are as important as the decision to be truthful."

~AFRICAN PROVERB

2 Samuel 18:31-32 "Then the man from Cush *arrived. He said, 'You are my king and master. I'm bringing you some good news. The Lord has saved you today from all those who were trying to kill you.' The king asked the man from* Cush, *'Is the young man Absalom safe?' The man replied, 'King David, may your enemies be like that young man. May all those who rise up to harm you be like him.'"*

1. Samuel records the conflict between David's army and forces of Absalom, the rebellious son of David. The king wanted a victory, but wanted to preserve the life of Absalom and gave instructions not to terminate him.

David loved Absalom; in fact, he loved him too much. In like manner, this nation has created an Absalom-like culture that they love too much.

The Absalom Culture: Money, Materialism and Selfish Avarice

An acronym for **A.B.S.A.L.O.M**. could mean (**A**varicious **B**ased **S**elfishness **A**nd **L**ove **o**f **M**oney) Absalom's name means "*my Father is peace.*" He symbolizes a cultural mind-set that is plaguing this nation; a false sense of peace and the thing they often refuse to let go, but that thing which will destroy them if they don't. For this nation, it is the love of money, materialism and greed.

The Absalom Cultural Mind-set Vigilantism and the murdering of Innocent People of Color

In addition, Absalom killed his brother Amnon to avenge an assault on his sister Tamar. He also represents a spirit of vigilantism or the "George Zimmerman syndrome" emboldened by a gun-happy culture, where people set themselves up as judge and jury, ignoring legal protocols.

Absalom's violent nature became a generational legacy inherited from his father David. As the king of Israel, he epitomized the hope of the nation, which is why his men often did not let him go out to battle, but his sin against Uriah came back to visit him in the generation of his son Absalom.

Uriah was a Hittite a descendant of Ham—the patriarch of the people of color.

America, like David because of past killing of "Uriahs," has a history of violence against innocent people of color and taking that which belongs to them (for Uriah *Bathsheba*, for African Americans their *freedom*, for Native Americans their *land* and *Latino Americans* their *dignity*),

They have consequently created an Absalom sense of false peace. That, like Absalom, is a mind-set of greed, ambition, and lust for power that has come back to destroy this nation in this generation.

Absalom had to die, but David was unwilling to let this happen. There are those in this country who will fight to preserve this Absalom cultural mind-set. To change this Joab became God's *instrument* for *judgment* of Absalom after he tried to escape on a mule, an animal associated with *stubbornness*.

Mules are supposedly smart. They are not as easy to train and what they learn is never forgotten. For the most part they are sterile and birth-wise unproductive.

Cushite people of African descent will get to our destiny by *riding* our God-ordained chariot and *not* by riding the back of Absalom *mule* of greed and materialism. That is why Proverbs 3:31 says:

"Do not envy the oppressor, and choose none of his ways;" NKJV

The word oppressor here is the original Hebrew word *hamas*, which means *strong fierce active force*, an *injustice* to some standard, implying severe or grievous *injustice* to a people, the ruining of a land or a people.

We Americans like a mule ride, thinking that we are smart, and our culture because of avarice and racism is moving on an inflexible path like a mule. In many ways, it has rendered us economically sterile.

`Thus, we are behaving in a manner much like the mule that Absalom rode to his destruction and the Scripture warns us in Psalm 32:9 (GOD'S WORD Translation)

"Don't be stubborn *like a horse or* mule. *They need a bit and bridle in their mouth to restrain them, or they will not come near you."*

Because of our *stubborn* pride as a nation, we will not come near to God. Thus, He is going to bit and bridle the mouth of our Absalom culture.

For the *mouth* has been the biased *media*, lying politicians, the corrupt government, greedy Wall Street and even pseudo-religious leaders. They have spoken for our culture, and together they represent the mule. They often present false images of African people and people of color. They are enabling our nations ride to national destruction.

That mule symbolizes a cultural *movement* toward God's *judgment*; a *ride* of *ruination* following a *course* to *calamity*. Given how much racial hate and xenophobia has *blinded* the minds of White America and given how *deeply* they are steeped in *denial* they are moving quickly to disaster.

Absalom rode this beast to his demise. There are many in this nation with an Absalom cultural mind-set who are acting stubbornly, refusing to be restrained from the destructive path they are going on, and are riding that thinking to their own hanging.

Because of riding this symbol of stubbornness, Absalom got hung up in a tree by his head probably because of his hair. The Bible says he was suspended between heaven and earth.

This Absalom culture is *hung* up, suspended between heaven and earth, stuck between not being righteous enough to be called heavenly, but too religious to be designated as just earthly.

The head and hair is a characteristic of *power*, and Absalom's long hair represents a long history of power, but God is going to allow this Absalom culture, to get hung up, ending this nation's ride on its stubborn mule course. Our nation is riding this mentality to a portending fate.

Absalom had to experience God's judgment on a tree for Judah to be saved. The tree he was caught on was an oak tree symbolizing *strength* and it was a *hard* wood tree.

This Absalom culture is going to get caught politically and economically in an oak tree situation—a *hard* situation so *strong* that it will bring the termination of the Absalom culture and alter our system.

In the same manner, the Absalom mind-set must be hung up on the tree of Christ; be crucified with him; be pierced by the word of God many times and then be buried so that this nation can experience a true victory for all its people.

> *Acts 5:30 KJV: "The God of our fathers raised up Jesus, whom ye slew and hanged on a tree."*

> *Acts 10:39 KJV: "And we are witnesses of all things which he did both in the land of the Jews, and in Jerusalem; whom they slew and hanged on a tree:"*

> *Galatians 3:13 AKJV: "Christ hath redeemed us from the curse of the law, being made a curse for us: for it is written, Cursed is every one that hangeth on a tree:"*

> *1 Peter 2:24 AKJV: "who his own self bare our sins in his own body on the tree that we, being dead to sins, should live unto righteousness: by whose stripes ye were healed."*

Now Joab's name means *Yahweh is Father*, or *God is his father*. God is raising up Joab situations to bring a fatherly retribution on the Absalom culture.

David was so busy trying to errantly father Absalom he forgot who his spiritual father was. Many in this nation in positions of power have forgotten who the real Father is, so God must send Joab political and economic scenarios to remind them. The near economic crash of 2008 was such a reminder. In order to judge Absalom he had to be pierced through with three javelins.

> 2 Samuel 18:14-15, NIV: "Joab said, 'I'm not going to wait like this for you.' So he took three javelins in his hand and plunged them into Absalom's heart while Absalom was still alive in the oak tree. And ten of Joab's armor-bearers surrounded Absalom, struck him and killed him."

In a similar manner, to bring judgment on the Absalom cultural mind-set of this nation, three javelins must pierce through the very heart of the culture. The *three* javelins are the *moral truth* of *Scripture, financial crisis*, and *growing racial diversity.*

The ten armor bearers are interesting. In Bible numerology ten is one of the numbers of the completion of *divine order*. The most obvious example of this was the Ten Commandments—God's law. Armor bearers were servants who carried the armor and weapons of the king into battles.

The ten armor bearers symbolize God's judgment that serves the agenda of God to bring things into *divine order*. The American culture is spiritually, politically, and economically out of order. God is sending a Joab chastening to the Absalom culture that will bring it into order.

Absalom was a recipient of God's judgment. His demise was a victory for David and the nation just as God's judgment of the Absalom cultural mind-set will be a victory for the U.S. The time came when the message of that victory had to be shared with David and the nation.

Someone had to run and tell the message. To begin with we had Ahimaaz who volunteered to run to take the message (2 Samuel 18:21). There are those who want to be first, who because of their status of privilege, and sense of entitlement feel that they should precede everyone else.

Ahimaaz was a good man, but he was ambitious and had a desire for rewards. This despite the reality that Joab told him that his desire to be the messenger of the hour was *untimely*, for he wasn't the one selected for the season.

Now Ahimaaz's name means *brother* of *anger* or *irascible*. There are those who operate out of the anger toward people of color and who believe they are more qualified.

One of the things the 2016 presidential political cycle has revealed is how much hatred and anger there is in this country.

These people want to be the first to carry the message of victory for this hour, but they are untimely and unseasonal. They also lack the heart to speak the truth about the Absalom culture (2 Samuel 18:20): so Joab said to Ahimaaz:

> *"You are not the one to take the news today," Joab told him. "You may take the news another time, but you must not do so today, because the king's son is dead."*

Like the tribe of Issachar people must be able to discern seasons and know when it is another ethnic group's time to be used for an important kingdom purpose. They must be willing to step aside and be enablers and not obstructers.

For example, there was a religious revival that swept Western Europe and came to the British American colonies called the "*Great Awakening.*" This movement was mainly out of Europe and was led and spread by mainly Europeans and Euro- Americans between 1720 and the 1740's.

It was followed by another revival known as the *Second Great Awakening* that began in New England in the 1790's.

These were basically European and Euro-American movements. God used them to be the main religious catalyst of those revivals.[220]

Today he is bringing a different revival and a much *greater awakening* and people of African descent, and other people of color will be the vessels God uses to spur this last day revival.

However, there are persons today who have largely not accepted that it is someone else's time to bring a special message for this hour. Those whose time has passed or not yet come must have the same humble attitude of resignation to the will of God that John the Baptist had toward Christ. An attitude that says:

"He must increase, but I must decrease.*" John 3:30 KJV*

Instead of Ahimaaz Joab chose and sent a man of *Cush*—a Sudanese *African*—*a black man,* as the messenger, He was most likely a foot soldier under Joab.[221]

This Cushite Sudanese African man was probably an unnamed archer mercenary in David's army. Cushite archers of-

---

220 The Editors of Encyclopedia Britannica, "Great Awakening American religious movement," Encyclopedia Britannica, https://www.britannica.com/event/Great-Awakening.

221 David H., "Good news / Bad news - The Run of Ahimaaz," 18 February 2011, http://www.runningwithhorses.com/2011/02/good-news-bad-news-run-of-ahimaaz.html.

ten served in armies as mercenaries. The use of mercenaries had been a staple in organized warfare since ancient times.

Cushitic Africans had served as mercenaries in Israel under both David and Solomon.[222] They were widely known throughout the ancient, fighting for both sides in Egypt, Assyria, *Israel*, Persia and Greece.

I established in an earlier chapter that there was a close association between ancient Cushite Africans and Israel.[223] They would have been part of David's forces under Joab in 2 Samuel 18 and in 2 Samuel 11:1: (GW)

> *"In the spring, the time when kings go out to battle, David sent* Joab, his mercenaries, *and Israel's army* [*to war*]*. They destroyed the Ammonites and attacked Rabbah, while David stayed in Jerusalem."*

One other translation of this passage warrants mentioning:

> *"It was spring. It was the time when kings go off to war. So David sent* Joab *out with the* king's special troops *and the whole army of Israel. They destroyed the Ammonites. They went to the city of Rabbah. They surrounded it and got ready to attack it. But David remained in Jerusalem." NIRV*

Thus, God's Word Translation uses the term *"mercenaries"* and the New International Reader's Version uses the phrase *"the king's special troops."*

There was a contrast between Israel's general army and the mercenaries. The King James translation uses the term *servant*

---

222 David A. Latzko, "THE MARKET FOR MERCENARIES," David Latzko's Web Page, Penn State, http://www.personal.psu.edu/~dxl31/research/presentations/mercenary.html.

223 Boyne

from the original Hebrew term *ebed*, which Euro-centric scholars like to translate as "slave" when applying the term to Africans in the Scripture, but depending on the context of the word the overwhelming translation of the word is *servant*. It translates as "servant" 744 times, "manservant" 23 times, "bondman" 21 times, "bondage" 10 times, "bondservant" once, and "on all sides" only once as slave.[224]

It means a *servant*, i.e., one who helps in the service to another, but *not* necessarily the *possession* of another.

It can also mean *officer, official*, one who *has authority* in *government* who is referred to as a "servant of the king."[225]

To reiterate the Cushite African official who helped Jeremiah was named *Ebed* Melech, which means *"servant* of the *king,"* a designation of some status but *not* the title of a slave.

Therefore, the Cushite African in 2 Samuel 18:29-30 was a *warrior* with a *word*, a *combatant* with a *communiqué*, and a *mercenary* with a *message*.

Although once again many Euro-centric commentators want to make him a slave. His name is unknown but his ethnicity is identified; for he symbolizes a people as opposed to an individual. He is a metaphor for the destiny of the people of African descent.

For they will be war-like soldiers who not only fight triumphantly in the battle, but will run with a victorious message.[226]

---

224 "2 Samuel 11:1," The Bible, King James Version- Enhanced Strong's Lexicon, Miklal Software Solutions, Inc., 2011.

225 Swanson, James A., The Dictionary of Biblical Languages with Semitic domains- Hebrew (OT), Libronix Digital Library System.

226 Felder, "Blacks in Biblical Antiquity"

Joab ordered this African soldier to take back the good news that Absalom forces were defeated and the bad news for David that his son Absalom was dead.

> *2 Samuel 18:21: "Then Joab said to a* Cushite, *'Go, tell the king what you have* seen.' *The Cushite* bowed down *before Joab and ran off." NIV*

> *"Then Joab said to a man from* Sudan, *"Go, tell the king what you* saw." *The messenger bowed down with his face touching the ground in front of Joab and then ran off." GW*

This Cushite is a personification of the people of African descent. Several aspects of his story represent our destiny. We will review the responses of this Cushite African for they are clues to our reactions as a people in fulfilling our prophetic fate. To understand this, we need to discuss two factors; the *commandment* given to the African and his *commitment* to compliance.

The Commandment to the Cushite African
"**GO**" Mobilization
"**TELL**" Proclamation
"**WHAT YOU HAVE SEEN**" Revelation

The Commitment of the Cushite African
"**BOWED DOWN**" Subordination
"**RAN OFF**" Acceleration
"**ARRIVED and SAID**" Destination

"GO" Mobilization

The original Hebrew word translated **GO**: *yalak* /yaw•lak means to proceed, or move. This is the season where Cushitic Africans are receiving a '**GO**' commission of divine prompting from God to bring deliverance, for throughout Scripture and throughout history Cushites and Cushitic Africans heeded this commission call to go heip others:

- To *rescue* Moses from a life-threatening ministry stress, Jethro a *Cushite* had to **GO** from Midian to the Wilderness.[227]
- To *save* the Israelites *from* getting lost, **Hobab**, a *Cushite* scout, had to **GO** with Israel to be their guiding eyes. (Numbers 10:29-34)[228]
- *To endow Solomon with precious gifts Cushite Queen Makeda had to **GO** from Kush to Israel adopting the Jewish religion along the way. (2 Chronicles 6:1–11)*
- To *liberate* Jeremiah Ebed-Melech a Cushite *African official* had to **"GO"** from the palace to a pit getting permission from the king to free the prophet Jeremiah. (Jeremiah 38:1–13)[229]
- To *help* deliver Hezekiah from the Assyrians, Tirhakah, a *Cushite African* Pharaoh, had to **"GO"** from Egypt (Khemet Africa) to the Jerusalem region. (2 Kings 19:9; Isaiah 37:9)[230]
- To *relieve* the weariness of our Savior, Simon a Phutite North African related to *Cushites,* was compelled to

---

227 "Exodus 18:13-27", The Bible, Winston's Original African American Heritage Study Bible Encyclopedia, edited by James W. Peebles (Nashville: James C. Winston Publishing Company, 1996) 394.

228 Winston's p.338.

229 Winston's p.185.

230 Taharqa from Wikipedia, the free encyclopedia Ibid.

> *"GO"* from a crowd to carrying the cross the remainder of Via Della Rosa route. (Matthew 27:32)[231]
> - To *take* the *gospel* back to his queen and to Africa a *Cushite African* official had to *"GO"* from Jerusalem back to his country of Kush. (Acts 8:27)[232]

Now in these latter times once again God is telling Cushites and people of African descent to **GO** be agents of deliverance to the nation and world. We are the Cushite African runners of this hour.

"TELL" Proclamation

This original word for tell *nagad*/naw•gad means to declare, announce, report, to make known, expound, to inform of, to publish, and proclaim.

Cushites and people of African descent are being called to be heralds of the good news of the kingdom of God. They are being sent to go bring this gospel not just within their national borders, but beyond to other nations.

To places that are spiritually dry and that need a refreshing. Cushites will take the refreshing of spiritual revival from their foreign countries to other nations. Thus, the following passage:

> Proverbs 25:25 NIV *"Like cold water to a weary soul is good news from a distant land."*

There is a message that God has given to them, it is a message that is good news plus it will also be a message that speaks the truth concerning God's judgment of this Absalom culture.

---

231 Winston's pp.643-644.

232 Ethiopian eunuch from Wikipedia, the free encyclopedia.

Proverbs 25:11 "Like golden apples set in silver is a word spoken at the right time" ISV

Proverbs 3:7 "There is a time to be silent. And there's a time to speak"

The Cushite African's message was the right message for the right time. God is saying today it is now time for the Cushites; the people of African descent—the people of color to speak. They have a message for the present.

The African gave a positive message of good news and victory, but it was a message of the complete truth. It was not the word David wanted, but it was the exact message he needed.

Africans of this season who have been selected by God will be humble people with a positive message of Good News, but they will be people of integrity who are truth tellers about God's judgment of this nation's Absalom culture, and the consequence to those that follow it.

The African runner had to demonstrate a certain courage when he told David the truth, because he was in jeopardy of losing his life, but the truth he did tell, for truth no matter how hazardous is the key to liberation. Jesus said in John 8:32 that:

"You will know the truth, and the truth will set you free." GW

His message set off a chain reaction of events in the nation. David was forced to bring closure to his issues with Absalom; the nation could lament with the king; and move on, Joab could rouse David from his melancholic state challenging him to man up accepting his son's death, and finally a divided nation could begin healing as warring segments began to reconcile.

Healing will not occur until the negative effects of the Absalom culture, the related effects of racism and xenophobia, are properly judged. All of this was the residual benefits of an Africans message for a kingly political leader.

"WHAT YOU HAVE SEEN" Revelation

The word *seen* in this passage is from the original language, which means to perceive, consider have vision, learn about, observe, watch, look at, give attention to, discern, and distinguish. The Cushite African was instructed to go and tell what he *saw*.

Therefore, he had to have *vision* to see what happened, and the plan of God for the nation. As people of African descent, we Cushites have developed a God-endowed vision that has become a byproduct of our oppression.

Our suffering has heightened our discernment, increased our spiritual awareness, honed our perception skills, and deepened our spiritual intuition.

There are things in the spirit realm that the Holy Spirit will enable us to see that others cannot see, or unwilling to see. There are things we willbe able to sense that others cannot sense.

In the past, Satan has sought to exploit this spiritual sensitivity through the occult, but in the last days God will use that vision for his purpose as the means of fulfilling his will.

"BOWED DOWN" Subordination

The original Hebrew word for *bow* is *shachah* /shaw•khaw, which means to take a bowing stance, it is a position of *submission* to a superior. This African bowed before Joab this gesture was symbolic of African people submitting to the Father's will to bring the timely message to this nation.

He showed respect for authority. The destiny of people of African heritage is so pivotal, God will not permit rebels to ruin it. Those who have issues with Godly authority will be removed; for they would have disqualified themselves. More importantly, rebellion is like witchcraft.1 Samuel 15:23:

> "For rebellion *is as the sin of witchcraft, and* stubbornness *is as iniquity and idolatry.*" *KJV*

God will not permit stubborn rebels and witches to control the outcome of God's agenda for us; our *submission* will follow God's *commission;* our people are to strategic to God's plan.

"RAN OFF" Acceleration

> "*Every morning in Africa, a gazelle wakes up. It knows it must run faster than the fastest lion or it will be killed. Every morning a lion wakes up. It knows it must outrun the slowest gazelle or it will starve to death. It doesn't matter whether you are a lion or a gazelle. When the sun comes up, you better start running.*" (*African Proverb*)

> Ran: *The word in the original Hebrew for ran is* [*ruwts/roots/*], *meaning to hurry, to move quickly, and pursue.*

When it comes to fulfilling the last day purpose of the people of African descent time is of the essence. We cannot afford to waste it; we must be doing the right thing, and do it expeditiously.

There is the urgency of God's intent for this hour that will require an acceleration of our steps. Although, we must run steady, we must not run anxiously. Hebrews 12:1:

> *"Therefore, since we are surrounded by such a huge crowd of witnesses to the life of faith, let us strip off every weight that slows us down, especially the sin that so easily trips us up. And let us* run *with* endurance *the race God has set before us."* NLT

God will facilitate our speed for in the words of the Psalmist. Psalm 119:32

> *"I run in the path of your commands, for you have broadened my understanding."* NIV

The challenge was Ahimaaz would not accept no for an answer. He pleaded with Joab to let him run even though Joab told him he shouldn't. Some folk will settle for running in an untimely fashion in God's permissive will.

> *2 Samuel 18:22: "Ahimaaz son of Zadok again said to Joab, 'Come what may,* please *let me run behind the Cushite.' But Joab replied, 'My son, why do you want to go? You don't have any news that will bring you a reward.'"*

Joab rightly discerned that Ahimaaz's motive was financial reward and a political payout from King David. Unlike the African who just wanted to fulfill the assignment for which he was chosen and be compliant to the authority figure who sent him.

There are many in the church they are seduced by the financial reward for giving the message of the Good News. The love of money has permeated their motives for their religious activity.

Joab gave him permission to run, Ahimaaz stated that he would run *behind* the Cushite, but the Scripture says he took a shorter, less-demanding route.

There are those who sense that this is the time of Cushites, but who are anxious about it. They claim they are willing to run behind them, but if the truth be told their prejudice won't allow them to let a person of color outrun them to be first. So, like Ahimaaz, they want to take shortcuts to success.

> *He said, "Come what may, I want to run." So, Joab said, "Run!"*
> *Then Ahimaaz ran by way of the plain and outran the Cushite."*

Joab gave permission to Ahimaaz to be the *"also ran,"* but he took a shorter route. In taking the shortcut through the plain, Ahimaaz ran ahead of this Cushite African which was his real aim all along. Sure, enough he arrived before the African. David was familiar with Ahimaaz and knew he was a good man and therefore, assumed he had good news.

However, just because one is presumed to be a good person does not necessarily mean they have good news. Because good news must encompass the whole truth and nothing but the truth.

Ahimaaz was spotted by a watchman running ahead of the Cushite, but he also spotted the African running behind him. This nation needs true spiritual watchmen who can see who is running with a message of good news, and not discount a runner because he is behind or because he or she are of a different race.

Just because a person is well-connected to the system, has familiarity with political leaders, is from the majority race, has status, and is ahead of others on the road to success does *not* mean they have the message of victorious deliverance for this time.

Therefore, *watchmen* are the prayer intercessors who must be elevated enough on the wall of prayerful vigilance to discern those running with good news for this time.

> *2 Samuel 18:24–27: "While David was sitting between the inner and outer gates, the watchman went up to the roof of the gateway by the wall. As he looked out, he saw a man running alone. The watchman called out to the king and reported it. The king said, 'If he is alone, he must have good news.' And the runner came closer and closer. Then the watchman saw* another *runner, and he called down to the gatekeeper, 'Look, another man running alone!' The king said, 'He must be bringing good news, too.' The watchman said, 'It seems to me that the first one runs like Ahimaaz son of Zadok.' 'He's a good man,' the king said. 'He comes with good news.'" NIV*

The watchmen witnessed familiarity with the first runner's stride. He called down to the gatekeeper to open to the runner. Today there must be a call to pastors who are the *gatekeepers* of this hour to receive those who genuinely carry a message.

When he arrived Ahimaaz said all the right things and followed all the protocols. He had a positive message of victory, but when asked about the primary thing David was concerned about, the fate of Absalom his message was inadequate lacking vital information. He wanted to share the good news, but he did not want to share the *truth* about the *judgment* of Absalom.

Today there are many well-meaning evangelical conservatives and all they want to do is share the good news, but because of their political leanings they also want to exclude the truth about the fate of the nation's Absalom culture.

They are engaging in a game of denial as in the story of the Emperor's new clothes—pretending that someone is clothed when they are naked, or like the child who plays with an imaginary friend that does not exist.

Ahimaaz said he did not see what happened to Absalom; he only saw *confusion*. His message lacked clarity of vision; and it was not the truth. When proclaimers lack vision, clarity and veracity for this hour they will report a self-serving half-truth out of confusion.

> Then Ahimaaz called out to the king, "All is well!"
> He bowed down before the king with his face to
> the ground and said, "Praise be to the LORD your God!
> He has delivered up those who lifted their hands
> against my lord the king." king asked, "Is the young man Absalom
> safe?" Ahimaaz answered, "I saw great confusion just as Joab
> was about to send the king's servant and me, your servant, but
> I don't know what it was."

Now Ahimaaz used the term servant *ebed* to refer to himself, the word Eurocentric scholars want to translate as slave when they relate it to Cushite Africans; but was Ahimaaz a slave? I don't think so. No, he was a trusted official known to David.

Ahimaaz told the king what he wanted to hear, "*All is well*," like Ahimaaz many evangelicals and religious conservatives want to tell politicians, corporate leaders and their supporters what they want to hear, that the Absalom culture of America is alright. They lie to themselves and engage in demagoguery.

Dr. Frederick D. Haynes, III of Texas says that the 51st state of America is the state of *denial*. So, when Ahimaaz gave his message to David the king was less than impressed. His response to Ahimaaz this first runner was 2 Samuel 18:30:

> "The king said, 'Stand aside *and wait here*.' *So he* stepped aside
> *and stood there*." NIV

Ahimaaz was commanded by the king to *step aside* and stand where he was told to stand. Those who wanted to be the first in line, who sought to steal the limelight, and seize an opportunity to be the main voice of victory for the nation will be moved aside, placed in a waiting mode to make room for God's Cushite African messengers who have the timely message of victory, but a message that will be told with the whole truth.

The circumstances of the king and the nation afforded the Sudanese African the timely opportunity to tell his message to the leader. He arrived last even though initially he started out first. Although overtaken by Ahimaaz ultimately his message was *first* in the *truth*.

People of African descent like the Cushite in the text started out first, but over time and due to advantages, we were overtaken by Europeans and Euro-Americans, but also like the Cushite there will come a time when we will *catch up* deliver our message and fulfill our divine destiny.

> Matthew 20:16 *"So the last shall be first, and the first last: for many be called, but few chosen." KJV*

One could say that in the context of 2 Samuel 18, Ahimaaz was called, but it was the Cushite African who had been *chosen*.

In like manner, in these end times it is the people of African descent who have been chosen for a special message.

"ARRIVED and SAID" Destination

> 2 Samuel 18:31–32 *"Then the* Cushite *arrived and said, 'My lord the king, hear the good news! The LORD has vindicated you today by delivering you from the hand of all who rose up against you.' The king asked the* Cushite, *'Is the young man Absalom safe?'*

> *The* Cushite *replied,*
> *'May the enemies of my lord the king and all who rise up*
> *to harm you be like that young man.'"*

> 2 Timothy 4:7: *"I have done my best in the race, I have* run *the*
> full distance, *and I have kept the faith." GNT*

The Cushite fulfilled his assignment, arrived at his destination, and proclaimed his message. In a similar way, people of African descent in the Americas, Africa, the Caribbean, and Latin America throughout the world will also arrive at their destination, fulfill their assignment, and proclaim their message.

Fulfilling one's race in the natural is not the same as fulfilling one's race spiritually. To finish the race spiritually means that one runs the race God has chosen, by the rules God has set, in the season God has ordained, and accomplishes the purpose God has predestined.

Through persevering determination people of African descent will fulfill their purpose, and mission.

Case in point: Blacks who trace their ancestry to Africa, and African Americans, hold more than 95 percent of the top times in sprinting; athletes from Kenya make up more than one-third of top times in middle and long-distance races; including top performances by East Africans (most from Ethiopia).

That *domination* swells to almost 50 percent. North Africans do well at middle distances. These African runners didn't win these races taking shortcuts; they ran by the rules and they won their prizes.

Just like the Cushite in this story who also did not take shortcuts. He stayed the course and accomplished his assignment. Likewise, Cushites today will accomplish their purpose.

Just as people of African descent are virtually dominating different types of races naturally, they are replicating this same feat spiritually.[233]

Just recently an African man from Ethiopia won the Boston Marathon and an African woman from Kenya won the female portion of that same race.[234]

They are two of the latest living symbols of God's intent for black people. I believe this marathon race has significance not only in the natural but also in the spiritual.

Our run with the message God has given us is not just a sprint; it is a cross country run. It is a run that will encounter some highs and lows that will require endurance. Ecclesiastes 9:11 says:

> *"The fastest runner doesn't always win the race, and the strongest warrior doesn't always win the battle."*

Running with the message God has given us, means we will be running with a last day message and mission, a very significant mission; it is a mission to be the *Kopher* covering to the body of Christ and to humanity in general.

Discussion Questions

1. How does the Cushite runner symbolize the last day message and messengers of people of African descent?
2. What key words in 2 Samuel 18:21 represent key components of the message process of African-blooded people in the last days?

---

233 Jon Entine, "The Story Behind the Amazing Success of Black Athletes," Rundown.com, 2000, http://run-down.com/guests/je_black_athletes_p2.php.

234 Lori Riley, "Ethiopia's Desisa, Kenya's Rotich Boston Marathon Winners," Hartford Courant, 20 April 2015, http://www.courant.com/sports/hc-boston-marathon-0421-20150420-story.html.

CHAPTER 18

We Got You Covered — Our Mission

✥

A man's actions are more important than his ancestry
~ AFRICAN PROVERB (KENYAN)

> *Isaiah 43:3–4 "For I Yahweh your God, the Holy One of Israel,*
> *and your Savior, give* Egypt *as a* ransom *for you,* Cush
> *and* Seba *in your place. Because you are precious in My sight*
> *and honored, and I love you, I will give people in exchange*
> *for you and nations instead of your life." HCSB*

God's love for his people Israel is the subject of these verses. He
mentions three other groups of people all related to Africa. The
nations mentioned in these verses are Egypt (Kemet), which was
northern Africa, Cush, which was Sudanese Africa, and Seba, related to Cush of Africa.

> *Isaiah 43:3–4 "I am the LORD your God, the Holy One of Israel,*
> *your Savior.* Egypt *is the* ransom *I exchanged for you.*
> Sudan *and* Saba *are the* price *I paid for you. Since you*
> *are precious to me, you are honored and I love you.*
> *I will exchange others for you. Nations will be the price*
> *I pay for your life." GW*

"I gave Egypt for thy ransom, Ethiopia and Seba for thee. Since thou wast precious in my sight, thou hast been honourable, and I have loved thee: therefore will I give men for thee, and people for thy life." KJV

We have devoted the bulk of this book to focusing on Cushites of African descent, but two other nations besides Cush are highlighted, namely, Egypt and Seba.

Egypt is a Greek designation for the North African nation that was known in ancient times as *Kemet* and in the table of nations in Genesis 10:6 and 13 as Mizraim, a name being interpreted as *"black."* It was one of the most renowned of African nations; the achievements of this great African nation are too numerous to cite in this space. Egyptians (Kemite Africans) were black people of color.

Many Western historians and media portrayals would have us believe these Africans were white, but such was not the case. Only in the very late centuries when European Greeks and Romans intermarried with these native Africans were there white or light-complexioned Egyptians.

Further corroboration of the Blackness of these Egyptian North Africans is found in Psalms 105:23, 27 also Psalms 106:22, Egypt is called the land of Ham, referring to Noah's son and patriarchal progenitor of the people of color.[235]

According to the celebrated historian Cheikh Anta Diop, the ancient Egyptians referred to themselves as *"Black people,"* or "they used words the root of which was translated as *"Kham"* or "Ham," which refer to black people in the Hebrew tradition.

---

235 The Bible, Winston's Original African American Heritage Study Bible Encyclopedia, edited by James W. Peebles (Nashville: James C. Winston Publishing Company, 1996).

The ancient Egyptians themselves referred to their home-land as "Khemet." Diop, William Leo Hansberry, and Aboubacry Moussa Lam have argued that the word they used to describe themselves was derived from the *skin color* of the Nile Valley people, who they say were *black*.[236]

Secondly, there is Seba, or Saba, also called Sheba, the place where the famous Makeda queen of Sheba ruled. A nation whose name was derived from the first son of Cush in Genesis 10:7, It was a nation in Africa included in Cush located on the Island of Meroe lying at the junction of the blue and white Nile and having a name and power in King Solomon's time (Psalm 72;10).[237]

The word "gave" is *nawthan,* which means give, put, deliver, employ, devote, consecrate, dedicate and, it is translated as give 1,078 times, put 191 times, and deliver 174 times. The Hebrew word for Ransom is *kofer,* which has the basic meaning of *covering;* Kofer" was the term for, *price of life, (bitumen) pitch,* the *Henna plant*, and an *unwalled village*. This original word kopher from Isaiah 43:3-4, its meaning and implied metaphors, are prophetic concerning God's mission and purpose for people of African descent.

Five meanings covering 'kopher' denote the Fivefold Mission of people of African Descent:

1. *Salvation*
2. *Preservation*
3. *Vegetation*
4. *Population*
5. *Reconciliation*

---

236 Fani-Kayoke

237 The Bible, Winston's Original African American Heritage Study Bible Encyclopedia, edited by James W. Peebles (Nashville: James C. Winston Publishing Company, 1996).

1. **Salvation: (*price of a life, ransom*)** The first meaning of *covering kopher* is *ransom* and *price* of *life* it is the most important meaning, and the one I will spend most of the time on. People of African descent are today's *kopher* because they will be used as vessels of salvation. *Kopher* (ransom) was the legal term for the *price of life*.

Isaiah 43 says they were a *ransom* to God's people in the Old Testament times. The use of this word *ransom* about these Africans in Isaiah is fascinating and somewhat ironic because the New Testament speaks of Christ as one who gave his life *ransom*. By his own admission, he stated that giving his life as a ransom was the reason for his being. In Matthew 20:27-28 he states that:

> "Whoever wants to become first *among you must serve the rest of you like a slave. In the same way, the Son of Man did not come to be served. He came to* serve *others and to give his life as a* ransom *for many people.*" NCV

The ransom purpose of Christ was confirmed by the Apostle Paul in 1 Timothy 2:5-6:

> "For there is one God and one mediator between God and men, the man Christ Jesus, who gave himself as a ransom for all people. This has now been witnessed to at the proper time." NIV

In this season, African-blooded people are poised by God to become *first* in a lot of areas, for in the context of this verse in the history of the Americas, Africa, and the transatlantic; they have served as *slaves*, and like Christ they have given their lives as a ransom for others.

Although the ransom of Christ was *voluntary* despite his momentary struggle in Gethsemane, the ransoms of Cushite people of African descent has been *involuntary* and seemingly thrust upon them.

The Greek word translated *ransom* in Matthew 20:27–28 is *lutron* (loo•tron), meaning the *price for redeeming*, the *ransom paid* for captives, for the liberation of many from misery and the penalty of their sins.

The word ransom in Isaiah 43:3–4 is *kopher* and one meaning is to *cover* over sins—hence, to make an expiation for sins, or to atone for transgression, and the *price of life*.

Thus, the Greek term *lutron* has a meaning similar to that of the Hebrew term *kopher*. People of African descent have been the *kopher*, and as a people and have lived through sufferings like Christ, which is why an African like Simon of Cyrene from North Africa carrying the cross of Christ is such a powerful prophetic symbol. Luke 23:26 (EXB):

> "*As they led Jesus away,* Simon, *a man from* Cyrene [*a port city in* North Africa (*modern Libya*)], *was coming in from the •fields* [*countryside; country; Simon may be a Jewish pilgrim visiting Jerusalem for Passover or an immigrant living there*]. They forced *him to carry Jesus' cross and to walk behind him.*"

This passage says that they (the *Roman Europeans*) laid on a Simon (the *North African*) the cross of Christ, and made him, that is forced him to, carry that cross and walk with Jesus.

I wonder why of all the people in the crowd they chose Simon. Was there something conspicuous about him, say like maybe his *color*, that made him stand out?

It can be said that Euro-Americans and Europeans have laid on people of African descent the social cross of the suffering of Christ. Just as Christ was falsely accused by witnesses, people of

African heritage have often been the victims of bogus court testimonies and false evidence.

Just as Jesus was subject to an illegal trial, people of African descent have encountered inequities in the criminal justice system.

Just as Christ was beaten by Roman guards, black people have endured a long period of beatings by law enforcement.

Just as our Lord was *hung up* from a tree, people of African descent have had their people *hung* from *trees* in numerous lynching episodes.

Thus, the Simon incident is more than just a historical event. It serves as a spiritual metaphor for the destiny of the people of African descent. For the cross is a symbol of both suffering and salvation.

Just as an African was compelled by Europeans to carry the cross of Christ and follow in his footsteps, people of African descent have been compelled by Europeans and Euro-Americans to carry the cross—enduring Christ-like suffering—and follow him.

In the same way, our pain-filled odyssey as a people has been a means of salvation. Just as a *crucifying cross* is the symbol of the suffering of Christ. Our suffering is also symbolized by crosses.

The diagonal *St. Andrew cross* of the Confederate flag and the *burning cross of the* KKK—symbols of the sufferings of black people. The cross Simon carried was inevitably released from him to Christ, where it became the means to the salvation of people.

Similarly, people of African descent will release their social cross to Christ, who will then use it to save others, and transform nations.

Therefore, whatever cross people of African descent have carried over the centuries, whatever burden they have borne through time, and whatever pain they have suffered over the generations was not for naught. It was purposeful; it had a divine agenda attached to it. This cross of suffering was released to the plan of Christ and the Father for the ransom of others.

Just as Christ gave his life as a ransom to save all humanity, and paid the price spiritually, African Cushites as a people have given their lives as a ransom to save nations socially.

It appears that the bloodshed of black people has been the price of social justice: moral change to America, and nations beyond. Such was the case with the killing of nine productive citizens and Christians of Emmanuel AME Church, and of that South Carolina community.

Thus, what had offended black folks for decades, and fueled debate—the Confederate flag—suddenly changed. South Carolina's leaders first flew the Confederate flag over the Statehouse dome in 1961 to mark the 100th anniversary of the Civil War.

It remained there to represent official *opposition* to the civil rights movement. What began as a smattering of calls for removing the Confederate battle flag from a single state capitol, intensified with striking speed and scope into an emotional, *nationwide* movement to remove symbols of the Confederacy; from public parks and buildings, license plates, Internet shopping sites, and retail stores.

Rev. Clementa Pinkney and the eight other blacks who died *accomplished* in death what they could not accomplish in life— the removal of a symbol of hatred, bigotry, and white supremacy.[238]

---

238 Campbell Robertson, Monica Davey and Julie Bosman, "Calls to Drop Confederate Emblems Spread Nationwide," The New York Times, 23 June 2015, https://www.nytimes.com/2015/06/24/us/south-carolina-nikki-haley-confederate-flag.html?_r=0.

Sadly, many Southern white Christians are following a legacy of coupling religious beliefs with their conservative politics concerning the flag, to justify its non-removal under the veiled notion of the heritage of their ancestors.

There were nine deaths at Emmanuel AME Church, and in that South Carolina community. In biblical numerology, *nine* is the number that symbolizes divine *completeness* or conveys the meaning of *finality*. It also represents the fruit of the Spirit.

Therefore, the nine deaths symbolized finality since they represented the final act of Rev. Pinckney's work that was needed to bring down an emblem of bigotry and hatred. It represented that he completed his work, which not only changed South Carolina, but also the nation.

Lastly, it represented the nine fruits of the Spirit, which is what the nine people showed when they welcomed the white stranger to their Bible study with open arms. Also, when the families of the nine victims showed remarkable forgiveness like Jesus showed from the cross. The result of the nine deaths was the fruit of love was produced.

Firstly, a national conversation about race, secondly, the mass removal of the Confederate symbols around the country, thirdly, both the South Carolina Senate and House voting to remove the flag that had flown over the state house for 54 years. Fourthly, Gov. Nikki Haley signed the legislation on Thursday July 9, 2015, permanently removing the Confederate battle flag from the state capitol grounds; the flag was removed from the grounds July 10, 2015.

For the first time since the civil rights movement, the Confederate flag was removed entirely from the South Carolina Statehouse, in a brief ceremony before thousands of witnesses who cheered as the Civil War-era banner was lowered and removed from a 30-foot flagpole.[239]

There was yet a fifth positive consequence arising from those tragic nine deaths in Charleston after Russell Moore, president of the Ethics & Religious Liberty Commission of the Southern Baptist Convention, called for Christians in the South to forsake their cultural ties to the Confederate flag.

This was a significant response from a white conservative evangelical, given the history of Southern white Christians. Moore, who is a descendant of Confederate soldiers, stated that, "The Confederate battle flag was the emblem of Jim Crow defiance to the civil rights movement, of the Dixiecrat opposition to integration, and of the domestic terrorism of the Ku Klux Klan and the White Citizens' Councils of our all too recent, and all too awful history."

He further stated, "White Christians ought to think about what that flag says to our African-American brothers and sisters in Christ, especially in the aftermath of yet another act of white supremacist terrorism against them."

After much soul-searching many other white Southern and religious conservatives came out in the support of *removing* the flag—challenging the legacy of the Southern tradition of using the Bible to justify the true meaning of that flag. These outspoken voices ended years of silence from white Christians who would not speak out on racism against their black Christian brothers and sisters.

---

239 Jeffrey Collins and Meg Kinnard, "Confederate flag taken down in South Carolina after 54 years," Seattle Times/AP, 10 July 2015, http://www.seattletimes.com/nation-world/south-carolinas-confederate-flag-comes-down-friday/.

Christ gave his life and shed his blood to save mankind. People of African descent have given their lives, and shed their blood to save others, as well as transform the culture of their countries.

Whether it was that peculiar institution of slavery in the Americas inclusive of lynching of black men by white mobs,[240] the killing of unarmed young black people by civilians and police, the massacre of nine beloved church members by a hate-filled supremacist, the segregating fatal shootings of the apartheid regime in South Africa, or genocide atrocities from other nations, people of African descent have paid a price with their lives to bring major change to their nations as natives or immigrants.

Yes, they have been the **R.A.N.S.O.M.** (**R**edemptive **A**fricans **N**obly **S**acrificing **O**ur **M**asses). This acronym aptly describes the redeeming contributions that people of African descent have made to the national, international, and social salvation of others. The shedding of their blood has proven to be the ultimate price paid to transform nations, and they have done so nobly.

The question is why Africans and Cushites had to give their lives as a ransom for God's chosen people. Well, one could also ask why God chose Christ to give his life to ransom us; the answer is in either case, those whom God sought to save were so precious to God that he chose the *best most valuable* thing that he had, Christ was the best and most valuable thing from heaven, for only the most valued expensive item could pay the high price of our redemption 1 Peter 1:18-19 states that:

> *"knowing that you were* ransomed *from the futile ways inherited from your forefathers, not with perishable things such as silver*

---

240 Wikipedia contributors, "Peculiar institution," Wikipedia, The Free Encyclopedia, Wikipedia, The Free Encyclopedia, https://en.wikipedia.org/wiki/Peculiar_institution.

or gold, but with the precious *blood of Christ, like that of a lamb
without blemish or spot." ESV*

Furthermore, one could argue the African Cushites represented the best, most-valued nations on the earth of their time,
but the payment of ransom is not the end of this story. For it not
only brings a benefit to those who were ransomed, but there is a
direct return to the ones that gave themselves as the price.

God used our suffering to curtail our idolatry. Our *oppression* has prepared us for our *progression*. It ended *our insurrection*
against God, so we could receive *our resurrection* from God. The
good news is Christ's *resurrection* followed his *ransom*.

In like manner, the resurrection of the people of African descent is scheduled to follow the hundreds of years of paid ransom
in the last days.

African-related people have followed a Christ-like pattern
of suffering because they gave their lives to fulfill the purpose
of God, which was the salvation of others, but giving up of life
would yield a receiving of life, and one even greater than what
they gave up.

Just as the cross was followed by the empty tomb, the ransom that African people have paid will be followed by an empty
tomb spiritually, politically, economically, and socially.

Hence, we are in a PRS (Post Ransom Season). This is our time,
our *kairos* of undergoing resurrection. This is the right time, our
opportune time to come back to life. We have followed a Christ-
like pattern of suffering, but we are also following a Christ-like
pattern of resurrection. There is a sevenfold process of resurrection we have gone through, and to some extent are still going
through:

A. *Burying* (*Laid in the tomb*): The enslavement of Africans was a form of the entombment of Africans. The Atlantic slave trade, or transatlantic slave trade, occurred across the Atlantic Ocean from the 16th through the 19th centuries. Out of about 20 to 22 million Africans who were taken from their homes and sold into slavery, about half didn't complete the journey, most of those dying along the way. Their numbers were so massive that Africans who came by the route of the slave trade became the most numerous Old-World immigrants in both North and South America before the late 18th century.[241]

B. *Reanimating* (*Coming back to life*): This is a time when African Americans started coming alive—a time that included slave revolts, the abolitionist movement, and the work of the Underground Railroad; in 1838 Frederick Douglass escaped from slavery in Baltimore. He later published his autobiography, and became a leading abolitionist. In 1839, led by a West African named Cinque, slaves transported aboard the Spanish ship Amistad staged a mutiny, demanding to be sailed back to Africa. Instead, the captain sailed to New York. The activists eventually won their freedom in a landmark Supreme Court case in which they were defended by former president John Quincy Adams. In 1849, Harriet Tubman escaped from slavery in Maryland. She became one of the most notable "conductors" on the Underground Railroad, returning to the South 19 times and helping more than 300 slaves escape to freedom. Thomas Garrett, a white Quaker abolitionist and a station master on the Underground Railroad, was a friend of Tubman who worked with

---

241 Wikipedia contributors, "Atlantic slave trade," Wikipedia, The Free Encyclopedia, Wikipedia, The Free Encyclopedia 28 January 2014, https://en.wikipedia.org/wiki/Atlantic_slave_trade.

William Still to help to free over 2,700 slaves. Roughly 75,000 slaves escaped to the North and to freedom through the Underground Railroad, an operation that brought together free African American and white "conductors," abolitionists and sympathizers to help guide and shelter the escapees.[242]

C. *Emancipating* (*Removal of the grave clothes*): This period covered permitting blacks to serve in the Union army. In May 1863, the government established the Bureau of Colored Troops to manage the growing numbers of black soldiers. By the end of the Civil War, roughly 179,000 black men (10% of the Union Army) served as soldiers in the U.S. Army and another 19,000 served in the Navy. Black soldiers served in artillery and infantry performing all noncombat support functions that sustain an army.[243] President Lincoln signed the Emancipation Proclamation, which was an executive order issued on January 1, 1863, as a war measure during the American Civil War, to all sections of the executive branch (including the Army and Navy) of the United States. It proclaimed the liberty of slaves in the ten states that were still in rebellion, thus applying to 3.1 million of the 4 million slaves in the U.S. The Thirteenth Amendment to the United States Constitution abolished slavery and involuntary servitude. It was passed by the Senate on April 8, 1864, by the House on January 31, 1865, and adopted on December 6, 1865. On December 18, 1865, Secretary of State William H. Seward proclaimed it to have been adopted. It was the first of the three Reconstruction

---

242 "Slave Rebellions a Timeline," Independent Lens, PBS, http://www.pbs.org/independentlens/natturner/slave_rebellions.html.

243 "The Fight for Equal Rights: Black Soldiers in the Civil War," The U.S. National Archives and Records Administration.

Amendments adopted following the American Civil War.[244] After the Civil War during the period of reconstruction from 1863 and 1869, Presidents Lincoln and Johnson upgraded the rights of the freedmen (former slaves). President Ulysses S. Grant enforced the protection of African Americans in the South using the Force Acts passed by Congress. Grant used both the U.S. Justice Department and the U.S. military to suppress white insurgency. The deployment of the U.S. military was central to the establishment of Southern reconstructed state governments and the suppression of violence against black voters.[245] In 1888 Frederick Douglass at the Republican National Convention received one vote as a nominal candidate for president of the United States. In 1904 the National Negro Liberty Party asked Judge George Edwin Taylor to become their candidate for the office of president of the United States. In the 1940s Marcus Garvey was a civil rights activist and proponent of the Black Nationalism and Pan Africanism movements.1940 Benjamin Oliver Davis, Sr. became the *first* black Brigadier General in the United States Army. The significant work but contrasting styles of Booker T. Washington and W.E.B Du Bois on how to remove the grave clothes from our mind was prominent.[246]

---

244 Wikipedia contributors, "Thirteenth Amendment to the United States Constitution," Wikipedia, The Free Encyclopedia, Wikipedia, The Free Encyclopedia, https://en.wikipedia.org/wiki/Thirteenth_Amendment_to_the_United_States_Constitution.

245 Wikipedia contributors, "Reconstruction Era," Wikipedia, The Free Encyclopedia, Wikipedia, The Free Encyclopedia, https://en.wikipedia.org/wiki/Reconstruction_Era.

246 Wikipedia contributors, "African-American candidates for President of the United States," Wikipedia, The Free Encyclopedia, Wikipedia, The Free Encyclopedia, https://en.wikipedia.org/wiki/African-American_candidates_for_President_of_the_United_States.

D. **Rising** (**Standing-up**): Ralph Johnson Bunche was an American political scientist, academic, and diplomat who received the 1950 Nobel Peace Prize for his late 1940s mediation in Israel. He was the *first* African American, and person of color to be so honored in the history of the prize. This segment of American history also encompassed African Americans rising up to take a stand for their rights which marked the end of Jim Crow laws; thus, in 1954 Thurgood Marshall won the Brown v. Board of Education case, in which the Supreme Court ended racial segregation in public schools. African Americans began in the south to use legal suits, mass sit ins, and boycotts to stop segregation and *stand up* for equality. In 1963, over 200,000 mostly African Americans with a few whites marched into Washington D.C. which started the movement to end the life under Jim Crow. The civil rights movement of the sixties was active, spurred by the incarceration of Rosa Parks, especially the work of Dr. Martin Luther King and the influence of leaders like Malcolm X. In 1966 Edward William Brooke III became the *first* African-American popularly elected to the United States Senate. In 1967 Thurgood Marshall was appointed to the Supreme Court. The black consciousness movement was prominent in the late 1960s and early 1970s, emphasizing racial pride.[247] The black awareness movement of the seventies started, where African Americans began to "stand up" for their black racial identity.

E. **Accessing:** (**Rolling away the stone**) Shirley Chisholm became the first black candidate for a major party's nomination for president in 1972. Chisholm was the first black woman elected to the

---

247 Wikipedia contributors. "Black Power." Wikipedia, The Free Encyclopedia. Wikipedia, The Free Encyclopedia, https://en.wikipedia.org/wiki/Black_Power.

U.S. Congress in 1968. This period also involved a number of legislative changes which enhanced our status and rolled away the stone of social encumbrances; such legislative actions as the Voting Rights Act, Economic Opportunity Act of 1964, the Voting Rights Act of 1965, the Civil Rights Act of 1968, and the Civil Rights Act of 1982 President Jimmy Carter appointed Andrew Young to serve as the Ambassador to the United Nations. All these events worked together to remove the barrier stone of discrimination and access.

F. *Exiting: (**Walking out of the tomb**)* politically and economically, blacks made substantial strides in the post-civil rights era. On November 2, 1983, President Ronald Reagan signed a bill, proposed by Representative Katie Hall of Indiana, creating a federal holiday to honor Martin Luther King. It was observed for the first time on January 20, 1986.[248] Civil rights leader Jesse Jackson, ran for the presidential nomination in 1984 and 1988, and brought unprecedented support and leverage to blacks in politics. In 1989, Douglas Wilder became the *first* African-American elected governor in U.S. history. In 1992 Carol Moseley-Braun of Illinois became the *first* black woman elected to theU.S. Senate. There were 8,936 black officeholders in the United States in 2000, showing a net increase of 7,467 since 1970. In 2001 there were 484 black mayors. Moreover, The Million Man March was a gathering en masse of African-Americans in Washington, D.C. on October 16, 1995, called by Louis Farrakhan. A parallel event called the Day of Absence, organized by female leaders in conjunction with the March leadership, occurred on the same date. These events

---

248 Wikipedia contributors. "Martin Luther King Jr.." Wikipedia, The Free Encyclopedia. Wikipedia, The Free Encyclopedia, https://en.wikipedia.org/wiki/Martin_Luther_King_Jr.

signaled that African Americans were walking out of our political tomb.[249]

G. *Manifesting:* (*Putting in Appearances*) This period of time was marked by African Americans putting in more significant appearances politically as evidence of the notion that our resurrection was in full swing; there were a number of significant political *firsts*. Among them were Colin Powell who became the *first* black to serve on the Joint Chiefs of Staff in 1989, and the *first* black Secretary of State in 2001. In 2004, Al Sharpton became a first black Democratic presidential candidate of the 2000 era, Condoleezza Rice became the *first* black woman Secretary of State in 2005; Deval Patrick was the *first* African American who was elected 71st Governor of Massachusetts in 2007.[250] In 2008 Eric Holder became the *first* African-American attorney general designate in the United States; in 2014 Michelle Howard became the *first* female and African American in the Navy's 236-year history to hold the rank of four star admiral.[251] Loretta Lynch became the *first* black female attorney general designate in the United States in April of 2015;[252] but the most significant change was the election of Barack Obama the *first* African American pres-

---

249 Wikipedia contributors. "African-American history." Wikipedia, The Free Encyclopedia. Wikipedia, The Free Encyclopedia https://en.wikipedia.org/wiki/African-American_history.

250 Wikipedia contributors. "Deval Patrick." Wikipedia, The Free Encyclopedia. Wikipedia, The Free Encyclopedia, https://en.wikipedia.org/wiki/Deval_Patrick.

251 JC Sevcik, "U.S. Navy promotes first black woman to four-star admiral," UPI Top News, 1 July 2014, http://www.upi.com/Top_News/US/2014/07/01/US-Navy-promotes-first-black-woman-to-four-star-admiral/8151404241128/.

252 Mike DeBonis, "Loretta Lynch confirmed by Senate as attorney general," The Washington Post, 23 April 23, 2015, https://www.washingtonpost.com/politics/loretta-lynch-confirmation-likely-today-in-senate-after-5-month-wait/2015/04/23/d8a3d9a8-e96d-11e4-9a6a-c1ab95a0600b_story.html?utm_term=.97f51b365bb9.

ident of the United States who was overwhelmingly elected in 2008, and convincingly re-elected in 2012.

People of African descent in other nations have experienced a similar journey. The saga of the Africans of South Africa and the election of Nelson Mandela comes to mind.

He was a South African anti-apartheid activist, politician and philanthropist. Mandela served 27 years in prison for his activism against Apartheid initially on Robben Island, and later in Pollsmoor Prison and Victor Verster Prison. This sparked internationally outcry and protests for his release. Like African Americans many South Africans lost their lives in the struggle for freedom.

An international campaign resulted in his release which was granted in 1990. This notable African man lost twenty-seven years of his life, but experienced the ultimate vindication when he became and served as President of South Africa from 1994 to 1999. He was South Africa's *first* black chief executive, and the first elected in a fully representative democratic election. His government focused on dismantling the legacy of apartheid through tackling institutionalized racism, poverty and inequality, and fostering racial reconciliation.[253]

There were other important events and other significant personalities concerning our story that I did not cite, my purpose here was to simply provide a general review of our progress as people and not to chronicle every event, or report every important person of our history. Admittedly, I have focused largely on those who were Christians.

---

253 Wikipedia contributors. "Nelson Mandela." Wikipedia, The Free Encyclopedia. Wikipedia, The Free Encyclopedia, https://en.wikipedia.org/wiki/Nelson_Mandela.

Our resurrection is not yet complete as there are still other pivotal appearances we have yet to put in and other significant accomplishments in this century yet to be yet to be done. There is presently an attempt to crucify us afresh due to the resurgence of racism and the rise of xenophobic rhetoric from religious and political ultra conservatives, the rise of hate groups, the epidemic of black men especially young people killed by law enforcement, the emergence of the Tea party, and the Supreme Court's decision to gut the Voting Rights Act. This will not impede those appearances which will come, but until that time we must be focused on our mission, and prophetic destiny of being the *kopher* covering for humanity in various ways.

2. **Preservation:** (*Pitch*) *Secondly*, people of African descent are today's *Kopher* that is the asphalt, pitch as a covering. Asphalt and Bitumen could be used interchangeably. The first use of kopher in the Bible was in Genesis 6:14, where it is translated *"pitch."* Noah used bitumen for Ark waterproofing in 2370 B.C.E.[254] It relates to the covering of the ark by Noah; that is pitch, asphalt or bitumen in its soft state, was found in pits near the Dead Sea. It was used for various purposes, as the coating of the outside of vessels and in buildings.[255] Pitch was Bitumen, a *black* sticky tar-like substance as a residue from petroleum. It was used in the bible as a water proofing, bonding, *adhesive,* and *preserving* cement.[256]

---

254 Wikipedia contributors. "Asphalt." Wikipedia, The Free Encyclopedia. Wikipedia, The Free Encyclopedia, https://en.wikipedia.org/wiki/Asphalt.

255 "Pitch," Bibletools.com, Easton's Bible Dictionary, http://www.biblestudytools.com/dictionary/pitch/.

256 Todd Helmenstine, "Definition of Bitumen," Thought Co., https://www.thoughtco.com/definition-of-bitumen-608746.

People of African descent will be God's spiritual pitch, His Bitumen to the body of Christ and the nations. It is not by accident that the color of this substance was *black* or that its purpose was to *protect, preserve* and *bond* elements together. For just as it was used to do those three purposes, God is going to utilize a black people to *protect, preserve* and *bond* the spiritual house.

For thousands of years before the first civilization in Sumer, the bitumen substance was already valued for its adhesive bonding properties—the result was an ancient hunter's discovery that he could attach his flint arrowhead to a shaft with a sticky dark substance found in a nearby spring.

Several thousands of years later, that same substance cemented one of the wonders of the ancient world, a man-made mountain built to ascend "to heaven"— the notorious Tower of Babel.

In Egypt, in ancient times, bitumen in oil form was flammable. Similarly, people of African descent are a fluid people, and in that state they are a flammable people with the spiritual potential to set the world on fire for God - burning up the enemy's fortifications.

3. **Vegetation:** (*the Henna plant*) the *third* meaning of Kopher is a *Henna* plant, people of African descent are *Kopher* because they are like the *Henna plant*. As in the Song of Songs 4:12–13 verses, that refers to the perfume of the Henna flower;. It was used for cosmetic purposes in ancient North *Africa*, and the Horn of *Africa*, it was also used as a dye to add a *color* to something. The powder from the plant is used in skin and hair dyes, such as *black* henna. In staining the skin to get great color the stain gradually oxidizes to a *reddish-brown* tone over 48 hours, and on the palms

and soles of the feet it *darkened* to a nearly *black* color. It is a plant that is native to *Northern Africa.*[257]

Henna was grown as a hedgerow around vineyards to hold soil against wind erosion in Israel and other countries.

Its dense thorny branches also protected a vulnerable valuable crop such as a vineyard from hungry animals. It was (six to twenty-five feet) and it was glabrous and multi-branched, with spine-tipped branchlets.[258]

In like manner, people of African descent will be crucial in protecting the Body of Christ against that hungry devouring lion mentioned in 1 Peter 5:8 Expanded Bible (**EXB**)

> *"Control [Discipline] yourselves and be careful [alert]! The devil, your enemy, goes around [prowls] like a roaring lion looking for someone to eat [devour]"*

The hedge, which protected the vineyard, also had clusters of fragrant flowers.

Like Henna, people of African descent will enable the church to resist erosion from the winds of adversity—Like *henna* they are *native* to or *came* from Africa—like Henna, they add color to a mostly Eurocentric colored body—and like henna, in the last days they will produce *fragrant* flowers. That is the sweet *fragrance* of worship, and forgiveness which will deodorize the racism in the church.

> *2 Corinthians 2:15 HCSB "For to God we are the fragrance of Christ among those who are being saved and among those who are perishing"*

---

257 Catherine Cartwright-Jones, The Henna Page, 2000, http://www.hennapage.com/henna/ccj/.

258 Wikipedia contributors. "Henna." Wikipedia, The Free Encyclopedia. Wikipedia, The Free Encyclopedia, https://en.wikipedia.org/wiki/Henna.

This passage is true for every authentic Christian, but we need to be reminded what the label Christian means. The word *"Christian"* is used three times in the New Testament (Acts 11:26; 26:28; 1 Peter 4:16). Followers of Jesus Christ were first called "Christians" in Antioch (Acts 11:26) because their behavior, activity, and speech were like Christ.

The word "Christian" literally means, "belonging to the *party* of *Christ*" or a *"follower* of *Christ."* And the evidence of a follower of Christ was demonstrating the *love of Christ.* That love has an aroma and fragrance. People of African descent especially with their ability to forgive their oppressors will emit a sweet-smelling scent.

Moreover, like Henna they will be used as a spiritual hedge to protect Christ's vineyard and to keep out predator attacks of the enemy—just like the Tuskegee airmen were used as an aerial escort to protect American bombers in warfare.[259]

4. **Population:** (*An Unwalled village*) the *fourth* meaning of *Kopher* is *village*, people of African descent are the *Kopher for* they are a village minded people—a clustered human settlement or community.[260]

In the African value system, it is the responsibility of the family, the clan, the tribe, the *village* to take care of those who have a deep need. Villages in ancient Africa were more than communities. They were teams that were communal - all pitched in to take care of the children.

---

259 "The Tuskegee Airmen," Tuskegee University, https://www.tuskegee.edu/support-tu/tuskegee-airmen.

260 Wikipedia contributors. "Village." Wikipedia, The Free Encyclopedia. Wikipedia, The Free Encyclopedia, https://en.wikipedia.org/wiki/Village.

They believed in working *together* for the *common* good. People had possessions, but if they owned something that everyone could use for the betterment of the whole village, then those possessions were *shared*. Which is part of the reason why African Americans coming from that African communal culture cater more to the notion of the commonwealth of government making adequate provision for all its citizens—especially the needy.[261]

As stated earlier the African village operated similarly to the early Christian church in Acts 2:44–45 (NIV) They too had a *village* mentality and a *communal* interaction with each other:

> *"All the believers met together in one place and* shared *everything they had. They sold their property and possessions and* shared *the money with* those in need"

God will use people of African descent to change the culture of the church—dominated by the Euro-centric ideology of *individualism*—to a church that is more *communal* as they bring their village mindset with emphasis on corporate unity. The body of Christ will learn how to function with a *village* mentality more conducive to the kingdom culture.

5. **Reconciliation:** (*Atonement*) the fifth meaning of Kopher is *reconciliation*, people of African descent are the *Kopher* because they will be agents of reconciliation in the last days. *Kopher* comes from a root word *Kaphar* which also means to *cover*, to make *reconciliation*, to make atonement; the Hebrew word *kaphar* means *"to cover over,"* and is the word for the lid of the Ark of the Covenant.

---

261 Dunn

The word atonement is an abstract word, and to understand the word we must look to the concrete meaning. If an offense has been made the one that has been offended can act as though the offense is covered over and unseen. We relay this idea through the word of forgiveness. Atonement is an outward action that covers over the error.[262] King James Word Usage—atonement 71, purge 7, reconciliation 4, reconcile 3, forgive 3.

People of African descent will show love and forgiveness despite the treatment they have experienced. They will atone —that is cover over the offences of oppressors with forgiveness.

This does not mean the oppressors are absolved of their onus to repent and change. For if they remain obstinate in their racism and xenophobia- fail to truly repent, they will experience the severe judgment of God, as well as a myriad of harmful consequences.

Nevertheless, what they do will not hinder the people of African descent's actions to cover with love. Because to not forgive would drain too much energy from us fulfilling of our purpose, and because of our strategic position as agents of unity in the body of Christ that is too high of a price to pay. And too much of a distraction to our mission.

Fortunately, with few exceptions African Americans have shown themselves to be a forgiving people, which qualifies them to be vessels of reconciliation to the Church of Christ. Dr. Martin Luther King, President Nelson Mandela and the families of the nine victims of Charleston were models of that forgiveness. The numerous people of color which have pardoned their persecutors despite years of maltreatment are also examples.

262 Jeff A. Benner, "Atonement, Ancient Hebrew.org, http://www.ancient-hebrew.org/vocabulary_definitions.html.

Now that does not mean that they continue to tolerate acts or attitudes of racism; suffer in silence or shun responsibility of direct loving confrontation. Not at all, they must continue to challenge this issue in all its manifestations while covering the offenders with love. So in 1 Peter 4:7-8:

> "The end of the world is coming soon. Therefore, be earnest and disciplined in your prayers. Most important of all, continue to show deep love for each other, for love covers a multitude of sins" NLT.

People of African descent truly have a special mission, but it will require spiritual warfare to accomplish it. Because of the *message* and the *mission,* they will experience a counter attack from the enemy. To respond to this `assault, they have been endowed with special *munitions*—weapons to fight and accomplish this assignment. They are archers in worship, and are armed.

Discussion Questions

1. What does the Hebrew word Kopher mean and how does the five meanings of the word relate to the mission concerning people of African descent?
2. How has the experiences of people of African descent simulated the resurrection of Christ?

CHAPTER 19

Come Out With Your Hands Up — Our Munitions

❧

Isaiah 18:7 (GW) "At that time gifts will be brought to the Lord of Armies from a tall and smooth-skinned people, a people who are feared far and near, a strong and aggressive nation, whose land is divided by rivers. They will be brought to Mount Zion, the place where the name of the Lord of Armies is".

Jeremiah 46:9 "The Message (MSG) "Run, horses! Roll, chariots! Advance, soldiers from Cush and Put with your shields, Soldiers from Lud, experts with bow and arrow"

Ps 68:31 Nobles shall come from Egypt; Cush shall hasten to stretch out *her* hands *to God. ESV*

The first passage cited in this segment is a translation of the prophecy of Isaiah 18:7. This prophesy refers to God being the *God of Armies*. When the situation calls for it, our God is a God of war. In addition, He is referenced in his military name plus the Cushitic Africans mentioned in the text are identified as a *strong aggressive* people.

This all alludes to warfare about to take place, and these warrior *Cushites*, have been selected to be a group gift of combatants to battle under the command of the Lord of Armies in the last Days. They will battle through the army of spiritual Mt. Zion which is the last day church. Hebrews 12:22-23 New King James Version (NKJV) states:

> *"But you have come to* Mount Zion *and to the city of the living God, the heavenly Jerusalem, to an innumerable company of angels, to the general assembly and* church *of the firstborn who are registered in heaven, to God the Judge of all, to the spirits of just men made perfect"*

Furthermore, we have a second passage from Jeremiah 46:9 which mentions, *warriors* from *Cush*, Put and Lud all African related nations.

Although this passage is in the context of God's judgment, it does provide insight into the warrior nature of these people. Lud or Ludim were descendants of Mizraim, (Egypt- Genesis 10:13) dwelling in Africa, probably near Cush; they were famous bowmen, (Isaiah 66:19) and are mentioned as soldiers with the Cushites, Libyans, and Tyrians, (Ezekiel 27:10; 30:5) Easton's Bible Dictionary says that Lud or Ludim was probably associated with *African* nations as mercenaries of the king of Egypt.

The Libyans: Put occurs in combination with Lud, as with Ludim, (in Ezekiel 27:10; Ezekiel 30:5). This appears to be the Somali country on the east coast of *Africa*, opposite to Arabia.[263]

These passages describe the combatant nature of Cushitic related Africans. Just as they have engaged their enemies naturally they will also engage the enemy spiritually. They are a people who are armed, and dangerous to the adversary.

For this task they possess special munitions, military weapons, and specialized ammunition. Besides the whole armor of

---

263 "Easton's Bible Dictionary," Bible Hub, http://biblehub.com/dictionary/eastons.htm.

God, they are armed with bows and *arrows*; for they are archers of spiritual warfare.

In the natural realm Cushites were expert warriors, they served other nations as auxiliary *archers*.[264]

The bible says in Ephesians 6:11-16 English Standard Version (ESV)"

> *"Put on the whole armor of God that you may be able to stand against the schemes of the devil"*

The armor metaphor referred to here is that of the Roman soldier, but there were *African* soldiers in the Roman army just as there are people of African descent who will display the whole armor of God based on the Roman soldier.

The Africans in the army served particularly between AD 193 and 211. Anthony Birley, in his work The *African Emperor: Septimius Severus*, explains that the Roman Empire embraced a *multicultural* mix of peoples from Syria, Germany, Britain, Spain and *Africa*.

There were three Roman legions in Britain for most of the period, each consisting of 6,000 men. The legions were made up of different ethnic groups from Spain, *Africa*, and other nations.[265] They would have represented an army of *diversity* in ethnicity.

Assuredly, several Africans ascended to high positions in the army. Also, the Romans employed auxiliary troops, *non-Romans* who occupied roles that the heavy infantry focused Roman mili-

264 Stephen Charles Mott, "From The Word A Black Power in the First Testament," CSCOweb, http://www.cscoweb.org/mott5-9.pdf.

265 A. R Birley, The African Emperor: Septimius Severus (New Haven: Yale UP, 1989).

tary could not fill effectively, such as *archers*.[266] This was especially so for the Cushitic African Nubians who were prized for their archery skills.

Throughout history, pictures of Nubian warriors show them holding *bows*. In the graves of Nubian men, archaeologists often find their skeletons holding bows and lying beside quivers of *arrows*.

In later centuries, men were sometimes buried wearing stone rings on their thumbs. These rings allowed them to pull back the *bowstrings* without cutting or hurting themselves. About 2600 BCE, the Egyptians began hiring thousands of Nubian archers.

Moreover, one black soldier named Maurice typified their military talents. He was a Roman soldier who was martyred for the Christian faith in the late third century. By the early 10th century, he had become the patron saint of the Holy Roman Empire. His military prowess and stalwart faith exemplified the warrior nature and strong conviction of the people of African descent. The personification of the empire by a *black* man reveals a virtual lack of racial prejudice in Europe before the slave trade.

Just as significantly, it relates to the multifaceted ethnicity of the empire.[267] The reason for employing the skills of Cushites was because they were known to be great fighters, highly skilled archers, and a formidable war-machine.

In African warfare, archers generally opened the battle, followed by masses of infantry in a general hand-to hand engage-

---

266 "An African community in Roman Britain?," Evo and Proud, 16 July 2010, http://evoandproud. blogspot.com/2010/07/african-community-in-roman-britain.html.

267 "The Root: Black Warrior Roman Soldier," Black in Western Art Archive, Harvard University's W.E.B. Du Bois Institute for African and African American Research.

ment.[268] A key role in the strengthening of Egyptian forces was played by archers from Cush. Officials often requested the services of the archers, or *Pitati*, to provide security.

The *Pítati* (pí-ta-ti) were a contingent of archers often petitioned and dispatched to support the Egyptian vassalage in northern Canaan. This force was from the African "land of Kush" in the 18th century. These troops had a reputation for archery into this period.[269] They were the *most* important force element.

Herodotus describes the Cushites in Xerxes' army as wearing the skins of animals such as lions. Again, Satan is referred to as a roaring lion in 1 Peter 5:8–9. Just as Cushites wore the skins of dead lions in the natural, people of African descent will exhibit the defeat of Satan as a lion spiritually.

Excavation of a tomb 2500–2052 BC in Kerma the early Cushite capital revealed a young *archer* lying on his side with his bow and bowstring in his hand. Models of 40 Cushite soldiers all archers carrying bows, were discovered in a tomb in North Africa from roughly the same period. These Cushite archers have been described as the king's *elite bodyguards*.[270]

As a parallel, Cushite Africans today are the King of Kings elite warriors - that is the exceptionally skilled archers to defend the body of Christ. Indeed, a part of the Cushite territory was called *"Ta-Seti"* or *"Land* of the *Bow"* by the Africans of North Africa. Psalms 18:34 says:

---

268 Sanders

269 Wikipedia contributors. "Pítati." Wikipedia, The Free Encyclopedia. Wikipedia, The Free Encyclopedia, https://en.wikipedia.org/wiki/P%C3%ADtati.

270 Boyne

> *"He trains my hands to fight every battle. My arms can bend a* bow *of bronze"* (*NIRV*)

We must remember that in the book of Genesis from the outset the first mighty *archer* on earth was the *Cushite* Nimrod (Genesis 10:8-9); He is the archetypal archer, and consummate bowman.[271]

> Genesis 10:8-9 *"Cush was the father of Nimrod, who was the* first *of the great men of the earth. He was a very* great bowman, *so that there is a saying, Like Nimrod, a* very great bowman" BBE

In the spirit realm, we Cushites are to continue Nimrod's *archer legacy,* but not his idolatry legacy.

From the beginning the *most* powerful archer on earth naturally was a *Cushite,* and in these last days the *most* powerful *archers* on the earth *spiritually* will be Cushites. They will become the experts in the *archery* of *Yadah* praise.

The Arrows of Yadah Praise

> *"A hunter with one arrow doesn't shoot with a careless aim"* (*Nigerian Proverb*)

The African Cushites are **A.R.C.H.E.R.S.** (**A**rrow **R**eleasing **C**ushitic **H**igh **E**lite **R**ecruits **S**piritually) just as the Cushite Archers were an elite warrior unit naturally, Cushite Archers today are an elite warrior unit spiritually. They are God's special bowmen with a worship specialty in "Yadah" praise.

---

271 "Nimrod"

In the spirit realm, they wear the whole armor of God, but they also carry a special weapon of a bow and arrow of praise. When they corporately praise God there is a barrage of arrows released against the enemy.

Therefore, Yadah-praise is associated with warfare and leadership.[272] This kind of praise does two things; it *exalts* God and *assaults* Satan.

Jesus is closely related to this mode of praise since he is referred to as the *"Lion of the Tribe of Judah,"* (Genesis 49:35, 49:8) the tribe whose name comes directly from the Hebrew word *Yadah* meaning *"praise"*.

Just as Cushite Africans in the past worshiped the pagan god Apedemak the *Lion headed* god of victory; in the last days, they will revere Jesus Christ the *Lion-hearted* God of victory from the tribe of Judah (*Yehudah* or *Yadah*); the true lion of victory. Hebrews 7:14 (HCSB) says:[273]

> *"Now it is evident that our Lord came from Judah, and Moses said nothing about that tribe concerning priests"*

This is significant because Cushitic Africans related to Judah and with the tribe of that name. As stated earlier Jews were linked to West African communities who were to known Jewish communities from the Middle East, North *Africa*, Spain and Portugal.

Various historical records attest to their presence in the Cushitic African Ghana, Mali, and Songhai empires, then called the *"Bilad as-Sudan"* from Arabic meaning *"Land of the Blacks"*.

---

272 Tim Miller, "Leading Worship: Hebrew Worship Words YADAH – Ground Zero," Worship Ministry, 6 February 2012, http://worshipministry.com/leading-worship-hebrew-worship-words-yadah-ground-zero/.

273 Miller

Jews from Spain, Portugal, and Morocco in later years also formed communities off the coast of Senegal and on the Islands of Cape Verde of Africa. These communities existed for hundreds of years, but have since vanished due to transitioning social conditions, migration patterns, and the Trans-Atlantic Slave trade.[274] Albeit, the name *Judah* comes from Hebrew word *Yadah* which extols God's goodness, mercy, and exalts His wonderful works.

> *Psalm 9:1 "I will give thanks (Yadah) to the LORD with my whole heart; I will recount all of your wonderful deeds" ESV*

In addition, Psalms 107:15 exclaims **"Oh that men would praise (yadah) the Lord for his *goodness*, and for his *wonderful works* to the children of men"**

In Acts 2:4 when the African mother language was restored it manifested at Pentecost in Yadah praise because it says those who gathered at Pentecost acknowledged **"We do hear them speak in our tongues the *wonderful works* of God"** They were hearing them speak a confession of Yadah Praise.

If Pentecost was a reversal of Babel then the purpose of the restoration of the original African mother tongue was that all nations in unity through the Holy Spirit would celebrate God's name, not make a name for themselves, and not just speak in different languages for the sake of doing so, but in the oneness of spirit they would speak through a diversity of ethnic tongues to confess God's *wonderful works.*

---

274 Wikipedia contributors. "Jews of Bilad el-Sudan." Wikipedia, The Free Encyclopedia. Wikipedia, The Free Encyclopedia, https://en.wikipedia.org/w/index.php?title=Special:CiteThisPage&page=Jews_of_Bilad_el-Sudan&id=776624493.

Yadah Praise is used in receiving the God of Deity

It is a praise that welcomes the presence of God a confession both of the name of God, but also includes a confession of sin. 1 John 1:9 says:

> *if we confess our sin he is faithful and just to forgive us of our sin and cleanse us from all unrighteousness.*

Yadah praise enables us to not only receive God, but forgiveness from him. It has this two-fold meaning: the confession of God's attributes, and the confession of our shortcomings.

It also carries the meaning of absolute surrender as a young child does to a parent; to utter or proclaim a confession of thanks in an audible voice.

It involves the *extension* of the hands heavenwards toward God. Eventually it also came to denote songs of praise—to lift the voice in thanksgiving—to tell forth and confess his greatness.

Moreover, Yadah yaw-daw is a verb with a root meaning, to *stretch* out the *hand*, to throw out the hand. The word pictures associated with the root word for this type of praise is *shooting an arrow*, to extend the hands, to worship with extended hands.[275]

The Hebrew word comes from two root words. *YAD* which means the open *hand*, direction, power, and *AH* which has reference to *Jehovah*.

---

275 "Strong's #3034: yadah (pronounced yaw-daw)," Bible Tools, http://www.bibletools.org/index. cfm/fuseaction/Lexicon.show/ID/h3034/page/2.

Coupled together they are rendered *"Hands* to *God."*[276] Lifting the hands in praise is almost always equivalent to a Yadah whether literally or figuratively.[277]

The free King James word usage rendering totals are: 114 praise, 53 give thanks, 32 confess, 16 thank, 5 make confession, and thanksgiving 2.[278]

Yadah: Term used in Conceiving Progeny (Leah)

The first time this word appears in scripture is in Genesis 29:35 when Jacob was married to Leah and Rachel.

However, Leah was the wife rejected by Jacob, she was the *black* sheep in the marriage. Her name contributed to her issue for it means to be *weary, tired, grieved,* and *offended.* When the Lord saw that Leah was *unloved,* He opened her womb, but Rachel was barren proving once again that God works on behalf of the *rejected* people.

The fourth-time Leah conceived, and bore a son she said, *"Now I will YADAH the Lord".*

Therefore, his name was called *Judah—Praise.* Judah also means *celebrated* (3063 Yehuwdah).

This was the first time anyone was recorded raising their hands in praise and celebration for their blessings:

More importantly, she produced a Judah tribe; a Yadah people of praise through which the savior Christ would be born.

---

276 "7 Hebrew Words of Praise – Yadah," Rockin with the Cross, 13 June 2011, https://rwtc.wordpress.com/2011/06/13/7-hebrew-words-of-praise-yadah/.

277 Wikipedia contributers, "Yadah"

278 "Yadah," Bible Tools.com, http://www.biblestudytools.com/lexicons/hebrew/kjv/yadah.html.

Leah was the rejected one that even though she was not selected by Jacob she was the one ordained by God to produce the tribe of Judah (Yadah) from which the "lion of Judah" Jesus Christ would come. A *rejected* woman was chosen to birth the *savior*.

Ironically Christ did not come from the accepted preferred Rachel, but rather from the *rejected* disenfranchised Leah. She was the *last* selected by Jacob, but the *first* chosen by God to give birth. She represents a rejected unloved people who out of their pain birth Yadah praise and bring forth salvation to the masses.

It is a type of praise that is born from the deep spiritual womb of an *oppressed* people. It is given despite one's unfair treatment; it still extols the goodness, greatness and mercy of God.

It is a praise which has the optimum effect when it is emitted from the spiritual core of a persecuted people. It is a confession from the soul pregnancy of a mistreated populace.

Yadah praise is dear to the heart of Christ firstly because he is a descendant from the tribe of Judah that derives its name from Yadah. Secondly, like his ancestor Leah the matriarch of Judah he was *rejected*, so Isaiah 53:3 (NKJV) reminds us:

> "He is despised *and* rejected *by men, A Man of sorrows and acquainted with grief. And we hid, as it were, our faces from Him; He was* despised, *and we did not esteem Him*"

Yadah praise makes Christ both Yadah *sensitive* and Yadah *responsive* especially to the rejected forgotten people dealt with like they were Leah. People of African descent have been the "*Leahs*" of the earth. For like her they have been the "*black* sheep" —the rejected of humanity literally by their *color* and the treatment accorded them.

Furthermore, like the meaning of her name they have been weary, tired, grieved and offended from their long plight of oppression, and have been the unloved and unwanted people of the world, but a people chosen to birth salvation.

Leah's birth of Judah as her fourth child is symbolic; since *four* is the number of the *earth*. This tribe was destined to impact the earth.

Likewise, the people of African descent would become those who would affect the earth. Like Leah they would travail in birth pangs, conceiving in pain, but achieving in birth; bringing forth a Judah-Yadah like praise; a stretching forth of their hands to God in worship.

Yadah was used in Achieving Victory (Judah Worshippers)

The second significant use of Yadah was 2 Chronicles 20:19–21 when king Jehoshaphat of Judah placed a choir before his army to publicly confess praises concerning the goodness of Yahweh.

> *The Message* (MSG) *"After talking it over with the people, Jehoshaphat appointed a choir for GOD; dressed in holy robes, they were to march ahead of the troops, singing, Give thanks to GOD, His love never quits. As soon as they started shouting and praising, GOD set ambushes against the men of Ammon, Moab, and Mount Seir as they were Attacking Judah, and they all ended up dead. The Ammonites and Moabites mistakenly attacked those from Mount Seir and massacred them. Then, further confused, they went at each other, and all ended up killed"*

The king instructed singers from the priestly class to go out before the army, and to say, Praise the Lord, (that is, *YADAH*); for He is good and His mercies endureth forever."

What the group did was to lift their hands to God in Yadah Praise thereby thoroughly exposing their vulnerability to the vicious nations gathered around them. This praise brought a quick, decisive, and thorough victory in their war contest.[279]

People of African descent will be like the priestly singers selected by King Jehoshaphat that went before Judah's army with Praise. For they will be stationed by the ultimate king; the Lion king of Judah to the forefront of the last day battle under the "Lord of Hosts". Yadah praise created division, and confusion in the army of the enemies of Judah; it will have that same effect on the spiritual enemy today.

There was another event in scripture where Yadah praise proceeded the army according to Ami Yisrael—a Hebrew roots of Fellowship, this event happened nearly 300 years earlier. Shortly after Joshua died, there were still more conquest to be done in regards to purging the land of the pagan Canaanites. Without a human leader to advise them, the Israelites went directly to God and asked in Judges 1:1 "Who shall be first to go up for us against the Canaanites to fight against them?" God replied "*Judah* shall go up! "(vs. 2).

According to God, Judah would be the first to go up for the battle. They would be the one to lead the armies of Israel. Why would that be? As mentioned before, Yehudah (Judah) comes from the word Yadah - praise. What God was saying is "*Praise*

---

279 Michael McBuba, "UNDERSTANDING THE SUBJECT OF 'PRAISE' FROM THE HEBREW LEXICON," Faith Writers, 21 January 2009, http://www.faithwriters.com/article-details.php?id=93200.

should go up before the battle." When the people of God begin their spiritual warfare with praise, He fights their battles for them"[280]

In another passage of scripture concerning Judah Zechariah 9:13 states that the Lord said

"For I will bend Judah as My bow",

God likens himself to an archer and Judah as his bow and we know the purpose of which is to shoot arrows, the imagery of Yadah is the *shooting* of *arrows*. It is a praise that is both *worship* and *warfare*; it is both a praise act and a warrior attack. This is the kind of praise that was exercised by King Jehosophat's army.

In like manner, God has placed worshippers of African descent at the preceding position of the spiritual battle of the Lord's army, they will lead the fight similarly to the worshippers of Judah. They will help defeat the enemy by releasing the arrows of Yadah praise.

Because of this; God's hand was moved against the enemies of Judah. When the people of African descent move their hand in worship, God will move his hand in warfare. For this type of praise prompts God to action causing Him to take on His role as the Lord of Armies.

As the people of African descent *stretch up* their hands, God will *stretch down* His hand against the adversary. Their stretched-out hand will move God's hand. Their *adoration* will invoke the Lord of Hosts to *Confrontation*.

---

280 Ami Yisrael, http://www.amiyisrael.org/.

Yadah was used in Perceiving Destiny (African Related People)

As mentioned, Yadah means the extending of the hands, and the imagery of the word is that of an archer shooting arrows.

As previously stated Yadah worshippers are spiritual archers and successful archers require clear vision, and they must effectively extend their hands. With one hand they must extend the bow forward from their body and with the other hand they must extend the bow string and arrow back in a pulling motion.

So, hands become very important to an archer. The natural archers extend their hands *outwardly* and spiritual archers extend their hands *upwardly*.

In the same manner hands become very effective in Yadah as part of the destiny of Cushite people of African descent; Yadah "Hands to God" will be prophetically significant in the last days so says Psalms 68:31

> *"Ambassadors will come from Egypt; Cush will stretch out its*
> hands *to God" HCSB*

Michael Brown was an 18-year-old who was fatally shot multiple times by a Ferguson Missouri police officer August 9, 2014 allegedly while his *hands* were *lifted* in the air in a surrendering.

This image became a rallying cry for blacks nationally with people raising their hands and chanting *"hands up don't shoot."*[281]

It became both iconic and prophetic. For as the mostly African American protesters were *stretching* their *hands* up in a symbolic act of surrender to law enforcement, people of Afri-

---

281 Sarah Kessler, "Hands Up Don't Shoot and Growing Power of Protests Memes," *Fast Company*, 15 August 2014, https://www.fastcompany.com/3034486/hands-up-dont-shoot-and-growing-power-of-protest-memes.

can descent globally will stretch their hands up to God in Yadah praise as a *real* act of *surrender*.

The arrows of these spiritual archers are not your ordinary arrows they are *flaming* arrows, for Ham is a North African word meaning "*black*"; a name which also means *warm* and *hot*.[282]

The Yadah arrows shot from the people of African descent are from a people that are descendants of Ham, and a people that are both *black* and *hot*.

They release praise from the very thermal core of their fiery ethnic temperament; as well as a people in the last days who have been set ablaze by the flaming fire of the Holy Spirit as in Acts 2:1–4.

They are a hot people that shoot hot flaming arrows to counter the fiery darts of the enemy. Their shield of faith will quench those darts, but the praise arrows from them will counter the fiery darts.

The releasing of these arrows will take away the enemy's advantage, and will make all who wield the sword in the army of Christ even more effective in combat.

I believe in the last days God is causing people of African descent in North America, the Caribbean, Latin America, Africa, and throughout the world to be his bow he will bend to release the arrows of Yadah praise; extolling the goodness, *mercy*, and wonderful works of God 2 Chronicles 20:21 "Give thanks (*Yadah*) to the Lord, for his loving kindness is everlasting"

> Psalm 107:15 "*Oh that men would praise* (Yadah) *the Lord for his* goodness, *and for his* wonderful works *to the children of men*"

---

282 "Ham," Bible tools.com, Easton's Bible Dictionary, http://www.biblestudytools.com/dictionary/ham/.

Psalm 136:1 "Oh, give thanks (Yadah) to the LORD, for He is good! For His mercy Endures forever"

There is a prophetic utterance concerning people of African descent and Yadah praise and its meaning related to the hands: Here we repeat this prophecy once again.

Psalm 68:31 (HCSB) "Ambassadors will come from Egypt; Cush will stretch out its hands to God"

This prophecy states that the Cushite's will stretch out their hands to God. I have said that Yadah means the *stretching* or *extending* of the hand.

In other words, this prophesy is saying, the Cushites will give God Yadah praise. To stretch out your hands symbolizes a yearning for God [Psalms 143:6]. There will come a yearning for God from black people that will be praise and warfare on the adversary.

These spiritual archers who will lead the battle are a gift to the body, and will enhance the war against the forces of darkness and enable them to capture the spoils of war from the conflict.

Our *message*, our *mission*, and our *munitions* will set us up for restitution for we will take back what we loss, and make a great recovery due to the great *mercies* of the Lord that we will receive.

Discussion Questions

3. What is the meaning of *Yadah* and how does it relate to God's agenda for black people?

4. How does Christ relate to *Yadah* and the destiny of people of African descent?

5. What weapon is *Yadah* like and how does it relate to the munitions of war for black people?

CHAPTER 20

Mercy Suits Our Case — Our Mercies

‌

"Lord have Mercy"
~ **AFRICAN AMERICAN PROVERB**

*"Kindness is a language which the blind can see
and the deaf can hear"*
~ **AFRICAN PROVERB**

*Jeremiah 39:16–18 "Go tell Ebed-Melech the Cushite: This is
what the LORD of Hosts, the God of Israel, says: I am about
to fulfill my words for harm and not for good against this city.
They will take place before your eyes on that day. But I
will rescue you on that day"—this is the LORD's declaration
—"and you will not be handed over to the men you fear.
Indeed, I will certainly deliver you so that you do not fall by
the sword. Because you have trusted in Me, you will keep your
life like the spoils of war." This is the LORD's declaration.*

The older black saints used to have an expression when they
prayed: they would say, "have mercy Lord because *mercy suits our
case*." The case that mercy suits is our condition as a people.

In a song sung by Marvin Gaye there is a phrase of lyrical repetition "*Oh mercy mercy me*". It captures our desire to obtain God's mercy, but is also a declaration of his agenda for us.

In the above passage on Ebed- Melech we see the mercies of God toward a Cushite and as we go over this passage we will find that there are ten mercies we will discuss little later.

Mercies defined are the compassionate kindly forbearance shown toward an offender, an enemy, or other person in one's power, compassion, pity, or benevolence.

The concept of mercy has several different Hebrew and Greek roots, which are rendered in other occurrences by other synonyms, such as '*kindness*', '*grace*', and '*favor*'. It is also *compassion* for the *miserable*.[283]

It is an attribute of both God and a righteous human being. In the Hebrew the most frequent word for mercy is *Chesed*, which means *loving-kindness, love, loyalty*, and *faithfulness*.[284]

Mercy then to the people of African descent would be God's loving kindness, compassion, forbearance, pity, grace, benevolence, and favor coupled with his faithful devotion to us despite having offended him in the past and suffered in a miserable state as a result.

God's mercy moves forward with our destiny. It is a factor that is key to our recovery and the essence of our restoration.

I have mentioned that Yadah praise extols the *mercy* of God, and that it was this kind of praise performed by Jehosophat's worshippers that preceded his army.

---

283 "Mercy," Easton's Bible Dictionary.

284 Achtemeier, Harper's Bible dictionary (San Francisco: Harper & Row, 1985).

It is a praise that proclaims those mercies despite one's oppressive condition. It does not focus on what others are *doing* against one, but what God is *being* to one.

It does not murmur, complain, or carry out vendettas. It is a praise from a merciful person extolling a merciful God.

It is nonviolent in the natural, but very violent in the spiritual. It confesses the mercy of God during the misery of life.

It does not allow an *adversary* to make it *contrary*. It does not seek the vengeance of God on the enemies, but forbearance from God for their enemies.

It exclaims from the cross of suffering *"Father forgive them for they know not what they do"*. It recognizes that people are blinded by ignorance, prejudice, and hatred and they don't know what they are doing to those they persecute, but more importantly what they are doing to themselves in the process, and the consequences they and their children will reap.

When we confess God's mercy during the battle it touches the *heart* of God and moves the *hand* of God. `The stretching of our hands to God will cause us to be major benefactors of the multiple mercies of God.

We have established earlier in this book that we are associated with Judah and the following prophecy relates to us concerning the mercies of our hope filled future.

> Jeremiah 29:11 (NIV) *"For I know the plans I have for you,"* declares the Lord, *"plans to* prosper *you and not to harm you,* plans *to give you* hope *and a* future"

God is planning a glorious hope and future for us as a people and that hope is found in his mercy. Psalms 147:11 (AKJV) declares:

"The LORD takes pleasure in them that fear him, in those that hope in his mercy"

A clue to the nature of our recovery is personified in a biblical black figure we have already discussed, namely Ebed-Melech. He received a prophetic word in Jeremiah 39:16–18. This passage has both historical and prophetic significance.

Ebed-Melech is a person, but he is also an Afroistic symbol representing Cushitic people. As we fulfill our destiny, part of which is to be the Kopher covering, our own deliverance will spring forth.

For God sent this prophetic word specifically to Ebed-Melech a Cushite African. There were three things that made him the right prospect for God's purpose; three things needed to fulfill his assignment. They are the same three things we need to fulfill our purpose as a people.

His Position: Ebed- Melech as I have said was an African official not a slave, a high-ranking official that had been exalted to that position by the king. His name Ebed Melech means *"servant of the king"*. He was a high ranking and highly respected person in the kingdom of Zedekiah.

Cushites today will become high ranking and highly respected people in the Kingdom of God. They will be divinely positioned to have major impact in this season.

As a people, we corporately bear the name *Ebed-Melech* for we will be servants of the king in the kingdom of God. To have the influence we need to fulfill God's purpose we will also see a promotion of black people by the King of Glory to positions of influence in business, politics, and the church.

His position in the kingdom explains his influence on King Zedekiah. No mere slave would have had that kind of influence on the king and received those kinds of resources.

His Petition: Ebed-Melech had to show mercy to Jeremiah before he received mercy from God. Out of compassion he made a petition to the king to rescue the prophet.

We Cushite Africans will engage in intercession to our king not only for our own people, but for other racial groups and people of color in a struggle for parity. Because of our struggle, we have developed an empathic side for those who are pursuing their racial equity. Which is why we can support what Latinos are going through, what Native Americans are fighting for and have endured, and what innocent Middle Eastern immigrants are experiencing.

So, the Cushite African was operating on a harvest principle that they who *sow mercy* will *reap mercy*. Jesus highlighted this idea in Matthew 5:7 ESV.

"Blessed are the merciful, *for they shall* receive mercy"

His Provision: The Cushite was provided with sanction and manpower to go and remove Jeremiah from the cistern. In a parallel manner God is equipping Cushite Africans of this hour with provision to fulfill their task of elevating the church from its perceived lowly place to a higher level of freedom. For where there is a God inspired *commission* there will be God transpired *provision*.

The message to this Cushite official is also a message to the people of African descent today. In Jeremiah 39:16–18" (HCSB) it says:

> *"Go tell Ebed-Melech the Cushite: This is what the LORD of Hosts, the God of Israel, says: I am about to fulfill My words for harm and not for good against this city. They will take place before your eyes on that day. But I will rescue you on that day"—this is the LORD's declaration— "and you will not be handed over to the men you fear. Indeed, I will certainly deliver you so that you do not fall by the sword. Because you have trusted in Me, you will keep your life like the spoils of war." This is the LORD's declaration.*

This passage is about two individuals, Jeremiah and Ebed-Melech, and how their destinies intersected. As previously stated the name Ebed-Melech means *servant of the king*. He was more than a servant of the natural king, he became the servant of the king of the universe.

On the other hand, Jeremiah means *"God will uplift or Yahweh will uplift"*. The events of Jeremiah 39:16-18 are about God uplifting these two men.

First, it is about how God used a servant of the king of the universe; a Cushite Sudanese African to *uplift* the prophet Jeremiah out of a cistern. Then in turn once Jeremiah was uplifted he then prophetically uplifted the Cushite African out of his spiritual cistern.

In the prophecy, we've studied as the Lord of Hosts gives the Cushite African a promise of ten mercies; they illustrate the ten mercies God extends to people of African descent related to their restoration in the end times:

1. *The Mercy of Identification*: vs. 16 "Go tell *Ebed Melech* the *Cushite*"

The first mercy extended to the African was the mercy of God's knowledge of his *identity*. Sometimes as oppressed people we think that God has forgotten us- this incident proves otherwise. He is keenly aware and intimately acquainted with who we are, and what we have gone through. He was very specific about the Cushite; he knew both his title name and ethnicity.

In fact, God is so particular in knowing who we are he has made a record of the physical days of our time here Psalms 139:14–16 (NIV):

> *"I praise you because I am fearfully and wonderfully made; your works are wonderful, I know that full well. My frame was not hidden from you when I was made in the secret place, when I was woven together in the depths of the earth. Your eyes saw my unformed body; all the days ordained for me were written in your book before one of them came to"*

Moreover, God has even accounted and enumerated the specific hairs on our head (and it does not matter if those hairs are straight, bushy or curly) so in Matthew 10:28-30 New International Version (NIV):

> *"Do not be afraid of those who kill the body, but cannot kill the soul. Rather, be afraid of the One who can destroy both soul and body in hell. Are not two sparrows sold for a penny? Yet not one of them will fall to the ground outside your Father's care and even the very hairs of your head are all numbered"*

For God to be so detailed concerning us that he would take the time to number how many individual hairs speaks to a God who is very aware of who and what we are, but who loves us.

The word from God through Jeremiah was not sent to a European, it was specifically to a Cushite Sudanese African. Such knowledge of us is in and of itself a mercy of God. People may forget us, but God does not. Our identity as a black person and as black people is well known to God.

2. *The Mercy of Communication*: **vs. 16 "This is what the** *Lord of Hosts*, **the God of Israel,** *says*"
Says: ['amar /aw•mar/] to speak, to answer, to promise, to intend, to avow.

In verse 16 God is introducing himself to a Cushite African as the "*Lord of Host*" the "*Yahweh* or *God* of *Armies*" This is a second time God introduces himself like this to Cushite Africans. The other was Isaiah 18:7.

The second mercy of God shone Ebed-Melech was God communicating to him. For the God of the universe to be so concerned about us knowing who he is and our fate that he would be purpose driven to get a *Rhema* word to us, is a mercy of God.

He has not ignored us, he wants to commune, talk and verbally interact with Cushites even if he is not speaking to others. His ear has been open to our cry and now in this season our ear must be open to his voice concerning our destiny. For him to even speak to us is a mercy.

In this season of history Cushite people of African descent are in his chat room of grace. We are a people chosen to receive his special word concerning who we are.

3. *The Mercy of Revelation*: **Vs. 16 "***I am about to fulfill my words* **for harm and not for good against this city"**
People of African descent like the Cushite in this story will be given a third mercy of God—a *revealing* of the judgment about to occur.

Revelation is crucial to our purpose for without it we will become unfocused, distracted and uncontrollable.

We will resort to fighting carnal battles with each other as well as others, and left to our own devices, but the good news is revelation has come, and due to being the spiritual people that we are we will readily receive it for Proverbs 29:18 (HCSB) states:

> "Without revelation *people run wild, but one who listens to instruction will be happy*"

Many are living in denial to the peril of our country and moving about blindly with eyes shut. Not so for people of African descent, we will see clearly what is about to befall the U.S. God says there is judgment coming and not prosperity. The presidential election is the beginning of that judgement

Several prominent Economists are predicting another major financial disaster to occur that will be much worse than the financial crisis of 2008.[285]

Just as God prophesied judgement would come to Babylon the city he is going to bring judgement to America—the Babylon as a nation—there are striking parallels. Babylon is mentioned in the Old Testament and New Testament. Could the "Babylon" in Revelation 18 be the USA? For In this chapter it is described in the following way;

1. It is a *literal place*, with *lots of wealth* and *products* to sell. Rev. 18:12-13
2. It is a *wealthy country* that even *sells its money* (*gold & silver*). Rev. 18:11-12

---

285 Adam Shell, "Doom saying experts who foresee economic devastation ahead," USA Today, https://usatoday30.usatoday.com/money/perfi/stocks/story/2012-02-26/stock-market-bears-doomsayers/53259742/1.

3. It is a country that *deceives* all other *countries.*
   Rev. 18:23
4. It *spreads* its *sexual immorality* to other countries.
   Rev. 18:3
5. It *lives* in *luxury.* Rev. 18:7
6. It *helps* others *get rich.* Rev. 18:19, Rev. 18:3
7. It is *'married'* to *another* country. Rev. 18:7
8. It is *responsible* for many *deaths* (*especially people of color*). Rev. 18:24

Also, the unhealthiest states also correspond with the most conservative and poor states, *Idaho, Alabama, West Virginia, Tennessee Oklahoma, Kentucky, Louisiana, Arkansas,* and *Mississippi.*[286]

Ironically, all these states are run by Republican governors, thus *Idaho, Arkansas, Louisiana, Alabama,* and *Tennessee* are such. I believe that the economies of the states are affected by their prejudice and that there is a correlation between the two.

Prophets of African descent will confirm what these economists are saying, but will not give economist explanations. They will receive revelation into the moral cause of this collapse; which will be God's judgment on the wealth of this nation because of the mistreatment of poor persons of color.

In addition to the financial disaster there will also be environmental disasters which will have a major impact on the United States. Greenhouse gas concentrations in the atmosphere will cause changes that will impact our food supply, water resources, infrastructure, and ecosystems,[287]

---

286 Kelly Dickerson, "These Are The 10 Unhealthiest States In The US," Business Insider Science, 11 December 2013.

287 "Climate Change: Increasing greenhouse gas concentrations will have many effects," United States Environmental Protection Agency.

A recent 331-page study, entitled *Climate Vulnerability Monitor*, was carried out by a non-governmental organization based in Europe, and the Climate Vulnerable Forum. It was written by more than 50 scientists, economists and policy experts commissioned by 20 governments, and it revealed climate change is costing the world economy more than $1.2 trillion.

Furthermore, by 2030, the researcher's estimate, the cost of climate change and air pollution combined will raise global GDP. For the U.S., adding up the effects to the farming industry and damages to property, we are faced with major losses.[288]

There has been a growing number of hurricanes hitting largely the *southern portion of US.*

It is interesting that most hurricanes begin in the Atlantic because of tropical waves that move westward off the *West African* coast, a major site in the past for the transport of African slaves. Some form in the vicinity of the Cape Verde islands and are known as *"Cape Verde"* hurricanes.[289] For three centuries, the Cape Verde islands were a setting for the transatlantic *slave trade.*[290]

Moreover, Hurricanes hit mostly *Florida, Texas, North Carolina, Georgia,* and *Louisiana.* All five states are among the states listed in the top ten *most* racist states today per research done by an independent cyber-geography group which among other factors looked at the number of racists tweets and the number of KKK

---

288 Fiona Harvey, "Climate change is already damaging global economy, report finds," The Guardian, 25 September 2012, https://www.theguardian.com/environment/2012/sep/26/climate-change-damaging-global-economy.

289 "Hurricane science and forecasting," USA Today, https://usatoday30.usatoday.com/weather/resources/askjack/archives-hurricane-science.htm.

290 "History," www.CapeVerde.com.

chapters in the state.[291] All five states were part of the southern Confederacy which fought to defend the slavery of black people.

Some have even suggested that hurricanes follow the same path that the *slave* ships did. For both started out on the African West Coast and moved west toward the Caribbean and onto southeastern North America from sub Saharan *Africa*.

In addition, parts of the U.S. are bombarded by devastating tornadoes. These storms are *more* common in the United States than in *any* other country. This nation receives more than 1,200 tornadoes annually—*four* times the amount seen in Europe. Violent tornadoes—those rated EF4 or EF5 on the Enhanced Fujita Scale—occur *more often* in the United States than in any other nation.

Most tornadoes in the United States happen east of the Rocky Mountains. The Great Plains, the Midwest, the Mississippi Valley, and the southern United States and are all areas that are vulnerable.[292]

Ironically, once again the states most *affected* are those which are touted as the most *racist*, and who were part of the confederacy during the Civil War. There is some speculation that the furious energy of these violent storms is fueled not just by atmospheric conditions, but by the soul cries of Africans who lost their lives on the slave voyage.

Albeit, people of African descent will receive revelation of the calamity coming on those who will be most affected by the predicted economic crisis—the wealthy. We will see failed busi-

---

291 A Moore, "Top 10 Most Racist States in America," Atlantic Black Star, 7 May 2015, http://atlantablackstar.com/2014/05/14/top-10-racist-states-america/.

292 Wikipedia contributors, "Tornadoes in the United States," Wikipedia, The Free Encyclopedia, Wikipedia, The Free Encyclopedia, https://en.wikipedia.org/wiki/Tornadoes_in_the_United_States.

nesses, bankruptcies, criminal arrests, successful litigations, IRS levies, suicides, tremendous lost revenue, fraud, and corruption exposed.

There will come surprising disclosures of financial improprieties from Wall Street and the corporate sector of America.

This revelation will usher us into the next mercy of God. For He will allow us to behold his severe chastening of those who engaged in oppression of the people of color. We will receive prophetic discernment of his judgment on those who participated in unjust practices against us which leads to the next mercy of God.

4. *The Mercy of Visualization:* **vs. 16 "They will take place *before your eyes* on that day"**
Before: [Paniym Paw-neem] in the front of, *before* your presence the word **day** *'yome'* can refer to a period from *sunrise* to *sunset* or an *age*. Historically it refers to that time but prophetically it refers this *age* of the *end times.*

God has witnessed the oppression of people of color and has been acutely aware of our plight. He has noted that the record of this American nation concerning oppressing others is described in Ezekiel 22:29 (HCSB):

> *"The people of the land have practiced* extortion *and committed* robbery. *They have* oppressed *the* poor *and* needy *and unlawfully* exploited *the* foreign resident. *"*

The word *oppressed* is the Hebrew word *o'-shek* which means to cause injury, cause fraud, to distress, to get by unjust gain, to act cruelly, to do extortion, or oppression, to deal deceitfully.

These have been notorious practices of the business community in their dealings with the poor.

The word *exploited yaw-naw' is* a primitive root; which means to *rage* or *be violent to*; by implication to *suppress*, to *maltreat*, destroy, thrust out by oppression, to vex, do violence to.

This word describes the treatment of people especially African Americans, Native Americans, Latinos, and people of middle Eastern heritage.

People of color will receive a fourth mercy; they will *see* the judgment of their persecutors with their eyes. Which is why the Cushite mercenary that Joab sent to David would *see* the judgment of Absalom with his *own eyes*.

Therefore, Joab could say to him "go tell what you have *seen*" or Ebed-Melech this Cushite official would *see* the judgment of God on Babylon *with his eyes.* Or the blacks in the civil war that witnessed the death of lives of the confederate soldiers of the South with *their eyes.*

Cushite Africans are visionaries—that is, people divinely endowed with special insight and foresight beholding the Lord's indignation. Yet God will supernaturally make provision for them that will astound the nation and puzzle the so-called experts Psalm 146:7-9 New International Version (NIV). They will *see* the destruction and yet *flee* the destruction.

> "*He (God)* upholds *the* cause *of the* oppressed *and* gives food *to the* hungry. *The Lord sets prisoners free, the Lord gives* sight *to the blind, the Lord lifts up those who are bowed down, and the Lord loves the righteous. The Lord watches over the* foreigner *and sustains the fatherless and the widow, but he frustrates the ways of the wicked*"

This passage says God frustrates the wicked—that is, those who wrongfully cause suffering.

It says the Lord gives *sight* to the blind and in this day, he is allowing Cushites of African descent to see, and visualize the judgment of God, just as he allowed Ebed-Melech to see the destruction in his day.

Cushite people of African descent will be given an enhanced vision of the present, and the future which will enable them to see the judgment, and His vindication of people of color.

They will witness the destruction of today's political Babylon. That ancient nation had done to the Jews of Jeremiah's time what was done to the people of African descent - in our time; the invasion of their homeland and the taking of many inhabitants into captivity.

This was not the end of the story for Ebed-Melech nor for Cushites of African descent today. For in both cases their salvation was forth coming.

5. *The Mercy of Salvation*: **Vs. 17 "I will *rescue* you on that day"**
The word Rescue in the original language is [*natsal* /naw•tsal/] meaning to deliver, to *snatch away*, to spare, *save*, being safe from danger, and so be in a *more favorable* circumstance.

The *fifth* mercy of God was his promised salvation to the Cushite, that he would rescue him on *that day*, the word rescue in the text meant the Lord would spare him, *snatch* him away from the situation, and place him in a more *favorable* circumstance.

It will mean being snatched out of America to other countries and for others it will mean being supernaturally snatched away from oppressive situations.

Like Ebed-Melech in this season God has heard our cry and is ready to respond and rescue us *snatching* us away to a more favorable place. Psalms 12:5 says:

"Because of the violence *done to the* oppressed, *because of the*
painful cries *of the* needy, I *will spring into action," says the Lord.*
"I will provide *the* safety *they so desperately desire. "NET"*

The word *safety* here is the original Hebrew word *"Yesha"* and
it means deliverance, salvation, prosperity, victory, and protection that produces freedom from a present danger.

He has and he will provide a way of escape from the judgment
awaiting the U.S. nationally. He will supernaturally save us from
his retribution of America.

Furthermore, this salvation will include us being put in a
more *favorable* place spiritually in victory, deliverance, and prosperity making our salvation encompassing of our restoration.

6. *The Mercy of Preservation:* vs. 17 "you will *not* be *handed over"*

The Hebrew word for *Handed Over* is [Nathan /naw•than/] defined as, to be *durable, healthy,* not be easily diseased or uproot-
ed, *last* a *long* time, continue in a state for a *considerable duration.*

Yet another mercy of God to the Cushite African was that
God promised that he would not permit him to be handed over
to those he feared, and the Hebrew word for *handed over* or *delivered* is *Nathan,*

To some extent we have suffered with anxiety about what people in power would do to us and to our families, we have feared
what the police would do to our black men especially our young
black males, what ultra conservatives would do with our rights,
what supremacists would do to our churches and what the banks
and Wall Street would do to our money. But we are reminded in
2 Timothy 1:7:

"For God has not given us the spirit of fear, but of power and of love and a sound mind"

God was saying to the Cushite African I will preserve you and not betray you to your enemies. He was assuring the Cushite African that he would be safe from the calamity coming.

Irrespective of any racial backlash that may come to people of African descent, God will not concede us to the hand of those we fear. Our struggle has made us resilient, strong, and in the process God has made us *durable*.

People of African descent have seemed indestructible, able to undergo great adversity and successfully survive it. They are the living miracle of the world resisting extermination as a people, surviving both homicides and genocides. Circumstances that would have wiped out others have strengthened us. We have proven to be a fortified people; that like a stamp can take a *licking* and keep on *sticking*. This also means that we will regain our health from physical and mental wounds. That we will be healed, and will go through a *rebirth*.

7. **The Mercy of Regeneration: vs.18 "I will certainly *deliver* so that you do not fall by the sword"**

The *seventh* mercy of God to this Cushite African was the promise that God would deliver him, but the original word for deliver is *Malat* which was different from *Natsal*. For it means to *give birth* to, the freeing of an object from the body, and to *deliver a baby*.

God is saying to people of African descent I will cause you to *escape* the captivity *womb* and I will *birth* you forth into a new life. I am pregnant with your purpose when it comes to your destiny; I am with child.

God is speaking out of the feminine essence of the El Shaddai mother. For after all, even though God is spoken of most often as a Father we need to be reminded that God is spirit and a spirit has no gender per se.

God is saying I am expectant with the life possibility which I have travailed over you for these centuries with the birth pangs of your struggle but I will birth you forth with new life.

Your delivery will be with some pain, but it will end with the joy of your rebirth, for you will come out a fresh and new generation. There will be no miscarriages, still births, or womb abortions.

You will be born a healthy generation. Don't be dismayed by this new insidious surge in this era of backlash, and racial animosity. God has a plan of rebirth for people of color.

Our deliverance and our restoration have been like a painful delivery of one pregnant. God said to Ebed-Melech you will not fall by the sword of judgment; you will escape death and you will embrace life.

He is saying the same to Cushite Africans of the present. We may experience the physical death of some of our people, but remember Ebed Melech was a total person with a whole body so he represents the whole body of Cushite people of color.

Just like in the natural body some cells die but the body regenerates new cells so the whole organism can continue to survive as a whole—as the body of Cushite people we will lose some people but the whole body will continue to regenerate and the body of people will survive.

One indication of this is the decline of birth rates of whites. Their deaths outnumbered births for the very *first* time in US history.

The census predicts that significant drops in birth rates versus death rates will be regular among them by 2025. Several demographers have pointed out that *no* other racial group in the U.S. experienced a similar drop.[293]

This decline is happening at a time when God is making people of African descent more bold, secure, and confident. Which leads us to the eighth mercy of God.

8. The *Mercy* of *Confirmation*: vs. 18 "You have *trusted* in me"
The original Hebrew word *Trusted* [*batach* /*baw•takh*/] means to have *confidence*, to be bold, to be *secure*, and to make secure.

The *eighth* mercy to Ebed-Melech was what Yahweh told the Cushite via Jeremiah. What God said He would do because the African had demonstrated great confidence, and placed his expectation in God; for he was convinced that Yahweh was reliable and worthy of trust.

> *Numbers 23:19 "God is not human, that he should lie, not a human being, that he should change his mind. Does he speak and then not act? Does he promise and not fulfill?" NIV*

Ebed-Melech was promised by Yahweh that his life would be spared when the Babylonians took over Jerusalem, because of his *trust* in the Lord (Jeremiah 39:15–18).

Likewise, as a mercy of God we will obtain our expectation from the trust we have placed in a proven trustworthy God. We will develop a sense of secure boldness, and a *confident fortitude* out of a *confident attitude*. We will make him the *shelter* and *refuge* of our trust. Psalms 9:9

---

293 Andrew Kelly, "'First time' in history: White deaths outnumber births in US," Reuters, 13 June 2013, https://www.rt.com/usa/us-white-births-census-613/.

> *"The LORD is a* shelter *for the* oppressed, *a* refuge
> *in times of trouble"*

People of African descent have developed an unswerving trust in the Lord, an unshakeable confidence in Yahweh. They will be bold in their conviction and secure in their faith even when others doubt.

Trust has become the legacy of our oppression, but also the anchor of our hope. It is the common thread of our history and the common denominator of our progress. Trust is the key to our survival and the essence of our revival. The suffering from our history has been purposeful according to the will of God and it has taught us to trust God

> 1 Peter 4:19 *"Therefore let those who* suffer *according to* God's *will* entrust *their souls to a faithful Creator while doing good".*
> ESV

It is this trust in God that will enable us to confiscate back what we have lost due to plunder of Satan. People of African descent are scheduled for a major recovery of the spiritual, social, and economic spoils that was taken from us - that restoration time is now.

9. *Mercy of Confiscation:* **vs. 18 "you will** *keep* **your life the** *spoils* **of war"**

This statement highlights the *ninth* mercy of God which I call the mercy of *Confiscation:* the act of taking or *seizing* someone's *property* with authority. The property being the very life of the Cushite African, but with residual benefits.

Here God promises the African that he would keep his life as the *spoils* of *war.* Not just keep his life, but keep it as the *spoils* of war. The meaning of *Spoils* is: Goods or *property seized* from a victim after a conflict, especially after a military victory.

It is the incidental benefits reaped by a winner, *seized* possessions, taking possession from a defeated enemy, booty: the plunder taken from an enemy in war goods or *property seized* by *force*. A valuable prize, award, or *gain* to the victorious army during war has been common practice throughout recorded history.

For foot soldiers, it was viewed to supplement their often-meagre income and was part of the celebration of victory. Spoils meant what was taken was often greater than what they had and it *increased* their resources.[294]

To reiterate, God introduced himself to Ebed Melech through Jeremiah's prophecy as the *Lord* of *Hosts* which means the "*Lord* of *Angel Armies*". This is the designation God uses as his combatant identity. It is the name he employs when He is about go to war, and engage in a military campaign. Jeremiah 39 is essentially about war. Ebed Melech was a warrior demonstrating the warrior nature characteristic of Cushites.

In his own way, he had fought for the life of Jeremiah, and in return Yahweh fought for his life. Yahweh gave him his life as a reward from the victory against Ebed-Melech's enemies. God gave him both the "*reward* of *life*" and a "*life* of *reward*". Yahweh granted his life as the booty (valuable stolen goods seized in war, goods or property seized by force) from God's military conquest.

Therefore, it was a life given from a victory, it was a *victorious* life. God won His war on the Babylonians (he never loses) the life

---

294 Wikipedia contributors, "Looting," Wikipedia, The Free Encyclopedia, Wikipedia, The Free Encyclopedia, https://en.wikipedia.org/wiki/Looting.

God granted the African came from a *winner* that made it a *winning* life.

Without the *toil* of the battle the African enjoyed the *spoil* of the battle which was his own continued existence. As an oppressed race God will find and exact justice for people of African descent. Psalms 103:6 ESV says:

> "*The LORD works righteousness and justice for all who are* oppressed"

In the same way God is giving a victorious life and a *winning life* to them. For He will wage war and engage in conflict for them.

The Lord didn't just promise the African his life; he promised him a *life as the "spoils of war"*. That is a life as a valuable prize, an award, or gain; a life more *abundant* because the word *spoils* implies the seizure of goods from a defeated enemy by force *enriching* the life of the recipient.

Which is what the savior stated as his goal for coming to the earth. He took us back from the thief who stole our life. He came to retrieve it back and to give us a rich *abundant* one so again he says in John 10:10 **"ESV**

> "*The thief comes only to steal and kill and destroy. I came that they may have life and have it abundantly"*

Thus, Yahweh's triumph over Ebed-Melech's enemies meant that the African's life was taken back forcibly by God from his adversaries and returned to him as a valuable prize, but returned with gain and incidental benefits.

Likewise, God has triumphed over our spiritual adversary and is giving back the life that Cushite people of African descent lost, but he is also returning that life with compensatory gain.

There is some debate as to whether people of African descent should receive reparations for slavery. The chances of that happening are slim to none. This nation has never even really come to grips with the horrors of slavery or come up with an adequate apology let alone financial compensation. For that would represent the ultimate admission of guilt and wrong doing in our nation's original sin.

However, God is going to send reparations to black people and he will do so creatively and supernaturally. He will invoke economic scenarios that will make this happen.

He has affirmed this with a prophetic declaration. The indicators of this divine reparation are starting to be seen and they are part of the prophetic signs of our restoration. Our *reparation* is per God's *declaration*.

10. *The mercy of Declaration:* vs. 18 "This is the LORD's declaration."

The word *Saith* (KJV) or *Declaration* (HCSB) is the Hebrew word which is an oracle a marker of prophetic discourse, found in the beginning, middle and mostly on the end of a discourse, or utterance.

This *tenth* mercy was more than God just communicating with the Cushite. This was a prophetic utterance from God. It was a word with authority behind it. It is mentioned twice in the passage in Verses 17 and 18. For God to make this statement twice means this prophetic declaration must be significant.

The utterance has both an air of prophecy, authority and there is a sense of certainty. God is very purpose driven in declaring this oracle to the Cushite African. He is divinely determined to make it happen.

When God is focused on doing his purpose to an individual or a people, it moves that declaration from mere *possibility* to *inevitability* and nothing in the earth or for that matter in the universe will stop it.

There may be challenges and delays, but they will not arrest the purpose of God. Such was the case with Ebed Melech and such will be the case for the people that he represents; the Cushite people of African descent. God's word will fulfill His work.

> Isaiah 55:10 *"As the rain and the snow come down from heaven, and do not return to it without watering the earth and making it bud and flourish, so that it yields seed for the sower and bread for the eater, so is my word that goes out from my mouth: It will not return to me empty, but will* accomplish what I desire *and* achieve the purpose *for which I sent it." NIV*

God's prophetic word to Cushites will not only come with *authority* it will arrive with *ability. For* the word spoken will also have the power to accomplish its aim. *When God "speaks" he "tweaks".* His word *transforms* a situation per the details of His promise. The word to the Cushite in verse 16 was a communication bringing a revelation of what was going to happen to the Babylonians. The word God spoke to the Cushite in verse 18 was a declaration concerning the African's fate.

The role of the Cushite Africans is of such value in the end times that Yahweh has prophetically declared a strong word concerning their restoration. God will *declare* to them a word that will bring a *recourse* for them.

This declaration in Jeremiah 39:18 is the ten mercies we have discussed in the discourse given to Ebed Melech. The number 10 signifies the completeness of order, and the fullness of a cycle.

They are completeness of the order, and cycle of the mercies that God will redress to us for our struggles.

Truly people of Cushitic African descent have been the consummate example of Psalms 9:9-10: For as a people we are Ebed Melech we are black servants of the King. We have received a prophetic declaration.

> "*The LORD is a stronghold for the* oppressed, *a stronghold in times of trouble. And those who know your name put their* trust *in you, for you O LORD, have* not forsaken *those who seek you*" ESV

Discussion Questions

1. How does Ebed Melech typify the salvation of black people?
2. What are the ten mercies God will bestow on black people in the last days?

Conclusion

❧

"A Worthy cause is worth pursuing to the end"
~ AFRICAN PROVERB

"Tomorrow belongs to the people who prepare for it today"
~ AFRICAN PROVERB

In white American history there was a belief called *Manifest Destiny* in the 1830's and 1840's that said the U.S. (essentially White America) had a "divine right" and was destined to conquer people and expand territory. This attitude helped fuel western settlement, *Native American* removal and war with *Mexicans*.[295]

This belief was used to justify the subjugation of people of color and the taking of their land. It was not confined to American coasts but permeated the belief system of those who took slaves from Africa.

Reginald Horsman's book *"Race and Manifest Destiny the Origins of American Racial Anglo-Saxonism""* is the first study to examine the origins of racialism in America and to show that the

---

295 History Channel: "Manifest Destiny."

belief in white American superiority was firmly entrenched in the nation's ideology by 1850.[296]

However, there is another manifest destiny which has not been discussed or acknowledged. It is a divine purpose of the Africans and other Cushitic people of color. I have prophetically cited that destiny in the prophecies from the Bible in this book such as Isaiah 18:1–7, Psalm 68:31, Isaiah 43:3–4 and others.

As it relates to people of African descent globally. God has worked our affliction for His Glory and our good, our *captivity* has brought *intercession, confession, aggression* and will culminate in *possession*.

It brought *Intercession* because like Israel it forced us to fervently engage in supplication crying out to God for deliverance. *Confession* because it made us specialize in *Yadah* praise.

First, *confession* of our sin of idolatry and pagan practices, but also a stretching of our hands to God in praise confession of God's name. Because it ultimately released our warrior nature rechanneling our *Aggression* toward the enemy, and not flesh and blood humans who are simply his pawns.

Finally, *possession*, for we will get our life back as the spoils of war, we will get our inheritance back, and we will recover our abundance. Once again, Dr. Martin Luther King prophetically proclaimed that we as a people will get to the Promise land.

Cushites from Africa, the Americas, the Caribbean, and other nations globally have a date with destiny and prophetically that time is now. They will be on the defensive as the spiritual guardians of the Body of Christ, but will also go on the spiritual offensive declaring war on the enemy.

---

296 Reginald Horsman, Race and Manifest Destiny (Cambridge: Harvard UP, 1986).

They will take back what was loss; they will take our health back, our families back, our prosperity back, our political power back, our influence back, our affluence back, and our history back.

Our loss has been great and our restoration will also be great. Our redress will commiserate with the suffering we have undergone. As a *multitude* of our people have the right *attitude* for our destiny it will facilitate the *magnitude* of our recovery.

For our movement will go forward, our *message* will be delivered, our *mission* will be accomplished, our *munitions* will prove effective, and our *mercies* will be received.

We are on God's timetable - his chronological calendar of historical events; we are on his divine clock and it is ticking down. Our *kairos* has come - our time has arrived. He has predestined us for this moment, he has chosen us for this season.

He has made us a people both resolute and resilient. We have and will continue to survive every assault on our identity, and every attack on our dignity with strength of character and nobility.

The dry bones will live again, the years that the locust have eaten will be restored. No demon of hell or man of the earth will stop this purpose. No weapon formed against God's agenda for Cushite people will prosper.

Every lie concerning us will be dispelled, every untruth regarding us will be revealed, every shackle that held us captive will be broken, and every significant door of opportunity closed to us will be opened. We are a people designed for and brought to the kingdom for this moment of human history.

Those who oppressed us can sense a change, they can feel it, and they *fear* it. The resurgence of overt racism is an indication of that fear. Even the election of Donald Trump to the White House is a manifestation of that fear.

There is a difference in the spiritual and social atmosphere. There is major shift in the paradigm of the nation's cultural venue. This change is not the Absalom mule riding to destruction, but rather a thoroughbred out the gate galloping to the victory finish line; too fast and too powerful to be stopped.

We have come full circle in our history, we will go back to our future, and forward to our destiny. The die is cast and the hand writing of God's purpose is on the wall. We are on schedule to fulfill Dr. Martin Luther King's prophetic annunciation for "we will get to the promised land".

The signs are evident, the indicators are present, and they point to a divinely orchestrated transition taking place. We will not be detoured by the resurgence of the renewed racial onslaughts, or the radical political extremism nor will we be distracted by the constant media episodes of activities which counter our purpose.

We have come too far from our past, and we are too close to our future. We have learned from our *history* and we will embrace our *destiny*. The time is now for our purpose to unfold.

Indeed, we are the *chariot riders* on a historic *movement*, the Cushite *runners* with a *message*, the fivefold Kopher *covering* with a *mission*, the elite *archers* of Yadah praise with war *munitions* marching from Mt. Zion (the Church), we are the *recipients* scheduled to receive the tenfold *mercies* of God.

We are a "*gift*" from the Lord of Armies to the church globally with our past behind us - our Christ with us - our armor and arrows on us - and victory before us.

We will be the catalyst for authentic racial reconciliation to the Body of Christ: We will be the fivefold *Kopher* to the church. God has purposed our destiny which we shall fulfill; and we will get to the promised land—to the flourishing place. We will over-come all challenges and surmount all obstacles.

So, let the people of African descent join with Pharrell Williams an African American song writer whose song "Happy" became an international phenomenon, impacting people of numerous cultures and say in the words of the "Happy" song.[297] **"Can't nothing bring me down, my level's too high to bring me down because I'm Happy"** Yes, we are happy. Happy for God's intervention, happy that our purpose will be fulfilled, happy that justice will be done, happy in Jesus Christ with the joy of the Lord as our strength, the weapons of the Lord as our victory, the horses of our destiny our direction, and the purpose of the Lord as our determined end.

Yes, once *we had it*, it is true that *we lost it* but thanks be to God through Christ and God's inevitable plan *we will get it back.*

Therefore, let the Cushites of African descent and oppressed people of color where ever they reside embrace their destiny — shout for joy, and exclaim I'm happy—we had it, we lost it, and now in this time we will get back. Amen, Amen and Amen!

Final Discussion Question

1. What did you learn about God's destiny for people of African descent?
2. What section of the book impacted you the most?
3. What biblical black character impacted you the most?
4. What will you do to spread the prophetic and historic message of the book?

---

297 PHARRELL WILLIAMS LYRICS.

Acknowledgements

There are many people to whom I am indebted to for this book first and foremost is my lovely wife of forty years, partner, queen and love of my life who encouraged me for thirty years to write and get this book published and provided me with much needed motivation to finally get this work completed. I am what I am today because of her invaluable influence in my life.

Secondly, I owe a heartfelt thank you to one of my best friends, Carl Jeffrey Wright, CEO of Urban Ministries who heard my tape on the subject and title of this book and called me from France to tell me "you have to get this published" and he provided me with the incentive to finally get it done.

My third acknowledgement goes to author Don Griffin who also listened to my tape with a group of African American men and got so inspired. He teamed up with psychologist Joel Freeman and let him hear my work and the two got inspired with my sanction to use the material to write a work largely based on my tape and message entitled Return to Glory.

Fourthly, Sister Patricia Ware who kept me motivated with her consistent communication and encouragement about writing this book. She was part of the impetus that made me push forward and bring this work to fruition.

Finally, I am indebted to Annette Leach who showed great professionalism in her quest to get this book published, her commitment to this project was greatly appreciated she was a timely godsend to this project.

However most of all I acknowledge my lord and Savior Jesus Christ the Messiah from the tribe of Judah and deliverer of oppressed people of color throughout the globe.

About the Author

Dr. Clarence Walker is the apostolic covering for over 100 churches in the U.S. and Africa supporting them with training, counsel and prayer. He received a B.A. degree in social work from Eastern University, his MSW degree in Community Organization from Temple University, and a PhD. in Biblical Counseling from Trinity Seminary. In addition, Dr. Walker received a post Graduate Certificate in Marriage and Family Therapy from the Marriage Council of Philadelphia and the University of Pennsylvania School of Medicine Division of Family Studies.

Dr. Walker served as a Community Organizer for Southwest Philadelphia with the United Methodist Neighborhood Services and was a Community Initiatives Liaison for the Youth Services Coordinating Office under the City of Philadelphia's Managing Director's Office. He was also a Marriage and Family Therapist in private practice for twelve years.

The author of *Breaking Strongholds in the African-American Family* and *Biblical Counseling with African-Americans*, Dr. Walker is a contributing author of *Biblical Strategies for a Community in Crisis*, *Called to Lead* and *It's Prayer Time*. He and his wife Ja'Ola developed *For Christian Lovers Only*; a marriage enrichment curriculum targeted to African-American couples.

As early as junior high school, Dr. Walker studied Black History and Black Literature. He continued with African Civilization studies at Community College of Philadelphia, Eastern University, and completed graduate work in the African-American experience at Temple University. A speaker at many churches, conferences, and courses on the African Presence in the Bible and the African-American Family, Dr. Walker wrote the Destiny of Hope Series concerning God's Prophetic Destiny of people of African descent. Ministering throughout the United States, the Caribbean, Africa, Korea, and Israel, Dr. Walker and his loving wife Ja'Ola of 40 years are the pastors of the Fresh Anointing Christian Center International (FACCI), a multinational congregation in Upper Darby Pennsylvania. He is the father of two sons, Justin and Arthur.

For more information about Dr. Walker, please visit clarencewalkerministries.com, thefacc.org, and marriage.urban ministries.com.

Selected Bibliography

"African-American Consumers: Still Vital, Still Growing: 2012 Report."
The Nielsen Company, 21 September 2012, http://www.nielsen.
com/content/dam/corporate/us/en/microsites/publicaffairs/
StateOfTheAfricanAmericanConsumer2012.pdf.

"African Ethics." *Stanford Encyclopedia of Philosophy*. Stanford U, 9 Sept
2010, https://plato.stanford.edu/entries/african-ethics/.

"America's Changing Religious Landscape." *Pew Research Center*, 12 May
2015, http://www.pewforum.org/2015/05/12/americas-changing-
religious-landscape/.

Aslan, Reza. *Zealot: The Life and Times of Jesus of Nazareth*. New York:
Random House, 2013.

Chatters, Linda M. et al. "Race and Ethnic Differences in Religious
Involvement: African Americans, Caribbean Blacks and Non-
Hispanic Whites." *Ethnic and racial studies* 32.7 (2009): 1143–
1163. *PMC*, https://www.ncbi.nlm.nih.gov/pmc/articles/PMC2962581/.

Chen, Stephanie. "Interracial Marriages at an All-time High, Study
Says." *CNN*, 04 June 2010, http://www.cnn.com/2010/LIVING/06/04/
pew.interracial.marriage/index.html.

"Christianity in the Caribbean Region." *Encyclopedia of Religion*, 2nd ed.,
March 2005.

Custance, Arthur C. "Noah's Three Sons: Human History in Three Dimensions Vol.1: Part IV The Technology of Hamitic People." *The Arthur C. Custance Centre for Science and Christianity*, 1988, http://custance.org/Library/Volume1/#Part IV - Volume1.

de Ngor, Mading. "Globalization and The African Kinship Network System: Will It Sustain?" *Sudan Tribune*, 27 July 2006, http://www.sudantribune.com/Globalization-and-the-African,16826.

Emerson, Michael O., and Christian Smith. *Divided by Faith: Evangelical Religion and the Problem of Race in America*. New York: Oxford UP, 2001.

Fieser, Ezra and Lise Alves. "Latin Evangelicals' Explosive Growth." *Catholic San Francisco*, 11 May 2012.

Freeman, Colin. "Nigeria hired South African mercenaries to wage a secret war on Africa's deadliest jihadist group." *Business Insider*, 15 May 2015, http://www.businessinsider.com/south-african-mercenaries-waged-secret-war-on-boko-haram-2015-5.

Fry, Richard. "Millennials overtake Baby Boomers as America's largest generation." *Pew Research Center*, 25 April 2016, http://www.pewresearch.org/fact-tank/2016/04/25/millennials-overtake-baby-boomers/.

Glaude, Eddie, Jr. "The Black Church Is Dead." *The Huffington Post*, 24 Feb. 2010, http://www.huffingtonpost.com/eddie-glaude-jr-phd/the-black-church-is-dead_b_473815.html.

"Global White Population to Plummet to Single Digit—Black Population to Double." *National Policy Institute*, 8 April 8 2008, *American Renaissance*. https://www.amren.com/news/2008/04/global_white_po/.

Gonzales, Suzannah. "More Mexican immigrants leaving U.S. than entering: Pew." *Reuters*, 19 November 2015, http://www.reuters.com/article/us-usa-immigration-mexico-idUSKCN0T82F220151119.

Heimlich, Russell. "Blacks Are The Most Religious Americans." *Pew Research Center*, 03 Nov. 2008,http://www.pewresearch.org/fact-tank/2008/11/03/blacks-are-the-most-religious-americans/.

Holland, Jesse J. "Pew study: Whites with Native American ancestry largest multiracial group in United States." *US News/AP*, 11 June 2015, https://www.usnews.com/news/politics/articles/2015/06/11/pew-white-native-american-adults-largest-multiracial-group.

"How did they get to Brazil?" *Exploring Africa*. Michigan State U, 2017, http://exploringafrica.matrix.msu.edu/module-fifteen-activity-three/.

Jenkins, Dr. Orville Boyd. "Peoples and Cultures Race and Ethnicity in the Horn of Africa." *Orville Jenkins*, 14 Mar. 2015, http://orvillejenkins.com/peoples/raceandethnicity.html.

Keener, Craig. "Dr. Craig Keener on the Historicity of the Book of Acts." *Seedbed*, 23 January 2013, http://www.seedbed.com/dr-craig-keener-on-the-historicity-of-the-book-of-acts/.Kendall, Timothy. "Racism and the Rediscovery of Ancient Nubia." *PBS*, 1999, http://www.pbs.org/wonders/Episodes/Epi1/1_retel1.htm.

Long, Richard. "Black Students Feeling Especially Crushed By Student Debt." *Our Future.org*, 29 April 2015, https://ourfuture.org/20150429/black-students-feeling-especially-crushed-by-student-debt.Menell, Richard. "How South Africa is helping deliver prosperity to all Africans."

World Economic Forum, 4 June 2015,https://www.weforum.org/agenda/2015/06/how-south-africa-is-helping-deliver-prosperity-to-all/.

Merritt, Jonathan. "Election 2012 Marks the End of Evangelical Dominance in Politics." *The Atlantic*, 13 November 2012, https://www.theatlantic.com/politics/archive/2012/11/election-2012-marks-the-end-of-evangelical-dominance-in-politics/265139/.

"Millennials: A Portrait of a Generation - Confident, Connected, Open to Change." *Pew Research Center*, 24 February 2010,http://assets. pewresearch.org/wp-content/uploads/sites/3/2010/10/millennials-confident-connected-open-to-change.pdf.

Mitchell, Russ. "The Top 20 Countries where Christianity is Growing the Fastest." *Disciple All Nations*, 25 August 2013, https://discipleallnations.wordpress.com/2013/08/25/the-top-20-countries-where-christianity-is-growing-the-fastest/.

Morgan, Timothy C. "Africa's Azusa." *Christianity Today*, 28 March 2006, http://www.christianitytoday.com/ct/2006/marchweb-only/113-23.0.html."New Grad Rate Data Show Gap between Minority and White Students is Closing."

Homeroom, 16 March 2015, The US Department of Education, https://blog.ed.gov/2015/03/new-grad-rate-data-show-gap-between-minority-and-white-students-is-closing/.

Oden, Thomas C. *How Africa Shaped the Christian Mind: Rediscovering the African Seedbed of Western Christianity*. Downers Grove: Intervarsity, 2010.

Olitzky, Rabbi Kerry M. "Was Abraham's Second Wife Really Hagar?" *My Jewish Learning*, http://www.myjewishlearning.com/article/abrahams-second-marriage/.

Passel, Jeffrey S., Gretchen Livingston, and D'Vera Cohn. "Explaining Why Minority Births Now Outnumber White Births." *Pew Research Center*, 17 May 2012, http://www.pewsocialtrends.org/2012/05/17/explaining-why-minority-births-now-outnumber-white-births/.

Radcliffe on November 2, Shawn. "More White People Are Dying at Middle Age." *Healthline*, 2 November 2015, http://www.healthline.com/health-news/more-white-people-are-dying-at-middle-age-110215.

"Religious Landscape Study." *Pew Research Center*, 2014, http://www.pewforum.org/religious-landscape-study/.

Robinson, Calvin R., Redman Battle, and Edward W. Robinson. *The Journey of the Songhai People*. 1st ed. Farmer, 1987.Waugh, Geoff. "20th Century Revivals." *The Revival Library*, 2015, http://www.revival-library.org/index.php/catalogues-menu/ 20th-century/20th-century-revival.

Whitaker, Morgan. " Census data reveals US immigrant population to top 51 million in 2023." *AOL.com*, 24 April 2015,https://www.aol.com/ article/2015/04/24/census-data-reveals-us-immigrant-population-to-top-51-million-in/21175968/.

"Whites no longer a majority in U.S. by 2043." *CBS News/AP*, 12 December 2012, http://www.cbsnews.com/news/census-whites-no-longer-a-majority-in-us-by-2043/.

Wicker, Christine. *The Fall of the Evangelical Nation: The Surprising Crisis Inside the Church*. San Francisco: Harper One, 2008.

Williams, Olivia A. "Effects of Faith and Church on African American Adolescents." *Michigan Family Review*, vol. 8, no. 1, 2003, pp. 19-27,https://quod.lib.umich.edu/m/mfr/4919087.0008.103/ --effects-of-faith-church-involvement-on-african-american? rgn=main;view=fulltext.

꙳ ꙳ ꙳

Destiny of Hope Series Profile

The Destiny of Hope Series mission is to provide faith to people of color, especially those who feel discouraged because of oppression, xenophobia, and racism. These messages, books, and CDs are designed to uplift the biblical, prophetic, and historical truth concerning people of color in general but particularly to those of African descent in the Americas, Caribbean, and Africa.